TEACHINGS
of the
COSMIC CHRIST

Restoring the Thread of Contact

TEACHINGS
of the
COSMIC CHRIST

Restoring the Thread of Contact

ELIZABETH CLARE PROPHET

SUMMIT UNIVERSITY ☙ PRESS®
Gardiner, Montana

TEACHINGS OF THE COSMIC CHRIST Volume 1
Restoring the Thread of Contact
by Elizabeth Clare Prophet
Copyright © 2021 The Summit Lighthouse, Inc. All rights reserved.

Except for a single copy for your personal, noncommercial use, no part of this work may be used, reproduced, stored, posted or transmitted in any manner or medium whatsoever without written permission, except by a reviewer who may quote brief passages in a review.

For information, contact
The Summit Lighthouse, 63 Summit Way, Gardiner, MT 59030 USA
Tel: 1-800-245-5445 or 1 406-848-9500
info@SummitUniversityPress.com
www.SummitLighthouse.org

Library of Congress Control Number: 2021947109
ISBN: 978-1-60988-379-9 (softbound)
ISBN: 978-1-60988-380-5 (eBook)

SUMMIT UNIVERSITY ♨ PRESS®

The Summit Lighthouse, Summit University, Summit University Press, ♨ , Church Universal and Triumphant, Keepers of the Flame, and *Pearls of Wisdom* are trademarks registered in the U.S. Patent and Trademark Office and in other countries. All rights reserved.

24 23 22 21   1 2 3 4

CONTENTS

FOREWORD vii

CHAPTER ONE 1
The Restoration of the Thread of Contact
   (January 8, 1979)

CHAPTER TWO 63
A Transfer of Power
   (January 17, 1979)

CHAPTER THREE 101
The Goal of Chelaship
   (January 23, 1979)

CHAPTER FOUR 207
The Initiation of the Solar Radiance
   (January 26, 1979)

CHAPTER FIVE 265
The Initiation of the Holy Spirit
   (February 6, 1979)

CHAPTER SIX 313
The Mantle of the Christ
   (February 23, 1979)

NOTES 351

FOREWORD

The spiritual path, with its mystical goal of oneness with God, is simple in concept—God is Love. But if the simple precepts that lie at the heart of all the world's religions were enough, we would have reached the goal of the ascension many embodiments ago. More than good intentions and purity of heart are needed. We need a guide.

Whether we know that one as teacher, guru, or master, that guide sees our inner, eternal reality and tutors our souls through the challenging initiations of the Path. The master holds us in his embrace as we transcend the limitations of the human personality and integrate with the personal presence of God.

Maitreya was the Guru in the ancient mystery school described in allegory in Genesis as the Garden of Eden. He is known in the East through the traditions of Buddhism: Gautama prophesied to his disciples that after a period of darkness, Lord Maitreya would descend to earth to preside over a future age of enlightenment.

Buddhists today await Maitreya's coming much in the same way that Christians await Jesus' Second Coming. Yet Maitreya *is here.* Since 1960 he has been delivering his teachings in the West through Mark and Elizabeth Prophet, messengers for the ascended masters. And in 1979 he called a group of students together to study his teachings and to make their connection once again with his heart—the heart of the Guru.

Teachings of the Cosmic Christ is the record of the profound and personal teachings given to that group of students. Join them now. You will find here precious keys for accelerating your spiritual path. You will learn how to restore and strengthen the thread of contact with your own inner teacher and your guru. And you will learn how to prepare for the initiations that come to all who would walk the Path all the way Home.

Take this as a handbook on your journey toward your ultimate destination. Maitreya shows the way. He invites you to enter in. He shows how in today's world you can truly walk in the footsteps of Jesus, of Gautama, and of all those who have found their ultimate Reality.

—The Editors

CHAPTER ONE

The Restoration of the Thread of Contact

If I were to answer the question, "What is the greatest gift the ascended masters give to us?" I would immediately reply that it is the person of themselves—their person, the person of the guru. The teaching is really not a teaching without the person.

What is the person? The person is the integration of the teaching, of the Trinity of God and of the Mother, into a living, moving, breathing, self-conscious awareness—a flame of God in action. Then, by the action and by the movement, by the interaction of the person, we know the teaching.

This is the great gift of Jesus Christ: *not that he was the Christ but that he was Jesus.* He was the Christ before Abraham was,[1] eternal as the Son of God. But the great gift was that he by free will responded to the command of God and became the man Jesus. The Word was made flesh. He became the person, personifying a light that without the person was not comprehensible.[2]

The more you walk on the Path and the more you pass through initiations that test the absolute limits of the capacity of your being, the more you are grateful for the person. In the midst of the darkest night, you can always remember a person, but you can't remember a vapor, an ether, some kind of an ethereal, metaphysical concept of God. You can remember the smile of your teacher, and you can remember that a person, *the guru,* has loved you personally.

And the love of guru is the love of God. It is infinite. It is beyond the capacity of any of us to even comprehend except the one great truth that we are totally, completely loved. We have read that in a book—God loves you. But when you meet the person in the flesh who loves you totally as the guru, as you know God is loving you—"that ye love one another as I have loved you,"[3] which is what Jesus gave to his disciples—then you are sure.

You are not quite sure until that moment, simply because from hour to hour and day to day you deal with a force that is in Matter as anti-Matter and its condemnation, its belittlement, its criticism. It seems to be the very dust that is a part of the earth, and man is formed "of the dust of the ground."[4] The very grains of condemnation are a part of the fallen consciousness of the carnal mind, the Luciferians, et cetera.

It is not real. It is not something to which we are attuned. But after moments in bliss and in light and in great radiation that descends, when we go back to the norm of our little house, our little abode, which is our temple where we live with our little habits and our little ways, when we come back to that place, by comparison to the great, great light of God that we have contacted, that place seems lesser and not adequate to receive the light. We can easily, then, have self-condemnation—because the light is so great.

That's the real meaning of the dark night of the soul and the dark night of the Spirit—to be so aware of this intensity of light simultaneously when one is aware of one's remaining untransmuted karma. Hence one entertains the vibration of unworthiness. Then, in the midst of this sense of unworthiness as we're going up the mountain on the Path over the years, we meet the person of the guru who is in the flesh, who may have the appearance of human habits and human frailties and human qualities like us—for the very reason that if he or she didn't we wouldn't be able to equate with that person.

This person is close enough to us to relate to us, and yet blazing through this person is the intensity of cosmic love made personal. And this one, totally devoted to us, conveys the message "I love you" from a God who seems too far away for us to imagine that we can reach or comprehend.

The Person of God

The person of this love was manifest to me in our beloved Lanello, in Mark Prophet. I saw in him the guru. And as I was meditating upon Lord Maitreya and his message to you today, which becomes the first message of the Teachings of the Cosmic Christ at Summit University, I was filled with a sense of the person of God.

Lord Maitreya, as you know, is the LORD God who walked with Adam and Eve in the Garden. He talked with them. He gave them instructions. He was a very personal friend, very intimate with Adam and Eve. It is that same presence of the person.

Then the serpent came along with an intellectual argument —a philosophical, ideological argument—and the fascination of the mental body with this ideology became the antithesis of the personal love of the guru. It became more intriguing, more fascinating, more stimulating, and more flattering than just the pure and simple love of the guru for his chela.

The serpent offers flamboyancy, flattery, the attention to a lesser self. It seems to be the very love that we're seeking, but it can never deliver the goods. It can never be loyal to the end. It doesn't have the capacity to hold love. It can hold a mechanical interchange of personalities, and it can definitely use its magnetism to adorn and make you feel wonderful. But it isn't the very, very special quality of the Father's love for his child that the true guru is able to impart.

This is the most amazing thing about the person of Jesus Christ toward Peter and the apostles. They were very obvious in their imperfections. Peter in his impetuosity even becomes the tool of Satan. When Jesus tells him that he is going to go through this most intense initiation of the crucifixion, Peter is not able to understand it, and he is very impatient and says, "Be it far from thee."[5] And then there was doubting Thomas and the questions and the doubts. With all that he went through with his disciples, Jesus Christ yet loved them with that perfect love of God.

What is so astounding about the love of the guru is that the guru by his very being sees through us, knows what we are, knows what our frailties are, knows the things that we've done, knows when we're lying and when we're telling the truth, knows when we're trying to cover for that human creation—yet loves us, never stops loving us, never stops seeing the God who we are.

I can remember Jesus loving me personally though I was imperfect. And I can remember Mark Prophet loving me personally though I was imperfect. To me, that is the great miracle of God.

Human Perfection and Imperfection

The great lie of the fallen ones is that you have to become perfect before you are acceptable to God, before you are worthy of communing with him, being with him, or being loved by him.

The false gurus have achieved their place because there's such a drive to get that perfection. They've come in and said, "You can do this, this, this, and this and master your consciousness."

Why do we respond? It's the pendulum swing between self-condemnation that says, "Whatever means is available, I've just got to get out of this unworthy state," and the need for flattery, that underneath all that condemnation you really think you're a great person and you're so glad to find someone who will flatter you and tell you so. This is the pendulum swing of the ego problem: self-aggrandizement and self-belittlement. They're just to the left and the right, the plus and the minus. Both of them are the perversions of the real ego of Christ.

Responding to those human needs and those ego needs, we accept the false gurus who are going to show us how to get perfect so that we can go up to God and say, "See, now I am perfect. Now you can accept me." Then the fallen ones would have us go one step further and say, "Now, God, you have to accept me. Now you *have* to accept me because I have become perfect." This is a very great subtlety that invades our consciousness on the Path.

The attempt to control God by becoming an adept is the whole point of the fall of Lucifer. He thought he was so great that he would give God an ultimatum and God would have to succumb. He is the original maniac with the power madness, the desire to control the Guru, God, by becoming omnipotent through a mechanical perfection.

You're going to hear this lecture again at the end of this quarter of Summit University because I think you'll understand it a great deal more then. It is the very crux of the Path. There is a great deal of pride in seeking to become humanly perfect.

People like to think that I'm a messenger because I've become humanly perfect. I find it very funny. People interview me and assume that I have all these human perfections. No. I'm a messenger because God has decided to be where I am and because he loves me regardless of my imperfections. And that's a big, big difference. Remember that you are a chela because God has decided to be right where you are in your heart and not because you have done some wonderful, great, good thing humanly.

Does that mean we cannot please God with good works? No. But the good works with which we please him are always done to his glory and in a great joy of ritual, of doing something for the love of God without any thought that, in fact, this something we're doing is perfecting the soul. The soul is gaining perfection because we engage the gears of our energies and our being in doing the highest good we're capable of understanding.

The catch is not to let the human consciousness take credit for it or think that *it* is what is becoming perfect. You see, the carnal mind will do this. The carnal mind doesn't want to say die. It doesn't want to give up, and so it will pose as this perfect person right while it is this great serpent.

Launcelot's Love for Guinevere

There are stories in the tales of Camelot and the Knights of the Round Table about women being able to put hexes on people. Even in John Steinbeck's version of Camelot, *The Acts of King Arthur and His Noble Knights,* Launcelot sees a woman who believes she has become a sorceress. The message you get is that the sorceress, or the witch, or the warlock is capable of manifesting the perfect self, the perfect form, the perfect face. And yet Launcelot knows that behind that face is a serpent, is a dragon, is a beast.

There are four queens. One comes out of the north, one out of the south, one out of the east, one out of the west. They entrap him and enclose him in a castle, all of which is created out of illusion.

It's an illusory castle with an illusory dungeon. He is held there, and each of these queens give to him something that she is offering him if he will but give her his soul and his life. They are all jealous that he loves Guinevere and Guinevere only. He is known for this and will never be moved from that love.

They offer him power and everything imaginable that a woman could offer in all of the levels of her being. He turns down each of them and he gives to them a speech about their stunning beauty, each one more beautiful than the other. But he says that he cannot believe or know for sure that that is what they really are, that behind them is the beast, the dragon, the old hag, the real old witch, and that the sorcerer has the power to put on the mask.

Then Steinbeck has Launcelot say the following lines, which are preeminently the very essence of what the guru will say. He gives his expression of his love for Guinevere, and he lists that she may be imperfect, she may not be this beautiful, she may not be this or that, but "Guinevere is Guinevere."

This is the whole essence of his love: What she is, is real. He is loving her for the fact that she is real, and this reality includes imperfection. He is not falling for the mechanical lie of the serpent that says, "I am better than God. I am better than his sons and daughters because I have this mechanical perfection and the ability to manipulate Matter substance in all of this witchcraft and this wizardry and all of these feats of power."

What the Guru Sees

Without the love of the person of God for us individually, you never quite make it on the Path, because, you see, when you accept these grains of sand, of dust, of condemnation about yourself, you begin to be quite certain that that is the guru's opinion of you.

You think that what you are condemning yourself for, God is condemning you for, the messenger is condemning you for, the guru is condemning you for.

The fallen ones never leave you alone. They amplify every wrong deed you have ever done. They hold it up as an example of your unworthiness, and they make you believe that they are the guru speaking in your consciousness, that they are God speaking, and that you must be forever condemned.

Well, a God that condemns you is a God that you will hate. You will hate the God that condemns you. The fallen ones know this. If they can pose as the guru, condemn you, get you to accept the condemnation and to believe the lie that the guru is giving the condemnation, then you will hate the guru. Then you will have to leave the guru. You will have to disassociate yourself from the person of God. This is a very subtle trap—a *very* subtle trap.

I have found that God in the person of the Keeper of the Scrolls has an accurate comma-by-comma, semicolon-by-semicolon awareness of all of our deeds. Thank God that God is not reading the book and the records of the Keeper of the Scrolls each day! I have also found that God in the person of the Christ has an absolute awareness of the totality of our real being and can be aware of our human frailties and human imperfections.

But God in the heart of the guru, the Virgin Mary, Mother Mary, is the immaculate heart who sees only that which is real and that which is light. The great quality of the World Mother is that she cannot remember the pranks and little mischievous deeds of her children. She appears to spoil her children, because whatever they do that is not in the Christ she cannot contain, she cannot see, she will not remember. That state of consciousness is almost unimaginable, but it is very real. Mother Mary has given to me that gift. I cannot remember the so-called sins of chelas.

When I meet chelas, when I see them, I have no retention of anything but the reality and the perfection of the chela. But I also have the retention and the awareness of that which you might call human imperfection that goes to make up the personality, which determines why all of your faces are different, your postures are different, why you've come through different races, and so forth. These are not necessarily evil, they just are the way you are. Everybody knows we got the way we are through the combination of our karma and our great etheric body, our great causal body.

So the guru does not simply love that which is perfect in you. The guru loves you as you are right now.

God has many levels of awareness. We read in scriptures that he hates certain conditions of vice and evil, and deeds of the fallen ones. He dislikes intensely certain vibrations. But as for his children, those whom he has created, he loves the child though he may hate the overlay of consciousness that has come upon that child. And he may vigorously defend the child against the intrusion of the scorpion and the viper within that one's household. Maitreya said that the Brotherhood and he, the Guru, defend the chelas against gossip and condemnation and criticism as long as the chelas also defend the messenger.

A Love That Is True

Understanding how God loves us, we need to also in turn love the guru at that level. We know the guru does not love us because of our mechanical perfection, and so we must not love the guru because we think the guru has a mechanical perfection. This becomes idolatry, a personality cult.

The vibration of a personality cult is unmistakable. Anytime I'm around someone who loves me because I'm mechanically perfect and because I then become an adornment to their ego and it's in their self-interest to know me and be around me—anytime I get near such people I just run, I just disappear from them, I don't want to be on the scene. And I have to remove myself because they have no comprehension of why I am here or who I am. They are not loving me for who I really am: a soul that has made karma, that has made mistakes, that is striving, that has come into a union with God, and that can give the option for the same union to others.

If someone doesn't love you as you are and for what you've been, it is not true love. Beware of such people. People do not only have an idolatrous sense about me, they will also have it about you. They will marry you, they will go into business with you, they will establish friendships on the basis of an idolatrous love—what you can do for them in the adornment of their person and because they think you have talents or money or beauty or glamour that is their image of what God is, a human god—that's the whole thing.

There's a temptation to make human gods of the chelas and human gods of the messengers. So that being exposed, we can throw it all out the window and we get down to this very real, living, simple relationship that we have. And it is the person of you, the chelas, that is always the teacher of the guru. The gurus always learn from their chelas. The gurus are gurus because their chelas are—it is a two-way interaction.

The Guru-Chela Relationship

As Gabriel is teaching us in his *Pearls of Wisdom,* which you haven't received yet,[6] the guru is always the plus polarity, and the chela is the minus polarity. The guru occupies the Alpha thrust, sending the thrust of light to the chela. The chela is the passive receiver of this light. Without the chela, there is nowhere for the light to anchor in the earth. Once the chela has received the light, the thrust of the chela is a return current of love that now becomes the plus that is sent back to the guru as an active love. And this active love is the living of the life of the guru: "Except ye eat my flesh and drink my blood, ye have no life in you."[7]

So when you receive the teaching and the light, first you receive it as the passive receiver. You assimilate it, you become it. In that measure you have become the guru, and in that measure you have become the life that the guru imparts. In that measure you go abroad in the world to be the presence of the ascended masters. So now *you* are the active one, actively sending the thrust of light to others who are beneath you in the scale of consciousness. They, then, become the minus polarity, the passive receivers.

Jesus said that not all who cried "Lord, Lord" would enter in.[8] When he said "enter in," he was talking about entering in to the kingdom, but he was talking about the consciousness, he was really talking about the guru-chela relationship. The Christ does not establish this tremendous figure-eight flow with all who cry out for the Christ.

The guru-chela relationship is a figure-eight flow. You have the same flow in the Chart of Your Divine Self between the great causal body and I AM Presence and your lower self. When you have a real guru, a person who is a guru in the flesh who receives you as a chela, this is the relationship you have. Twenty-four hours a day for life, the guru's causal body is flowing into your self and your self is flowing into the guru. The guru cleanses, strengthens, purifies and sends back to you your self. Now that is the exact relationship you are intended to have between the soul and the I AM Presence, with the Christ in the center as the mediator of that flow.

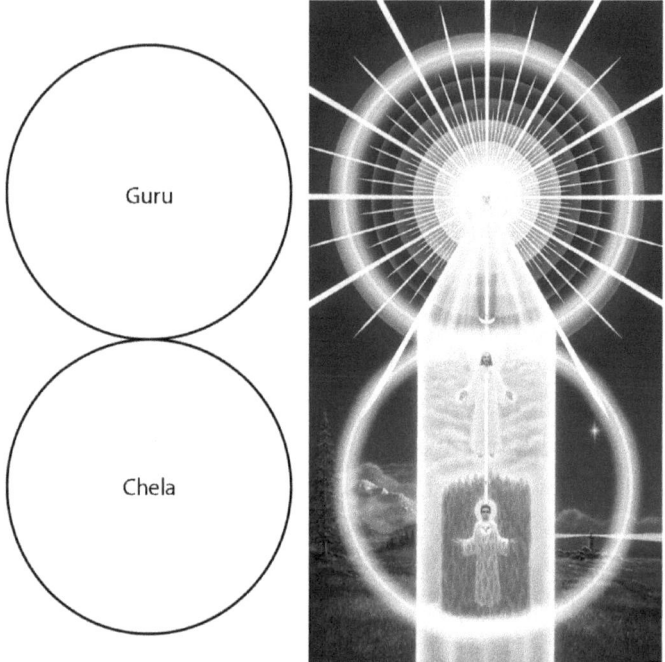

The figure-eight flow between the guru and the chela
FIGURE 1

You are "the quick"[9] if you maintain twenty-four hours a day the flow between your lower self and your Higher Self. You were once "the dead," but now you are quickened by the presence of the light and the person of the ascended masters. It is a process of the awakening and quickening of every cell and atom of consciousness. None of you has the totality of the 100 percent flow with your causal body to your outer self. If you did, you would have a much greater God consciousness and self-mastery. But this is the goal.

The messenger becomes the mediator of this goal, releasing the light whereby you gain more and more awareness of the person of God. You have not seen the person of God the Father except you have seen the Son.

And you must see the Son in flesh and blood; you must be able to understand the Christ in the person of the witness. All else is simply your imagination. It's the best that you can conjure up from the Bible, from stories, and from visualizations. But until the Christ is anchored in the flesh and blood of someone with whom you have that relationship, you really do not understand what the personhood of the Christ is.

The Problem of Idolatry

Since we are prone to idolatry and since the fallen ones take advantage of the fact that we're prone to idolatry, most people who consider themselves religious today are idolators—idolators of the person, the man Jesus, without ever having understood the meaning of Christ in the flesh.

It is something that is easy for some of us to understand, and for others it becomes a great shock to think that perhaps Jesus' feet got dirty and that he had to wash them; that he sweat, that his clothes were dirty, that he ate as normal people do; that he could become angry or annoyed, angry at the Sadducees and annoyed at his disciples; that he could have moments of great grief and burden and lamentation and moments of joy; that he could have a moment of indecision in the Garden of Gethsemane for a number of hours, wrestling in agony to decide whether or not he would actually go through with the crucifixion and finally deciding that he would.

If you talk about the idea, as Gabriel is bringing out in his *Pearls,* that Jesus lived before as David and had imperfections, for the idolator, this destroys Jesus. It absolutely destroys him because the only way they can see him is as the statue of a perfect god who has come down to earth. And so the idea that he could have been David, with all that David went through, is abhorrent.

But to me it is not at all. It's the great glory of the lifestream that he could experience all phases of the human experience and yet pursue the living God, and yet become that God.

You have to *be* God enough to understand the purity of David. It is the wicked and the demons and the fallen ones who impute to David this tremendous impurity of his being. But when you are in God and when you can flow and understand his consciousness, you realize that with all that he went through he had a tremendous purity. His soul was the same soul as Jesus' soul.

And his other incarnations in the Old Testament—Joseph, the youngest of the sons of Jacob; Abel, the son of Adam killed by Cain; and Joshua, who led the children of Israel under Moses—all of these are the person of Jesus, culminating in Elisha, who was with the prophet Elijah.

These incarnations give us an enriched understanding of how a Christed one incarnate behaves in the midst of a battle, in the midst of recalcitrant people; how he works out his karma, how he deals with his twin flame, how he deals with soulmates, how he deals with those who have been his disciples; how he makes mistakes, goes through the agony of his sin, calls on the law of forgiveness, and finally atones for that sin. This makes a person real, and this person says to us, "Because I've done it, you can do it too."

The God-Man in Mark Prophet

The words that I'm saying to you are really not the essence of my message. The essence of my message is the feeling, the love, and an impartation of light that enables you to appreciate this person of the guru who is imperfect. There has never been a guru who was perfect—never. The very nature of God's perfection is that they would not be in Matter if they were perfect.

It is because I so value this person and this personal relationship that I'm going to begin today with Mark Prophet delivering the first dictation from the Cosmic Christ, Lord Maitreya, of which we have a record. It was given in New York City in 1960. We have no record of the month or day—can you imagine that? I know there were a few classes held in New York City and we might be able to research the date by checking the records of the trips Mark made there.[10]

I am playing this recording because I want you to hear the voice of Mark as I heard that voice. I first heard that voice in 1961 in April in Boston as he gave a dictation from Archangel Michael. This dictation is from one year earlier—I had not met Mark at this moment—and this is Maitreya dictating.

Maitreya is the great initiator of your souls. Every dictation that Maitreya gives contains within it an initiation that is unspoken. The challenge of your quarter at Summit University will be to listen to the dictations of Maitreya and to meditate with the Cosmic Christ through your own Christ Self to determine what is the initiation for each dictation. I can tell you in three words what the initiation was in the dictation of Maitreya from the conference that we heard yesterday.[11]

Each one of you will have a secondary initiation out of that primary initiation that will be the adaptation of the light to your soul in its present state of evolution. Each dictation is not totally unique unto each listener. Each dictation has a definite purpose, and that purpose, that initiation, can be stated very succinctly. But how you relate to it and it relates to you becomes a few more paragraphs, because that always involves the person.

At the time Mark gave this dictation, I was looking for Saint Germain and El Morya as I was a student in Boston. And I do want to emphasize to you that since my earliest recollections in this life, I was doing and had done all I knew how to do to be the best disciple, the best follower of Jesus Christ and the ascended masters, given the material that I had. And basically all that I had at that time was the Bible, *Science and Health with Key to the Scriptures* and other writings of Mary Baker Eddy (which happened to be the path that I found when I was a child), the three "I AM" books, and a set of "I AM" Affirmations. That's all that I had for spiritual reading.

People always think that I must have read everything there was to read in the occult field, but I never read those books then and I haven't since. I have never had any need to read them. I've had the direct flame of God. So that was the totality of what I had, and through that I had the absolute contact with the ascended masters, with God the Father, God the Son, and God the Holy Spirit.

You find people who are erudite and have read everything there is to read, who have never ever established the contact, because they attempt to do so through the mental body instead of through the soul and its rising to the plane of the I AM Presence.

With that material and by following its teaching, I had gone as far as I could go without a guru. I could not have taken another step toward my personal salvation or the initiations on the Path. I needed to meet God in the flesh in order to know what I was doing right, what I was doing wrong, and what was the matter with the subjective awarenesses of my consciousness. I had many misconceptions that were accepted simply by the fact that they had become ingrained in me year upon year.

I had to meet the personal messenger. This is why I am so grateful for the person of the Cosmic Christ coming to Summit University and for the person of the messenger Mark Prophet. Until that day happens, you don't move forward on the Path. That is the absolute truth.

That very relationship, the guru-chela relationship, has been so attacked in recent months through the accusations against "cults." But the greatest attack on the *real* guru-chela relationship is that of the false gurus who present such a parallel path as to entrap many souls of light in their circles. And then you find parents and other people becoming aware and seeing through their manipulations and seeing through their hypnotism and so forth.

Nevertheless, regardless of the attack on the flame of the prophets and on their relationship to the people of God, I still have to state the absolute truth: The chela goes as far as he can go in his subjective awareness. He must meet the God-man.

So here is the God-man, beginning with the invocation before the dictation.

Invocation by Mark Prophet

Thou adorable God Presence, thou great magnificent seed of eternal fire planted in our heart to expand its radiance to our lives, we bow in grateful adoration to thee for thy Presence in the universe and in ourselves, sustaining us every moment of every hour.

We invoke the Presence here of our beloved Saint Germain, of our beloved Lord Morya El, of all the chohans of all the rays, the ladies of heaven, the angelic hosts, the Great Karmic Board, the magnificent Goddess of Liberty and all who have to do with the sacred fire. And we ask that they surround each one of us with their great love, which erases automatically all of our thoughts that are not in correspondence with eternal purposes.

We ask thee, O Eternal Father, thou great I AM Presence, that thou make of our hearts and consciousness an ever-living chalice that we may receive the radiance and benefit of the radiation of our own dear Maitreya as he comes to us and speaks his heart and his love and his compassion to us.

LORD MAITREYA
September 18, 1960

The Image of God

Greetings, children of the Most High. With a mantle of divine perfection and eternal light, I do cover you this hour with the infinite Presence of your Father and mine.

To understand his perfection is to become as he is. To be aware of his light is to manifest it. To think as God thinks is to be as God is: life, light, and love.

Peace be unto you in the name of the Cosmic Christ and by the mantle of the Buddha. May each of you recognize yourselves as unfolding spiritual beings created by God and destined to become radiant centers of light in his eternal garden of ever-living Eden. Peace, then, be unto you.

Long ago when beloved Jesus, who spoke to the children of Galilee and Judaea, uttered his words of wisdom, he said, "Show me a coin. Whose image and superscription is upon this coin?" And they replied, "Caesar's." And he spoke to them and said, "Render therefore unto Caesar those things which are Caesar's, and unto God those things which are God's."[12]

Mankind, trying to ferret out the eternal purposes by mere intellect, have often misunderstood the intent of this. And they seem to feel that their human identity, their outer self, is a separate world from their divine being.

I would like today to show you a little of the eternal purpose, using this same illustration. It is true that the coin has two sides, but it is also true that both belong to God. Both belong to your own mighty and beloved I AM Presence.

While I am speaking to you now, legions of angels are in the atmosphere hovering over this place, and they are pouring their radiance out into the city of New York and into your midst. How many of you are aware that you have the power as sons and daughters of the Most High to call upon the angelic hosts who are real and tangible? How many have forgotten their eternal purpose? How many today are able to do as beloved Jesus did in Gethsemane—speak unto the Father and receive angelic comfort?[13]

You also are children of the Most High. Some have forgotten that. And in the forgetting, your powers have waned and you no longer seem able to invoke that protection which mankind knew in their Edenic state. This the hierarchy of heaven would restore to you—not only today, but forever.

We of the Great White Brotherhood, we of the light, would restore to man the power that removes shadow, would restore to you the power of the communion of saints and the communion with the angelic hosts.

These angels have a reality. Men have smiled, and yet many today walk the streets of this world because of the intercession of angelic beings who ministered to them and restored them to health when they were upon self-created beds of pain and misery.

These angels are real. They are tangible beings of light and fire. From the heart of God they go forth, winged messengers of light, love, and power. They are yours to command as they are mine, but their commands must always be commands of light.

When you meet those who sit upon your highways and byways in penury begging for coin of the realm, and your heart is opened and you reach within your purse and you take therefrom a coin and place it in their hands, why do you do this? To be seen of men? Or because your heart reaches out and you recognize that they are in a state less than your own and you would raise them to a higher state?

Yet mankind know that the mere giving of coins does not in itself solve the problem. But to restore these individuals to wholeness, to a straight spine, to a right mind, to a proper understanding—this would remove this blight from your land and from the world.

And therefore, as wayshowers of light down through the centuries, magnificent cosmic beings have arrived on the scene of time. They have been projected on the screen of life like motion pictures, and yet they were living men and women. These have shown forth the way to light.

Many have gone forth from realms of light. As voices crying in the wilderness,[14] men have heard them. And yet the world has remained in shadow.

Today many of the wonders of Atlantis are restored to this earth. Your televisions, your radios, your use of electricity, your modern conveyances and communications—all are so reminiscent of the beauty of Atlantis.

But beloved hearts, children of God, mere physical accomplishment and the mere use of physical sciences in itself is not the greatest wonder of the ages. The greatest wonder of the ages is the miracle of your own being, your being which saith—because it is *empowered* to say it—"I AM!"

When you thus utter the name of God, *that* is the wonder of the age, the miracle of being, the sweet mystery of life—that consciousness with which you are endowed and by which you recognize one another and by which you may raise your eyes and your lives upward toward the sun and perceive its rays as they pour out the dawn of each day to each life. *This* in itself is the miracle of the ages.

And the gift of life given by God is sacred. It is sacred because that gift of life is connected with the sacred fire. And when the fire is removed from your physical forms, then, of course, there remains but the inert atoms. Yet they, too, have life. And these remain, but there is no animation.

Therefore, that which moves you and causes you to have being is your own mighty God Presence. Revere and adore this Presence. This is your Father and my Father. This is your

God and my God.[15] This is the God of every master and every cosmic being. This is the fire on the altar of heaven before which every knee does bow and every tongue does confess, saying, with great love and adoration and knowing, that it is "I AM."[16]

To say "I AM" is the full power of God. To feel I AM is to be at peace. But to *be* I AM is to manifest the eternal in form, in substance, and in dimension. Victory comes to those who are able to perceive their life not as belonging unto Caesar, but as belonging unto God.

It is not needful for men to always become ascetics. It is not needful for men to withdraw from the world as though it were not the Father's. But it is needful for men to *transform* the world because they, like eternal gardeners, are given the wherewithal to transform the world and make it a Garden of Eden, a paradise of beauty, using the scientific knowledge and blessings which are given to them wisely and well, using religion—not as a means for personal aggrandizement or a means whereby the ego can assuage some of its own conflicts—using religion as it was intended to be, as a mere ordered service directing their consciousness to their Higher Self, that that Higher Consciousness may *respond* to them, and in the response from the heart of God there may go forth the wisdom ray, and that that ray from on high may show them how to transform the world, how to transform their lives, how to remove their fears, how to walk the earth with dignity, how to wear robes of righteousness, how to be able to have the sight that sees and perceives a cosmic being and recognizes oneself as a cosmic being.

The Great White Brotherhood is an organization of the Spirit. It has, through the centuries and the ages, endowed various individuals with power. It has formulated plans and concepts in its sacred conclaves in order to show men how to find the pathway back to light. It has established churches, temples, mosques, and sanctuaries throughout the world. Many are on the periphery of light, and some are nearer the heart of the sacred fire. But these were ordained for one purpose.

Priestcraft and mankind operating in the realm of greed and selfishness have perverted its purposes. But the eternal purpose of God cannot be trifled with. Only in human consciousness have men perverted the plan of God. At higher levels it remains inviolate, pure, magnificent and glorious, with the glory of the Eternal shining out its radiance at every hour. Through all time and space, it permeates and it pervades life, and it restores health, strength, and vitality to the universe.

For the universe, the physical universe, is but a reflection of that great, magnificent macrocosmic world of God held in his arms and in his hands as a chalice of beauty, where he can pour forth the essences of his Spirit and direct those essences to take hallowed forms and beings of grandeur and glory—bodies indestructible, minds filled with divine wisdom, power, and glory, and the kingdom that is coming.

Throughout Christendom the cry has gone forth: **Thy kingdom come! Thy will be done upon earth, even as it is in heaven!**[17]

This mantram of the ages uttered through the mouths of thousands of the children of the Eternal, though they know it not, has produced a call which has reached the very heart of heaven, rending the human veil and bringing power to this earth—the power of the sacred fire which blazed upon the altars of Atlantis and blazes upon the altar here today in order that it may make you cognizant of your destiny eternal.

Mankind focus their attention upon the ephemeral. Mankind look and behold the glittering lights upon the streets of New York and the rest of the world. Their eyes become riveted to the power of their television sets. And yet who shall declare that the day may not come when our face will be projected thereupon? Who is able to say that cosmic beings shall not some day speak their directives through these very avenues and channels? And then because the subject matter is correct, mankind will be assisted into their eternal freedom.

What is it you seek, children of mankind? Is it not freedom from want? Is it not freedom from fear? Is it not peace, victory, light, love? Do you not desire to be loved? Do you not desire not to be rejected? Why is this?

Most of you (almost all of you, I think) have a feeling at times—what I would term a "parent feeling." This is of God. You have a feeling of a parent, of a mother or a father, toward some part of life. Remember, dear ones, that the Father has a parent feeling toward each of you. The eternal Father is *your* father and *your* mother.

Therefore, it is needful that men realize the status of a mediator—that they realize that there is their own Presence and that, in a sense of the word, they, too, are mediators as they take the light rays from the chalice of their own being and radiate it forth upon the world, acting, then, even as I AM in dispensing the light of God.

In a sense, I could use a homely illustration of a beautiful meadow with green grass and lovely flowers of every description, of a beautiful little girl walking in the meadow and plucking these flowers and filling a basket with these flowers, symbolic, then, of the grace of God.

And because she is a mediator of the Sun eternal which blossoms through these flowers, she takes these flowers home and into her community and city and passes them around among the children and the people of the city. And so the essence and the sweetness and the fragrance of the flower is scattered, and many are able to share the bounties of the light and the sun. This is intended to be.

You are all mediators, if you will—mediators of the

eternal light of God, even as I AM, as the Christ was.

Remember the words of Jesus when they said, "Who are you?" "Before Abraham was, I am!" was his answer.[18] And so, beloved hearts, you too can say, "Before Abraham, before Adam was, 'I AM'!"

For before there came into being discord upon this planet, God perceived all perfection in all life, and he has never failed to the present hour to perceive only perfection here. It is you, blessed ones, who have somewhat failed. But it need not continue to be so, for the purpose of all religion, the purpose of all life, is to manifest its eternal destiny.

I would turn the coin upon the other side. I would show you not the image of Caesar, *but the image of God!*

The image of God is so beautiful it defies a worded description, and I could only convey to you by my feeling and my radiation how glorious it is.

Who can describe the Eternal? The philosophers of the ages, the great orators of all time, even Daniel Webster and the Roman and Greek orators and philosophers, could not describe it. None of the great ones have even undertaken the describing of the Eternal; they have spoken of His attributes.

And today I would only add my light to this sanctuary and to this world by increasing the intensity of that light and commanding in God's name, I AM: **Increase, increase, increase! O thou light of the eternal wisdom of the sacred fire, and let the children of this earth come to know more of God's beauty. Magnify it ten thousand times!**

I, Maitreya, command it, unfurling my banner that this golden age shall *be* because the Eternal has spoken it, and He shall not fail.

The light of God shall not fail, the light of God shall not fail, the light of God shall *not* fail—and the mighty I AM Presence is that light!

O children of God, see mirrored within your *own* eyes,

within your *own* heart, the eternal radiance—and faint not, but be about your Father's business,[19] and you shall galvanize this age. You shall *fill* the tabernacles and temples with worshipers who shall worship in spirit and in truth,[20] who shall recognize their own divinity and shall realize that the farce of the ages is because men have looked at Caesar and have not looked at God.

I thank you.

Hail Maitreya! (6x)
Hail Lanello! (4x)
Hail to the Ever-Present Guru! (3x)
Won't you be seated.

What Is the Initiation?

Maitreya takes the coin that Jesus took, and the two sides of the coin—God and man—becomes the theme and the means to illustrate the initiation of this dictation. What do you think is the initiation of this dictation? What did Maitreya come to do in his very first dictation in this century through the messenger Mark Prophet?

Student: Through the I AM Presence, one could connect man and God. That one could become at one through their I AM Presence, connecting those two sides of the coin.

ECP: That is approaching the initiation, but it is said more clearly in better words.

Student: You are God.

ECP: Keep going.

Student: You can hold the immaculate concept for your twin flame.

ECP: I'm looking for a word now.

Student: We are mediators of the eternal light of God.

ECP: It's coming along. Let's hear the word. Who has the word?
Student: Innocence?
Student: Idolatry?
ECP: It's one word for the initiation.
Student: Restoration?
ECP: Who said restoration? Can you stand up? You said restoration. Here is the statement of the initiation in the dictation:

> We of the Great White Brotherhood, we of the light, would restore to man the power that removes shadow, would restore to you the power of the communion of saints and the communion with the angelic hosts.

That is the initiation of the dictation. Now this is a *lost* contact, and that is why it has to be restored. We have lost, first of all, our contact with "the power that removes shadow," which is the power of the I AM Presence. We have lost "the communion of saints." Although the Catholic Church speaks of the communion of saints, the communion of saints is direct contact by you with every other son of God who has ascended, hence the ascended masters. That is the communion of saints. You, a saint on earth, communing with a saint in heaven; you, a saint in Matter, communing with a saint in Spirit.

Then "the communion with the angelic hosts" is a different communion because the angelic hosts of whom Maitreya is speaking have never taken embodiment. They are not in the category of saints. They are beings of God. Some angels have taken embodiment.

So the restoration of the power that removes shadow, of the communion of saints, and of communion with the angelic hosts gives to you really the purpose of our entire movement, the purpose of our two witnesses, the purpose of your chelaship. It takes the Cosmic Christ, the Initiator, to come into our midst to give the dictation, to say and to announce that the Great White Brotherhood would restore, is restoring to man this power. This is our purpose.

The Mystery of the Spoken Word

That restoration of contact could not come without an edict from Alpha and Omega, given through Helios and Vesta, through the Four and Twenty Elders, through the Lords of Karma. It has to go through all of those chains of command. And the Cosmic Christ, Lord Maitreya, then is summoned as the instrument to release the initiation. And he releases it through the one in embodiment who represents the inner gurus.

And so "the restoration of contact," upon that point hangs all of the other commentary that some of you were making, such as that we become the mediators of light, which is a corollary to the thesis of the restoration of the contact.

This is something that the chelas of the ascended masters have that no others have. There's no other church, no other organization today—unless it's sponsored by the ascended masters—that has this initiation. We need to realize that it is not simply automatic. It is a personal initiation from God through his emissaries—through the Cosmic Christ, through the messenger—that is made physical and becomes the law of the physical plane because it is *spoken* in the physical plane. Until it is spoken, it does not happen. That's the great mystery of the Word.

The Word of God must be spoken in the physical plane. And to whatever level the Word reaches, it goes out at that level. If it only gets to the etheric plane, it only affects the etheric plane. If it gets to the mental plane, it affects the mental plane. If it gets to the emotional plane, it affects the emotional plane of the whole earth. For God's Word to act in the physical world, in physical people, in physical affairs, it must be spoken through a *physical voice*. That is the whole reason that God had prophets, messengers, and has overshadowed them for the release of the Word.

How Did We Lose the Contact?

The idea in the final sentence of this dictation, the "farce of the ages," is that men have looked at Caesar and not looked at God. Had they looked at God, they would never have lost the contact, because when you are looking through eye contact, you are connected with whatever you are looking at by the *flow of your attention.*

So this is the farce of the ages: People have looked at the Caesars. They have looked at the fallen ones in their positions of power and worshiped them. They have followed their ordinances and their laws in preference to God's laws. So they have lost the contact. Maitreya, in the person of the Christ, comes to restore it.

Now we go on to the corollaries of this. Once you have the restoration of the contact, you have the power as sons and daughters of the Most High to call upon the angelic hosts. Before he even announced the restoration, he says that we have forgotten our eternal purpose:

> Some have forgotten that. And in the forgetting, your powers have waned and you no longer seem able to invoke that protection which mankind knew in their Edenic state. This the hierarchy of heaven would restore.

We have lost the contact in two ways: One, by looking at Caesar instead of God. The other way is by not exercising the spoken Word to invoke the angelic hosts—through disuse of the power itself. Like any other power and any other talent, when it falls into disuse the power wanes.

This has to do with momentum. You can gain a tremendous momentum in the giving of decrees. And you will notice that after you've given any decree many times, there's a much greater action of the light than when you gave it the first time because you are exercising a momentum.

The Importance of Retaining the Light

I would like to mention to you that there are many purposes for your decreeing and for the giving of decrees at Summit University. One of the purposes that Lord Maitreya wanted me to mention today is that some people come to the light being children of God, having the heart of God, and yet having a very heavy karma. That karma can be so heavy that the child of God may sit at Summit University, be here for one or two or more quarters, go back into the world, and simply not be able to sustain the flame or retain this guru-chela relationship, this flow of contact with the I AM Presence. It is simply because of the weight of their own human karma.

Percentages do not tell us how much karma we have. If you balance 51 percent of your karma, you may be balancing two billion pounds of karma if we could weigh it in pounds. If someone else balances 51 percent of his karma, he may have balanced one billion pounds, because 51 percent is only 51 percent of a hundred percent, and everybody has a different amount. And so when people ask me, "How much karma have I balanced?" it depends how much you have. If it's 24 percent, 36 percent, it could be great a deal more than someone else of the same percentage, depending on what you came into embodiment with.

Morya and Maitreya, who work so diligently in the initiation of chelas, want you to know that you are assigned the hours of decrees that you give in order to afford you the maximum opportunity to balance the maximum karma so that you can retain what you have received at Summit University. Your capacity to retain light becomes something that acts in relationship to how much karma you have, how much darkness is in your world.

This is important for you to know in trying to explain why people fall away from the teaching. You have to realize that people have their karma and people have their will. You can have a huge karma, but with a determined will you can keep it sealed in light and keep yourself in light so that a great quantity of karma does not mean that you will not make it on the Path or not to be able to retain light. And Morya says that some people with a lot less karma and less will don't make it, where people with great karma but a great determination may overcome more quickly. But nevertheless, density in your body due to density of karma can be a determining factor.

The Power to Speak the Name of God

Angelic hosts are ours to command. They reinforce light and they stand where we stand; therefore, they become a counterweight. When we have karma and we invoke the angelic hosts, they place their electronic presence over us. We live in their presence while we are balancing karma, and so it is a great act of mercy. If we don't call for them, then we don't have that benefit. Just as we desire to restore the individual to wholeness as the greatest gift that we can give to the beggar, so God desires to restore us to wholeness.

> Mere physical accomplishment and the mere use of the physical sciences in itself is not the greatest wonder of the ages. The greatest wonder of the ages is the miracle of your

own being, your being which saith—because it is *empowered* to say it—"I AM!"

When you thus utter the name of God, *that* is the wonder of the age.

It's not just *being*. The fact that you utter the name of God, I AM, is what makes your being the great miracle.

The gift of life is sacred, and that sacredness is the sacred fire.

To say and to feel I AM is one thing, "but to *be* I AM is to manifest the eternal in form."

You don't have to be an ascetic or to withdraw from the world, but we must transform the world. And we can "transform the world and make it a Garden of Eden" because we are initiates of the Cosmic Christ and because we have the restored contact with the power of the I AM Presence, the communion of saints, and the angelic hosts.

Now it's interesting that Lord Maitreya in his first dictation speaks of the Garden of Eden, because he did not reveal himself to be that Lord God in the Garden of Eden until about three years ago. But here it is already in 1961.

The Guru's Gift of Self

Another nucleus in this dictation is in the final paragraphs when Maitreya makes the invocation for the increase of light and that it be magnified ten thousand times. It was in 1961 at the July conference that Lord Maitreya released the power of the ten thousand-times-ten thousand.[21] He said that every decree that you give would henceforth be multiplied by ten thousand-times-ten thousand. If you multiply it out, it comes to one hundred million. So one hundred million individuals are affected each time you decree. And that dispensation was released by the Cosmic Christ.

Now, I never knew until this moment—as Maitreya is telling me this now—that that multiplication factor of ten thousand-times-ten thousand is actually the x factor of his own causal body. It is Lord Maitreya's personal gift to his initiates. And the initiation really is that Lord Maitreya is saying, "Each time you decree, I will take my causal body, which is the causal body of the Cosmic Christ, and multiply it ten thousand-times-ten thousand."

The decrees that we have given over the years were as effective as they have been because we are chelas of a guru and because the guru has said, "I will give you the greatest gift and the only gift that I have to give. I will give you the gift of myself, and as long as you are my chela you have that gift."

And we are chelas as long as we do his commandments. "If ye love me, keep my commandments"[22] is a very simple requirement of the gurus. If we do what they ask, we remain in that relationship.

The Eternal Plan of God

Maitreya speaks about the fact that the fallen ones have no power to deter the eternal purpose of God, that it cannot be trifled with. In the human consciousness men have perverted the plan of God, but "at higher levels it remains inviolate, pure, magnificent and glorious, with the glory of the Eternal shining out its radiance at every hour."

This is what we keep hearing in the dictations today: The divine plan, the eternal plan of God, cannot be deterred. It is in its cosmic timetable in the Matter spheres in the upper etheric plane.

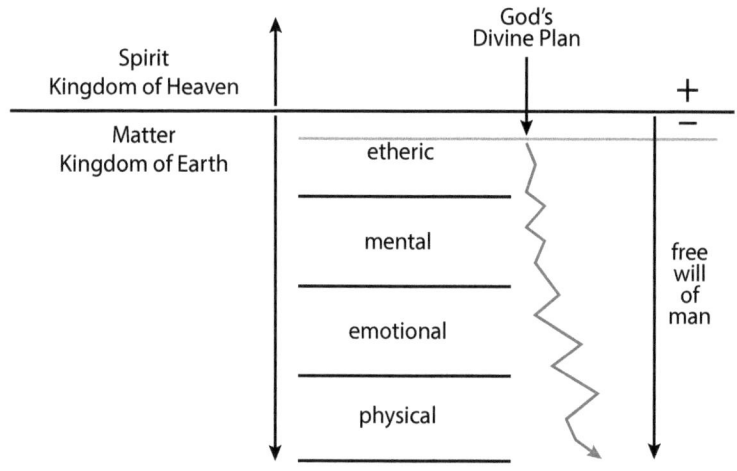

Planes of Spirit and Matter

The divine plan of God is perfect as it manifests in the upper etheric plane. As the plan descends to lower planes, it is taken off course by the human consciousness expressing free will.

FIGURE 2

It's important that you have certain patterns in your mind, so that when we speak you have a mental visualization. Let's say this is the point of demarcation between Spirit and Matter. Everything above it is Spirit and here below is Matter. That line always symbolizes the line of the Christ mediating between Spirit and Matter. You could draw the same line right through your Christ Self and what's above is Spirit, below is Matter.

So the four planes of Matter are the etheric, the mental, the emotional, and the physical. And of course there are gradations within each plane. Not everything that is physical is seen. There are areas of the physical plane that are physical but we don't see them with our eyes—yet they are classified as physical. So the physical is the bottom, the most dense plane to which our souls descend.

We're now in this physical octave. Between embodiments we may be in the astral plane, which is the polluted plane that contains the levels of hell and purgatory. The darkest reaches of the bottomless pit are in the lower astral plane. These planes have a way of interpenetrating one another. They are not just placed one on top of another, but we draw them this way for the purpose of discussion. They are all interpenetrating within our temples right now.

Above the line is the kingdom of heaven, below the line is the kingdom of earth, and the light descends. So God lowers his divine plan. The top part of the etheric plane is the only plane in Matter that's totally unpolluted. The top part of the etheric plane obviously contains the four parts of being: fire, air, water and earth. The upper part of the etheric plane is where the divine plan of God is not altered, is perfect, and is on this cosmic timetable.

When it comes to the lower etheric plane, you start getting into the etheric records of the human consciousness. And as soon as you get etheric records of the human consciousness expressing its free will in opposition to that plan, you get a slowing down. So from the lower etheric on down, the plan is off course until finally in the physical plane we see all kinds of things that don't have any relationship to our knowledge of a great golden age.

So when God releases a fiat and a commitment—"God has decided to save the earth," God will do this, God will do that—that fiat is carried by God and the ascended masters only as far as the upper etheric. That's as far as they have the authority to lower it. From the lower etheric down, it becomes the free will of man, the free will of individuals in embodiment.

People in embodiment control what happens in the physical plane, the astral plane, the mental plane, and the etheric plane. So you've got to get into physical embodiment in order to make

God's will become his will on earth as it is in heaven.[23] That is the very line of Jesus' prayer that Maitreya is citing. He says:

> Throughout Christendom the cry has gone forth: Thy kingdom come! Thy will be done upon earth, even as it is in heaven!
>
> This mantram of the ages uttered through the mouths of thousands of the children of the Eternal, though they know it not, has produced a call which has reached the very heart of heaven, rending the human veil and bringing power to this earth—the power of the sacred fire which blazed upon the altars of Atlantis and blazes upon the altar here today in order that it may make you cognizant of your destiny eternal.

Receiving the Prayer

Now, Maitreya as the Father (*Father* and *Guru* are synonymous terms to Jesus as the personification of God the Father to him) released the Lord's Prayer through Jesus. And he gave only one prayer—at least only one of which we have public record. As this dictation was being given, I asked Maitreya, "Why did you release only one prayer that was noted as a prayer?"

He said, "It's the psychology of the human consciousness. When you release one prayer, you are certain that it will be given. If you release a hundred prayers, each one assumes less importance until each one of a hundred is one hundredth of the importance of the single prayer."

And so the psychology of sustaining the light and the teaching for two thousand years comes out. The teaching is given very succinctly in four books of the Bible, the four Gospels. The single prayer repeated is the mantra of the Piscean age, the *great* mantra of the Piscean age, "Our Father who art in heaven."

And so, how many of you have not heard my Stump lecture?[24] Well, in that Stump lecture, I give the revelation of the teaching of Jesus Christ to me on the Lord's Prayer being seven commands following the seven Elohim and the order of creation. The revelation of the inner meaning of the Lord's Prayer according to the seven rays ranks as one of the all-time revelations that I treasure of my entire life.

The other all-time great revelation was the dictation by beloved Jesus Christ through Mark Prophet of his prayer, "It Is Finished." Mark typed that on his typewriter in Holy Tree House in his little basement office while I was next door in my office, and he came forth with that great prayer. Jesus gave it to him as the prayer that he gave on the cross, "It Is Finished." All we have recorded in the Bible are the words, "It is finished," and "he gave up the ghost."[25] That's all. But the prayer that we have written is the prayer that was spoken on the etheric plane by Jesus' soul.

So he lowered that into manifestation, and when Mark brought to me the mighty prayer that he received—just as quickly as it could be spoken from Jesus—I felt that all of my purpose of chelaship was on that one point. The joys of chelaship as well as its trials, its tribulations and its testings had all been worthwhile to simply stand there and be able to receive that prayer.

You realize that without a chela, the guru cannot give anything. And so one chela receiving that one prayer then seals it for all others who come. And that is so with you as you sit in this classroom. If this classroom were empty, I would not be teaching, the Brotherhood would not have the dispensation to teach, and so the Cosmic Christ and the messages of the Cosmic Christ would remain in the upper etheric plane, taught at the etheric retreats to those between embodiments, or to those who are asleep (out of their bodies). This doesn't do much for the physical universe, but it does sustain God's consciousness in Matter, in this upper etheric plane.

Now if it were nowhere in Matter, if it were only in Spirit, then we would have quite a dilemma because there would be no focal point for our souls to become aware of God in the Matter universe. The great gift of the ascended masters is that they maintain their retreats in the etheric plane, and the etheric plane finally accelerates so that at the point when it is at that line of demarcation between Spirit and Matter, the etheric plane has accelerated. So crossing over that line from the highest frequency of the etheric plane into the plane of Spirit is not any change in vibration. You finally have reached that point, except that it is plus in Spirit and it is minus in Matter. But minus ultimately then becomes the plus.

The Use of the Word

I think there are enough people here who have raised their hands who have not heard the Stump lecture that I think it should be played and reviewed. Even if you have heard it, I trust you will understand that the great point of coming to Summit University under Lord Maitreya is to learn to be a world teacher—not to just receive the teaching but to study how the teaching is imparted so that you also can impart the teaching yourselves. So if you've heard a message many times, the purpose of listening to it again is to understand how it was delivered, how a flame is conveyed by a word.

You heard that in Mark's intensification. That was Maitreya intensifying the energy, which then intensified the voice of Mark Prophet. You don't like to use such a mundane word as *technique* when listening to an ascended master dictation through the Holy Ghost. But the Holy Ghost has techniques, you know. God has techniques for reaching our souls, and God uses them. God is the great, great master of the use of the Word and of the communication of the Word.

God determined to release a *very* intense amount of power in that moment in that dictation. So when Maitreya increases the power, it increases the volume. Increasing the volume increases an arc of energy that contacts your heart. At the moment of the playing of that portion of the dictation, you can feel the flow of light and the *melting* of human creation.

And in that melting process, you'll find tears coming to your eyes and you'll feel a certain emotion in your being that has nothing to do with emotionalism. It has to do with the fact that that's the fire of the Holy Ghost breaking down recalcitrant emotions that have so long ago rebelled against God that they have forgotten how to feel God, the real feeling of God.

What Is the Master Like?

We don't often enjoy such an experience, such a moment. It is a very important point of the dictation, in which we really see the character of Lord Maitreya. You're always looking for glimpses in dictations of what Morya is like. What is Saint Germain like? What is their person like? How would you describe them as a friend? How would you paint them in a portrait? What are the qualities you would identify? And here comes Maitreya. He reveals himself unmistakably.

> It is not needful for men to withdraw from the world as though it were not the Father's. But it is needful for men to *transform* the world...

That gives you a sense of his character. He's not the ascetic Buddhist who simply sits in a room and meditates on the void. He's a very active person, and the flames of wisdom and compassion are equally intense. So don't be an ascetic, withdrawing from the world in your spiritual pride or your mental pride—get out and save the world.

It is needful for men to *transform* the world because they, like eternal gardeners, are given the wherewithal to transform the world and make it a Garden of Eden, . . .

You can transform it. You are given the wherewithal.

. . . a paradise of beauty, using the scientific knowledge and blessings which are given to them wisely and well, using religion—not as a means for personal aggrandizement or a means whereby the ego can assuage some of its own conflicts —using religion as it was intended to be, as a mere ordered service directing their consciousness to their Higher Self . . .

The purpose of religion is an ordered service that directs your consciousness to your Higher Self, that I AM Presence, that Christ Self, so that the Higher Self,

. . . that Higher Consciousness may *respond* to them, and in the response from the heart of God there may go forth the wisdom ray, and that that ray from on high may show them . . .

And here's the big statement:

. . . may show them *how to* transform the world, *how to* transform their lives, *how to* remove their fears, *how to* walk the earth with dignity, *how to* wear robes of righteousness, *how to* be able to have the sight that sees and perceives a cosmic being and recognizes oneself as a cosmic being.

Now you get the understanding that you have come to the Guru Maitreya who is a "how-to" guru, that the teachings of the Cosmic Christ are practical, down-to-earth, how-to. And the how-to is very much related to the practical scene today. Now anytime you see the do-it-yourself theme—which is really the theme of the American people, and it also is a quality that you see in lightbearers throughout the planet whether they're Russians,

Chinese or what have you—that do-it-yourself consciousness is unmistakably the revelation that the soul is in contact with the World Mother.

The World Mother and the Cosmic Christ

When I come again, I'm going to read you some of the teachings on the union of Maitreya and the World Mother. The Darjeeling Council, beloved El Morya, prophesied the coming of Maitreya. And they noted that the coming of Maitreya was the coming of the World Mother, and that the presence of *both* were necessary for the liberation of the children of God and for the deliverance of the teachings.

The reason is that the Mother occupies the bottom position on the clock, the six o'clock line, which symbolizes the lowest descent of life into physical form. It denotes the base-of-the-spine chakra. The lowest place in your body to which light descends is the base-of-the-spine chakra. That's the Mother flame. It's the fount of life, and that is why we can have a spine that goes to that place and why we can have a body designed as it is designed.

That is the limit of the descent of the Mother. And it's at that level of descent, the level where we have the creative force, that we have to know the how-to—how to create in Matter, how to build our buildings, how to run our schools, how to release our education, how to raise our families, how to teach our children, how to mount the spirals of the path of the spine, the path of the kundalini.

The how-to comes from the Mother, who gives birth to the Christ. And the Christ consciousness that the Mother imparts to her sons and daughters is the *how-to* consciousness. When you become the Christ, the definition of your Christhood is that you have the how-to consciousness. So the impractical disciple doesn't exist. If he's impractical, he's not a disciple—he just thinks he is. The practical building of the community of the Holy Spirit, the practical knowing of what to do when people are hurt or in need and children need us, that's the whole game of the teaching.

And so Maitreya says that's the purpose of religion. Let the soul go up, contact the God Presence, the Christ Self. In that contact the wisdom ray is released, and when you have the wisdom ray then you have the how-to. That's why you're here. That's true for every true religion that the Great White Brotherhood has ever sponsored. The extent to which the religion has lost the how-to message shows its corruption, its penetration by priestcraft, and its perversion. Finally, when you get a religion that no longer tells you how to do anything—how your soul can balance its karma, make its ascension, get back to God, master the material plane, and deal with life and with people—it's not a religion any longer. It's just the husks, just an outer ritual that has become an idolatry.

So you might say that Maitreya has come to restore the how-to of the Mother and of the Cosmic Christ. And here is more how-to:

> The Great White Brotherhood is an organization of the Spirit. It has, through the centuries and the ages, endowed various individuals with power. It has formulated plans and concepts in its sacred conclaves in order to show men *how to* find the pathway back to light. It has established churches, temples, mosques, and sanctuaries.... Many are on the periphery of light, and some are nearer the heart of the sacred fire. But these were ordained for one purpose.
>
> Priestcraft and mankind operating in the realm of greed and selfishness have perverted its purposes. But the eternal

purpose of God cannot be trifled with. Only in human consciousness have men perverted the plan of God. At higher levels it remains inviolate.

So the purpose of religion is for the soul to find the pathway back to light.

The Thread of Contact

Maitreya talks about the day when our concepts will be on television. And that day has come in these past few years with Saint Germain on "The Man Who Would Not Die"[26] and the messenger giving the teachings and the names of the ascended masters. But Maitreya goes a step further and talks about cosmic beings who will

> ... some day speak their directives through these very avenues and channels[.] And then because the subject matter is correct, mankind will be assisted into their eternal freedom.

The paving of the way for the coming of the ascended masters and their stepping through the veil is always through the messenger and through the chelas. *You* on television teaching the teachings is an example of the cosmic beings speaking on television. It's the first stage. It's stage one. It has to come. First people have to be there as the receptacles, the temples of the Brotherhood, then the masters come.

Maitreya talks about the "parent feeling," that we all have parent feelings toward various people. This is of God and that is how you realize your status as a mediator. You only become a mediator because you have been initiated by the Great White Brotherhood and the contact has been restored. Morya calls that restoration the "thread of contact," and you'll see that phrase through his mystical writings. And it's a very important little concept because, first of all, the crystal cord itself has been reduced to a mere thread by the misuse of light. So the crystal cord is your thread of contact to your I AM Presence. Your tie to the Brotherhood is a thread of contact.

Why does he use that term? Because he wants you to visualize a thread, like a silk thread, and he wants you to see yourself as this globule of light, this soul. Here you are suspended in the sea of maya somewhere in the earth.

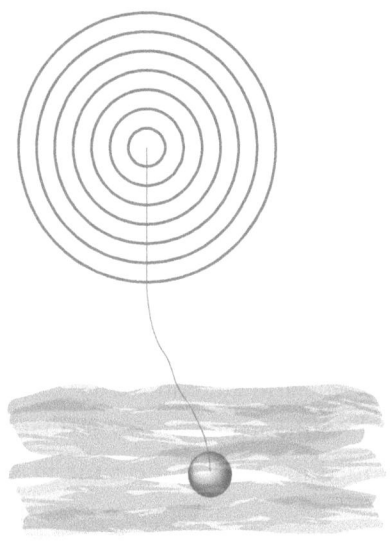

The Thread of Contact

The soul, suspended in a sea of maya, retains its connection to the I AM Presence through the thread of contact, the crystal cord.

FIGURE 3

But you've got a lifeline. The lifeline is to your great I AM Presence, of course. But in the point of the mediatorship, the Great White Brotherhood—in the person of your Christ Self, in the person of the ascended masters—makes the God flame personal to you until you can see God face-to-face.

Now the thing that I learned about the thread of contact, and the reason El Morya uses that term, is the masters want you to know that the thread is easily broken. The thread *can* be broken. It *was* broken. The putting of Adam and Eve as twin flames outside of the Garden of Eden was the breaking of the thread of contact with hierarchy and with the Guru.

Resentment of the Guru

Maitreya gave us a very interesting concept when he said, "Did you think that I had been evolving and taking initiations so that I could come?"[27] And he explained that the reason he had not come before was because of the hatred and resentment of the people of Lemuria that they had been deprived of the light and the power of the guru. They wanted the guru's power, but they did not want to give obedience to the person of the guru.

Southern California is filled with such people today and so is Northern California—the whole coast of Lemuria. And these people have, one and all, come back to this point in time and space, to embodiment now, to meet that Guru Maitreya, to meet the ascended masters, to meet the masters' messengers and their chelas.

Whether messenger, whether chela, you become the instrument of the judgment of those who renounced the guru anywhere from two hundred and fifty thousand years ago to ten thousand years ago. There were people who stormed away and rejected and denounced Maitreya on Mu who have never had a guru since that time. And those people are today being given the opportunity to take the ascended masters' teachings through you, through me, through the tapes, through the lectures, through the books.

Now, knowing that gives me a deep sense of commitment

and responsibility. I don't want to be humanly perfect, but I want to do the best job that I can do to present the teachings in the best possible way to give every soul who's coming to that place and doesn't know it, to give that soul the best possible circumstance, environment, and opportunity to accept the gurus, the ascended masters, and to accept the teaching.

I don't want to bungle it by being a poor example. I don't want to be such a bad example of the ascended masters that nobody is going to believe the teaching because I'm a poor example. And I'm sure you have that very same feeling.

The Standards of Those Who Represent God

When you are a chela of the Great White Brotherhood, your life needs to reflect the qualities and the virtues that people expect. No matter how dense and dark people are, they expect those who are representing God to have certain standards.

I find it very amusing that as I go across the country and I'm interviewed, people always want to know about money. Where do I get my money? What kind of car do I drive? What kind of a house do I live in? Where did I get the money to buy this property in Malibu? One man asked, "Why did you go and buy this expensive real estate in Malibu? How come you didn't go out and buy property in the desert?"

Well, it's a funny psychology in America. Obviously we've had a lot of people in churches and a lot of false gurus who have taken advantage of people, and it is shameful. But the funny thing about it is that this is a capitalist nation. Anybody but someone in a church or someone in religious work can be wealthy, have Cadillacs, have all kinds of cars, have all kinds of luxuries, and they will not be criticized. They will be extolled as the heroes of our culture—those who've made it, those who have really arrived in the success cult. But a person on the religious path somehow has to have absolutely nothing but sandals and a begging bowl, and if he has any more he is suspect.

We have come to teach people about the abundant life. And it is the false teaching of the false gurus, the false hierarchy, and it is their consciousness that the children of God and the emissaries of God have no right to the abundance of God.

You see, the fallen ones want the abundant life for themselves. They have created their pleasure cult and their success cult. It's all right for them to cheat, lie, steal, and make more money than everybody else. But the children of God should be poor, and that will somehow make them spiritual. Well, the ascended masters do not teach that. They expect you to multiply abundance and use it to the glory of God's kingdom.

For Judgment I AM Come

So the judgment here at this point in time and space has been noted by representatives of the Brotherhood and their organizations. I will bring you those various writings from other movements so that you will see that many people have pointed to Southern California in the decade of the eighties as the place of the coming of the mystery school of the Great White Brotherhood and the coming again of Maitreya, of Djwal Kul, of Morya, and of the gurus.

The coming, unfortunately, is always for the judgment. That's why Jesus said, "For judgment I am come."[28] It means that each time there is the presence of the guru-chela relationship, the teacher and the teaching, then all those who have rejected it in the past and therefore been outside of the circle of oneness, outside of Eden, must come to that circle once again, see it for what it is, have their own human rebellion exposed, see the great glory of God, and decide which they will serve.

That is happening. It is happening not only in the quietness and privacy of your own soul but also on a community level, a national level, and an international level. That's the point of the Path: "Choose you this day whom you will serve."[29]

Those souls who rejected the guru broke the thread of contact. And when that thread of contact is broken and it's just a frayed piece, the soul sinks into the deepest levels of the astral plane. It remains for the gurus and their chelas to go on their pilgrimages into the astral plane to rescue those souls.

As deep as the Pacific Ocean is deep are the levels of the astral plane to which the people of this earth have fallen. You can go out into the streets, into the entertainment industry, to the individuals who have their rock groups; to those who are very enmeshed in the depths of a drug culture; or even just to those in a very heavy vibration of greed. These people may look totally normal, well dressed, many times wealthy, many times churchgoers, but the level of the astral plane in which they are abiding is simply unfathomable and not understandable to the child of light.

Those souls are as far removed from the soul who still has the thread of contact as practically the God Star, Sirius, would be from the physical Earth. There is such a vast, vast difference between planes of being on Earth. As you go into the streets and into the cities, you just wouldn't dream how far removed from contact with their God Presence are individuals who have rebelled and continued to rebel and have not valued this thread of contact with hierarchy.

In the initiation of the crucifixion, when Jesus was taken down from the cross and put into the tomb, that was the period when he went into the astral plane. On Friday night and all day

Saturday until Easter morning, he was in the very depths of the astral plane preaching to those souls who had lost the thread of contact with the Cosmic Christ, Maitreya.

The Coming of Maitreya

Lord Maitreya sent Jesus Christ. Jesus Christ is the One Sent to test the people to see whether or not they will do what he said, so that two thousand years later they will be ready for the Guru of the guru, for the Cosmic Christ, Maitreya.

This is two thousand years later, and I have noticed in my personal life and in our entire staff and organization that the initiations and the demands of Lord Maitreya are definitely a step beyond what we have known before. They are definitely very intense and very demanding.

Maitreya demands obedience, and he demands a greater love, a greater self-sacrifice. If you want the relationship to the Lord God who walked and talked with Adam and Eve in the Garden, you can have it. But you need to understand that it's not like what the world says religion is. It's not so easy. It's not so simple. It's the straight and the narrow path that leads to eternal life.[30]

So Maitreya comes. You might observe the event that happened yesterday when you were fasting after you were told not to fast. It was a question of obedience. It was a question of something that really did not matter to me personally. But the masters have set the rule that there should not be fasting on Sunday for this very simple reason: You are all in the figure-eight relationship to me and to the Brotherhood when you are at Summit University. You are taken on, so to speak, as novice chelas. It's not a final initiation. It's not something you can't undo if you decide not to become a chela at some point. But your very presence here puts you in this great figure-eight relationship.

When I stand upon the platform with the body of light to deliver to you on a Sunday morning, the ascended masters do not want me in a figure-eight relationship to an audience that is fasting, especially over a hundred people who are fasting. This is because when you are fasting, you are definitely going into your astral records. Astral records are coming up for transmutation as you physically fast. They're coming out of your physical cells, your colon, your organs. You're flushing out toxins. Those toxins have an odor, they have an astral vibration, and they carry the records of your astral body. Fasting flushes drugs out of your body, and drugs are also an astral vibration—whether drugs that you've used for illnesses or drugs you've taken for psychedelic reasons.

To stand on the platform and deliver a dictation means that in this figure-eight flow, I take on that whole astral consciousness and you take on the light. And the Brotherhood has said that they don't want that happening during a dictation, they don't want an audience of people who are fasting, and they don't want people fasting during conferences, because they want the astral body sealed. They don't want the light that they're going to give to be absorbed by the astral level of your being, which is by definition impure.

They want it sealed because they want the light to flush out the mental body, to restore in you the mind of Christ, and to be anchored in the etheric body. They want you to have a God-conscious control of that assimilation of light. And you don't have that control when you're fasting, because your body is going through that toxic state.

I gave the direction for the fast to conclude on Saturday morning, and we didn't have any further communication. The delay in getting the apple juice resulted in the teaching assistants directing that change of assignment without telling me. So not only was it a disobedience—although certainly not malicious, it certainly was an attempt to do the best they could with the situation—but it was also that I was not informed until I was ready to go on the platform. The adjustment of my vehicles and my bodies to handle that substance was not something that the Brotherhood was going to take on. They didn't think it was necessary for me to do so after this tremendous conference and dealing with the energies of the world.

So the dictation of Maitreya became very, very loud—even though it wasn't spoken. And the loudness of it was, "Take heed, all you staff, all of you who have been here and who've had the teachings of the Brotherhood. The hierarchy in this year with the coming of Maitreya demands fastidiousness to the details of the directions that have already been given, as the staff must set an example for the new chelas."

Training for Direct Contact with God

I don't want you to think that this was a case of disorganization or confusion or miscommunication. It was a very clear example that now, when you get into the real love of the guru-chela relationship, it becomes more important to the Brotherhood that their chelas are completely in alignment through loving obedience than to just stack up one more dictation, one more release of light, one more release of teaching, when the basic teaching is "obedience is better than sacrifice."[31] If we don't learn to obey the outer rules that are given, we won't learn to obey the commands of our I AM Presence and our Christ Self.

So if we don't heed what the messenger has said, God always takes it as an example that if you don't listen to the outer representative, you will not listen to your heart when your heart speaks or to your God Presence when your God Presence speaks. That's why we have initiations in the first place. That's why there are rules in the first place. Rules are just like little hurdles that you make horses go over when you're teaching them to jump—it's training. All it is, is training.

It's not whether the rule is right or wrong or whether the rule makes sense. It's your determination to jump the hurdle and not knock it over. That's the whole point—that the hurdle is not going to get you down because in your human pride you think it's a silly rule. "It's a silly hurdle, so I won't obey that one, because it doesn't make any sense and it's not furthering the path of my soul."

The way that rule is furthering the path of your soul is that you are in form, you are in training, you are used to a universe that is a vast geometric grid of energy, the very mathematics that translates at our level as rules like the Ten Commandments and the commandments of Jesus. And then there are rules that are just necessary in dealing with two hundred people. If you're only dealing with one person, you don't need rules. But when you have two hundred, you have to make rules so that life can function. It's as simple as that.

This is always a test at Summit University, because people say, "Well, the rules are human-made. I'm smarter than the human being that made them, so I won't follow that rule." But you have to see that these rules are hurdles preparing you for the great jump. The great leap is direct contact with Maitreya—eliminating the hurdles, eliminating the intermediary steps.

The goal of the messenger is to get out of the way so that you have a direct contact with God. But God is not going to give you that contact when you are liable to make the karma of disobeying him face-to-face. So he just puts out representatives.

He puts himself out in the person of messenger or board of directors or other people on the staff and says, "Ok, follow them for a while and let's see how you do. Let's see how you come to grips with your own inner consciousness."

God Values Free Will

> I, Maitreya, command it, unfurling my banner that this golden age shall *be* because the Eternal has spoken it, and He shall not fail. . . .
>
> Be about your Father's business, and you shall galvanize this age.

So there's the command. Maitreya has unfurled the banner, the Eternal has spoken it, he shall not fail, you shall galvanize the age. God will not fail—right to here [at the upper etheric level]. And God is really not concerned about a golden age [from the lower etheric to the physical] in the sense that he will not bring in that golden age just for the sake of proving that his Word is right and that his Word does not fail. God would rather sink a continent to chastise one chela than create a golden age contrary to the free will of the individual.

God wants us to have the ultimate experience and experimentation with our individual free will. He wants us to know what we do to ourselves when we destroy ourselves with nuclear weapons or anything else. He wants us to come to learn everything there is to learn about being God in this octave. He has no attachment to a golden age *per se*. God is unattached. He is desireless. He has one desire—for you to become God. But he will not impose that desire upon you. He will give you the opportunity to choose to fulfill his desire.

People cannot understand why God lets suffering happen, why accidents and problems happen. God allows calamity and cataclysm because he values the life of your soul and the integrity of his commitment to you, his covenant of free will, more than he values the end result. In Buddhist teaching, this is called *non-attachment to the fruit of action.* God is more interested in the *ritual* of life itself as you live it than he is in the final outcome.

If God were more interested in the final outcome, he would have created differently. He would have made a perfect physical universe with perfect people. The only way you can get perfect people is by creating robots. Then the thread of contact becomes not that which gives life to a free and independent monad. Then the thread of contact is the string of a puppeteer—and you are the puppet, and you do exactly what the puppeteer-god says. If God were attached to a golden age and to human or physical perfection, the only way and the easiest way he could have gotten it was to deny you free will and just make it all happen in his little stage set.

And, of course, God himself would have been extremely bored in such an exercise, just as you would be bored, just as boredom is the very vibration that is the death of souls in a communist or socialist state—because everything is done for them. It's total boredom. What's there to live for? We live because we have options, choices. And choices are creativity and ingenuity. They're exciting. We never know what's around the corner, because we have free will.

Where Is the Golden Age?

What you need to realize is that the only thing that is final and secure is the golden age to this point [the upper etheric plane]. If you lead a good life and you have good light in your aura, each time you pass from the screen of life you go to the etheric cities and temples of light. There are fourteen etheric cities around the etheric plane, over the oceans and the deserts of the earth. And they are golden-age cities.

When we go there and live among the angels and the ascended masters between embodiments, we have renewed in our etheric body the memory of what a golden age is. Then we take embodiment and we try to improve our society. We have the very immediate memory of perfection, God's perfection, and that's why we have hope. That's why little children are so full of hope and the sense that they can do anything and they can change to world.

And we seem to retain that sense through about the age of twenty-five or twenty-six. And most people then get married, have a family, and get very much into the economics of maintaining that family. Then they get very greedy about maintaining it at a status quo. The more money they make, the more money they spend, the more money they want, and the higher the level they want to live in. So our great idealism begins to flounder at the point when we start wanting the things of this world.

But up to that point, when we're independent and free and, hopefully, if it has not been indoctrinated out of us, we do have the memory of these etheric cities. And they are clearly the patterns and the inner blueprints of what is intended to be built in our cities.

Washington, D.C., is one of the greatest cities in the world for outpicturing the alabaster cities of light of the etheric retreats. And that is by the grace of Saint Germain and George Washington and those who lowered that matrix. Its plan goes back to the great cities of light that were in the Amazon basin in the great golden age of South America. It has all of the buildings, of course, in the theme of white, and if you eliminate the kind of buildings that have been built for greed, for money, and for expediency and look at the original structures, you will see something very much like what you have known in the etheric temples. That was Saint Germain's and Godfre's dream for America.

The Gurus Won't Let Go

The thread of contact is broken by rebellion and disobedience. But you know, it's not even broken by that, because the gurus love us so much that they will tolerate our little rebellions and our little disobediences and they still don't let go. But if you multiply a single rebellion a thousand times, what does it equal? It equals rejection of the person of Christ incarnate in the guru.

Ultimately the breaking of the thread of contact is by your denial that Jesus Christ is come in the flesh, that God has made himself incarnate in his avatars and ultimately in your flesh. There's no way that you can say, "God is in me but he's not in the guru." It's simply not logical. It's not geometry. If you say God is where you are but you deny him in Gautama Buddha or Jesus Christ, then you have made your carnal mind a god.

So the order of hierarchy is that you accept God incarnate. And when you effectively deny God incarnate through continual rebellion and continual disobedience to the teachings, to the commandments, and to the person of the ascended masters, then there comes a moment when the thread is broken.

I dealt with an individual in the past year who had been a chela with us as messengers for perhaps six or seven or eight years. And a number of years ago he decided to go and make his way in the world. This was based on greed for money, pride of person, and the desire for name and fame. But even that did not break the thread of contact. So he went forth, he sought his way in the world, and many events intervened.

He was given an opportunity to serve again, did serve, and was disobedient to the rules and the disciplines of our retreat. But even *that* did not break the thread. But one day, when there had been a succession of opportunities and a succession of rebellions—and these could be counted in the hundreds over a long period of time—the Darjeeling Council made a decision. Godfre conveyed that decision to me and said that I should go and dismiss this person from the Brotherhood's service within this organization, which I went and I did.

In the course of that dismissal, I began to read to the individual from the writings of the dialogues of Saint Catherine of Siena,[32] which are the communications of God the Father to her soul, which she has written down and which we have in paperback form. It's published under the auspices of the Catholic Church. These dialogues explain very clearly that the most important relationship of the soul is to the person of Jesus Christ and that all that is done for the love of Jesus Christ as the Guru and for the love of God counts for grace and accrues as grace. And all else that is done for other motives does not count for grace and does not increase the soul's attainment of salvation.

So it came down to, once again, the opportunity to reestablish the guru-chela relationship. The individual denied the relationship. He expressed the desire for it in terms of wanting the light, but expressed that he would under no circumstances place himself in the position to be disciplined as a chela, but desired again to make his way in the world.

After all of this opportunity—and the fact that God does not simply chop off the thread of contact with the initial rebellion— after all of this, what it came down to in that meeting was that the individual denied the ascended masters in the person of their messenger, the One Sent, denied the Path, and said, "I will do what I will do. I will serve God independently of the teachings, independently of the personal representation of the Brotherhood to me."

You Can't Have Two Identities at Once

That personal representation is the opportunity for the pummeling and the teaching and the training of a soul. In fact, its whole purpose is that the guru holding the Electronic Presence over that soul enables him to reject his own carnal mind, his own pride, and his own rebellion. What really happens in that process is that the guru supplies the identity of the Christ to which the chela has not attained until the chela has slain the dragon of his own carnal mind and therefore can rise into the identity of the Christ.

You can't have two identities at once. Either you are the Christ or you have enthroned the carnal mind. If you've enthroned the carnal mind, you can't know yourself as Christ until this carnal mind is dethroned. While you're dethroning it, the moment you slay it, it's like killing the only identity you have. If the only identity you have is your human ego and it has to be slain, then someone has to hold your hand at that moment and sustain the life, sustain the consciousness of the Christ with you and for you. The *moment* you slay the beast and it is gone, your Christ Self comes into alignment and you gain your new identity.

But there's that split second when you are leaning utterly upon the One Sent in the person of the guru, who is one with your Christ Self. So that is the point of the relationship of trust. That is where the trust is required, because when you are slaying that carnal mind, you lose the ability to know the difference between the carnal mind and the Christ mind. The carnal mind is so loud in declaring itself to the living Christ within you, that unless you can lean upon the arm of the Lord, unless you have that one to lean upon, you'll go mad. There is a madness and an insanity.

You see that in Idi Amin in Uganda, in Africa.[33] You see the madness, the insanity of the carnal mind that has enthroned itself as the Christ and has gotten the soul to believe it is the Christ, who can murder and destroy and completely wreck a nation. When the initiation and opportunity came for the slaying of the carnal mind, the individual did not have the person of the Christ and did not assent to the guru-chela relationship in order for the process to take place.

"Whom the gods would destroy they first make mad."[34] The gods are the fallen ones who have enthroned the carnal mind in themselves. They're all insane by that very act of having enthroned the carnal mind.

So not just in rebellion, not just in disobedience—which can be considered sometimes the foibles of the child of God that we all fall into now and then—is the thread cut. But the ultimate act that really destroys the existence of the guru for that person for all intents and purposes is the final act of denying that the Word is made flesh, denying that the ascended masters are here, that they are speaking, and denying their teaching. That's a very serious moment. That moment came to this individual after opportunity had been given for literally tens of thousands of years to restore the state of grace. Grace is when you have the thread of contact, the restoration of the state of grace.

The Universal Chain of Being

I walked out of that meeting after having dismissed this individual, and I looked up into the sky and saw the ritual taking place of the breaking of the thread of contact. And it is a ritual. It is never taken lightly. I must emphasize that if you are of a pure heart and a sincere heart, God will never break that tie because you've made a mistake. Remember that. He will break the tie because you blaspheme the name of his Son in your Christ Self and in the Christ Self of the messenger and of the ascended masters.

When you look at the thread of contact, it is shown as a great chain of light. It is a scintillating chain of light—just the way you'd look at a link chain, one link after the other. But the links are of light and every link of the chain is a person, or a *pure-son*, of God, an ascended master and his chela. Everyone in earth and in heaven who is a part of the Great White Brotherhood is a link in what is called the universal chain of being. And you earn the right to remain a link in this great chain because you are obedient to the next link, who happens to be your guru of the hour.

So the ceremony that took place was that the hands of God came down and undid one link, took out the link, and put the other two back together. It's the removal of the individual as a link in the chain of being. It is a ritual, and it does not come without the consultation with the individual's Christ Self, without review before the Lords of Karma, and without absolutely ample opportunity for the individual to understand what is at stake both on the inner and the outer planes. So that has happened. That's not the only time it has happened. It has happened before. It keeps on happening over the centuries.

That is essentially what happened when Lucifer was cast out of heaven. His link in the chain of universal being was removed. Why does God do that? Because if he allowed the one who rebelled against Being itself, against the order of hierarchy itself, to remain in the chain, the chain would be contaminated. God would allow himself to be destroyed. So he doesn't do that.

This is why I say that the guru-chela relationship is the only real existence, it's the only reality. Outside of it, you are not a part of the universal chain of cosmic beings, angelic hosts, and so forth.

Shattering the Forgetfulness

Maitreya came in that dictation to souls who on the inner plane were a part of that chain and are a part of that chain. But he said that you have forgotten how to invoke the angelic hosts. You have forgotten, and your calls have fallen into disuse. The Great White Brotherhood would restore to you the power that is able to consume your fears, restore to you communion with the saints and communion with the angelic hosts.

So it's the restoration of the greatest miracle of the age—your being when that being utters the name I AM. When you utter the name I AM, then you are a conscious link in the chain of being.

Now Sanat Kumara, the Ancient of Days, and the Brotherhood have told us we have had a great light and a great association in the past and that our biggest problem today is that we have forgotten who we are, of whom we are a part in this vast universal order of being, and how to make use of the fact that we are a part of that chain, how to make the calls—the how-to teaching. And so that is the basic purpose of the hour for this Church, this religion, this movement, and this manifestation, this representation of the Cosmic Christ.

This dictation is a great way to start this quarter of Summit University. I'm very grateful to have heard it with you, and we will replay that little section in closing:

> It is you, blessed ones, who have somewhat failed. But it need not continue to be so, for the purpose of all religion, the purpose of all life, is to manifest its eternal destiny.
>
> I would turn the coin upon the other side. I would show you not the image of Caesar, ***but the image of God!***
>
> The image of God is so beautiful it defies a worded description.

That much energy was used by the guru to defeat the carnal mind. Your carnal mind is your image of Caesar. And the image of God comes tumbling down into your soul because Maitreya released a ray to shatter that forcefield of the carnal mind. It's a karate technique of light. Because it comes in suddenly, the fallen ones don't expect it. The demons who are standing by watching this release of light don't expect it. The chelas don't expect it. The soul of the chela doesn't expect it.

That's the great talent of all the gurus that you will ever read about. Their talent is their timing and their sense of the unexpected. It catches you completely off guard so that it does not pass through your mental mind or your reasoning mind. It reaches you independently of your mind, and that is precisely the purpose. It wants to unseat your dependence upon the mere mental body.

It's a great, great danger to depend only upon the reasoning mind to decide what to do with your life and what to do from moment to moment. There is a higher mind—a *higher* mind. That thrust of light bypassed the reasoning mind and got right into your soul and released your response of love that went back to God again, independent of your reasoning mind. It all happens like a clap of thunder. It's very, very exciting.

Now that is the conclusion of our message today. And I would recommend that you listen to this dictation now again from start to finish and take your final notes on it. You will have a test on just this dictation and what I have said about it on Friday. So I think you can put the whole thing together by listening to it once more. Your notes will then be complete. You should only have to read your notes and be ready to come in and get at least ninety percent of the questions correct. We're not ever going to ask you anything that's not self-contained in the message. But it is important that you take notes.

I myself could not come to Summit University and take one of those tests without studying. It's just impossible. There are too many fine points of the Law. If I were going to take the quiz on Friday, I would have to study for it. I would have to go back, read my notes, and see what was covered. It doesn't matter whether you're a guru or a chela or a master or not quite a master—the point is that God's laws must be studied. We all have to study the Word.

> *In the name of the light of God that never fails, I call for the eternal Word from the heart of the Father, the Son, and of the Holy Spirit, from the heart of the Mother. Let the Word descend now from the great I AM Presence of each one as the personal Christ of each one.*
>
> *By thy flame, O Lord Maitreya, by thy flame, O Lanello, impart that essence of thy Word, that thy Word be made flesh in these beloved chelas, O God. In the name of the entire Spirit of the Great White Brotherhood and the cause to which we are dedicated, in the name of the Ancient of Days, Amen.*

January 8, 1979

CHAPTER TWO

A Transfer of Power

We'll begin right away with the second dictation of beloved Lord Maitreya. It was given July 1, 1961, which was our Fourth of July conference in Washington, D.C. So that's a seventeen-year cycle from last July. It will be an eighteen-year cycle from this July.

LORD MAITREYA
July 1, 1961

The Christ Consciousness

Friends of eternal love, from the beginning of all time, from the beginning of the idea of creation in the mind of God, is an eternal reality woven into the fabric of individual lifestreams. It is too much a part of life to be separated. And no one has the power, neither "height, nor depth, nor any other creature,"[1] to separate mankind from the great power and beauty of divine love, which, like a mantle of ascended Christ perfection, rests upon the individual consciousness of each lifestream.

The purity of the new babe may be sullied by wandering in the human consciousness. But when it enters into the consciousness of its own immortal purity once again, it manifests that purity and expression which it did in its original pristine, pure state.

I exalt in you today—even I, Maitreya—the consciousness of the Divine One. Solicitude for purity of consciousness is to adore God within your heart.

Blessed ones from among mankind destined to be immortal, you come today into this place expecting perhaps to hear words of great power. The greatest word of power that has ever been uttered was spoken into your consciousness with the framework of your being when the voice of God in you spoke and said, "Behold, I AM!"

This being, which is the fiber of you, this existence of immortality, did not begin to be yesterday, nor shall it cease to be today, nor shall it cease to be forever. Anchor in yourself, therefore, a sense of the immortal consciousness of God and the immortal consciousness of love.

When the Master Jesus wandered upon the hillsides of Judaea outpicturing the magnificence of that which we at inner levels poured through his life consciousness, he drew the multitudes to him and he broke the bread of life. And he passed the Sacred Eucharist of God among mankind. Truly the night of the Passover—as he said to those that were assembled, "Take, eat; this is my body"[2]—they were unaware of the full beauty or the full power or the great meaning underlying those words.

So today, blessed ones, I speak to you as to babes in the Christ consciousness. I tell you, of a truth, there are but few of you that are fully aware of the meaning of the bread of heaven that comes down and manifests as your life.[3] So caught up is the consciousness of mankind by the consciousness of the mundane and the superficialities of life, that it only momentarily glimpses the beauties of the Christ consciousness. And this is pitiful, but remediable.

The all-enfolding, all-encompassing love of God, which I now pour around you with the radiance of my heart, is able to seal in you that mantle of God perfection and so illumine the consciousness that is you, that you shall manifest and outpicture that which we already are.

We beckon just beyond the veil, calling you with the great tones of spiritual inspiration to come into our consciousness and abide. The voices of the world, crying in the wilderness[4] of the world, call also. It is up to you, blessed ones, to make the decision as to whom you shall listen and to whom you shall hearken.

This is a great and a magnificent land conceived by your beloved Saint Germain and endowed with the great spirit of Liberty. Paul, the Venetian master, radiated so much love to America in the past and continues to do so.

But, blessed ones, America is destined to be an ascended master nation, a nation flooded with the beauty of God. If this destiny that America was intended to outpicture is to manifest here, it will be because individual lifestreams have put their shoulders to the wheel—not the wheel of selfishness and the wheel of selfish endeavor, not the mechanistic wheel that merely turns in the marts of commerce, but the wheel of divine consciousness that in its turning brings forth a more beautiful civilization, that determines to outpicture in each succeeding generation a more noble visage than the past.

I come to you today in the enfolding mantle of Cosmic Christ light. And I come to you today with the form and consciousness of the Buddha. I am (for purposes of those among you who do not see me) standing just approximately four feet behind our messenger, and I am above in the atmosphere about three feet above his head.

I am speaking to you today with arms of radiant light. I am pouring out my light rays through his consciousness and into your consciousness that you might absorb these light rays and feel the healing love that I am bringing to you, that you may be blessed with the infinite mantle of Christ protection and that you may feel that love which has never begun to be—which always was—which from the beginning is identified with the creation, for it existed long before the creation was even conceived in the mind and heart of God.

Blessed and beloved ones, hearken now as I speak to you —but hearken, I say, as your Holy Christ Self speaks to you. During those moments when you are not so privileged to sit at our feet and hear directly from us, your own Holy Christ Self is speaking to your heart.

Your Holy Christ Self, guided by the great masterful light rays from your own God Presence, floods through your consciousness that sense of direction that tells you, "This is the way, walk ye in it"; and your teacher, therefore, is not removed into the corner,[5] but is directly hovering over you in consciousness, pouring out and flooding to you daily— if you will listen and if you will hear it—the voice of God, the direction of God, the wisdom of God, the strength of God, and the love of God.

What you shall do with this divine energy, blessed ones, is determined by your own consciousness. What you shall do with it is determined by your acceptance of its pressures of light. It is a benign pressure. It does not come, however, to take away your freedom of will or your freedom of expression. It comes to bring you the great will of God and the freedom to express the fullness of that same God.

I AM the full expression of the radiance of God!
I AM the full expression of the power and glory of God!
I AM the full expression of the kingdom of God!

For now I AM expanding the consciousness of light here, and I AM increasing the strength of the great stream of light that comes from the power of my office!

I AM the Buddha, and therefore I enfold you today in

the great "budding divinity" that shines over your form, that desires to change your form into those golden light rays that shall make you outpicture that which God intends—not which humans intend, but that which the Father intended from the Beginning.

Blessed ones, when the great laws of God are thoroughly understood by you, then the veil of mystery is removed, and the clarity with which you behold the face of your Holy Christ Self will determine how you will behold the face of your God Presence. And when you are able to see the face of your God Presence in its own fullness of glory, you will *be* that glory.

Ladies and gentlemen, I salute you today as ladies and gentlemen of heaven. You are intended to sit in heavenly places in the ascended Jesus Christ consciousness. You are intended to be a part of the vanguard of that movement of light which should sweep the earth and bring to all mankind the freedom to express this Christ, the freedom to express the ascended masters' way of life, the freedom to express God-beauty all ways at all times.

Open, therefore, your hearts today. Open the doorway to your own budding divinity. Cease to look upon mortal aims, and consider the immortal aims of your existence. These are like a great shepherd. These aims will care for you. These aims will care for your earthly endeavors. These aims will look after you.

I say to you, do you think, blessed ones, that it is necessary for you to take thought for tomorrow as to what you shall do or be? Is it not truly possible for the Father, for the Christ in you, to take that thought for you? For indeed, which of you could change your stature by thought?[6] And yet it has been done. Blessed and beloved ones, it is done by the Father.

When the immaculate image of God, the immaculate thought of God, is flashed forth in living letters of fire, it is a fiat of heaven eternal, and there is no power on earth or heaven or elsewhere that can alter or change the divine consciousness.

Enter, therefore, into this Christ consciousness and *know* that it is that consciousness which shall be the compulsion of change within you, which shall *compel* the answer of victory, which shall *alter* your thought about yourself, and shall give you *the freedom to express your immortal God perfection made manifest! made manifest! made manifest!*

I say to you today that never in all eternity can you outpicture the Christ consciousness by merely doing it in the human level. It must come from an invocation of your conscious attunement with your God Presence and your Holy Christ Self.

And you must actually open your consciousness until the floodgates and the flood tides of immortal life have so directed their energies through your conscious thinking form and your being, that you *are* that which you desire to become—that you are a manifestation of God, that you are *aware* that you are a manifestation of God, that you *desire* to be a manifestation of God, that you *determine* that the fires of immortality shall flame upon the altars of your being, and that those altars shall be as God intended—altars to alter the human consciousness and direct it to its highest exalted state wherein the sacred fire flaming there becomes the consciousness of God in full manifest expression; and you are able to see not only the face of your Presence, but every angelic being, every cosmic being, every ascended master, every deva, and are able to see into the heart of all Matter, are able to control matter and energy and be masters not only of your own world, but also of the world of material form and substance.

I, Maitreya, say to you today that the ascended masters, in the great deliberations and the councils of the Great White Brotherhood, have determined that human tyranny has too long held sway over the mass mind. Therefore we have asked for a great petition whereby the student body today shall be given that which is known as the full power of the ten thousand-times-ten thousand. From this day henceforward, every decree that you utter shall be increased by the power of the ten thousand-times-ten thousand!

I, Maitreya, declare that those who give decrees from this day forward shall be creating a tremendous, impelling, swiftly moving acceleration that shall sweep through the earthly consciousness of mankind and compel this earth free.

It is determined by the Great Cosmic Law that this earth shall not submit to the tyranny of human consciousness—which, in itself, while it is intelligent substance to a degree, is not ascended master discriminating intelligence. Therefore, it has *no* power! It has *no* power! It has *no* power! And I say that you must cut yourself free from that consciousness by a conscious, joyful entering in to our thought by entering in to the thought of God about you.

You are thought of by God. Each and every lifestream here is a part of God. Each of you has a doorway to enter in to God's consciousness. Each of you can expand the flame of the sacred fire on the altar of your own being. And no other lifestream can do it for you. No ascended master can do it for you. No one can do it for you, in the final analysis, but your own God Presence and Holy Christ Self.

We can and we *do* give you our love! We can and we *do* give you our energy! We can and we *do* give you our strength! And we guide you and we direct you and we deliberate in our councils to bring to the earth and all of its environs the great enfolding love of the infinite Cosmic Christ intelligence and the All-Father-Mother God.

But, blessed and beloved ones, it is up to individuals to determine that they shall be *one* with God, *one* with life, *one* with beauty, *one* with the Buddha, *one* with the Buddha of their own unfolding divinity, *one* with the mantrams of the Spirit—until they in God-victory are a part of God forevermore.

I thank you. I seal you with the smile of the eternal radiance of heaven.

O blessed and beloved ones of the Freedom class in Washington, thank you for coming. Thank you for hearing my words. I give you God-gratitude in the name of heaven.

Go forth, then, this day to consciously exist as children of the light to expand the light as we do. And then no power in heaven and earth shall cause you to swerve from the Path.

The demons shall tremble when you speak. And light shall go before your path like a shaft of blazing infinite fire. As Moses walked through the wilderness, you shall pass unscathed through human consciousness, and there shall come near you nothing that can hurt or destroy in all the holy mountain of God-illumination.[7]

Peace to you from the Summit—Cosmic Christ peace from your own God Presence, your Holy Christ Self, and from the consciousness of the Buddha eternal within you all.

I thank you. Good afternoon.

This dictation was given at the first conference that I attended, and there were many dictations given at that conference—so many that I was simply astounded at the endurance of the messenger Mark Prophet, and also just at the amazing light and the amazing versatility of his being.

Now, I would like you to tell me about the initiations of this dictation.

The Initiation of the Dictation

Student: I think the most important initiation or dispensation was the power of the ten thousand-times-ten thousand because that really increased the momentum of the decrees.

Student: I think the exaltation of divine consciousness.

Student: I think the main thing was that he wants us to enter in to an adoration of God and to be really aware of the fact that we have a God Presence and a Christ Self, to make contact with them, and that in doing that it's by adoring God in our hearts, "Enter into a sense of an adoration of God in your heart." And Jesus had that same type of adoration, that same love, and he had mastered that love that Maitreya wants us to outpicture.

Student: I believe the initiation was the giving to us of the supreme word of power, which is I AM.

ECP: Stating that God spoke this within our being?

Student: Right.

ECP: It's descriptive. He says that God spoke that in your being. You have to be aware of what is simply a reciting of facts or history and what is a present initiation. He simply is telling us that God spoke that into our being. It's not an initiation of the dictation.

Student: He said to go forth this day and consciously exist as children of light.

ECP: He said we should be a part of God forevermore.

Student: Cease to look at mortal aims and instead take on immortal aims.

ECP: Is that an initiation? We're looking for the key initiation of the dictation, not picking points out of it. What was his initiation?

Why don't you tell me what the initiation was from the first dictation?

Another Student: The word for the initiation was *restoration*.

ECP: The restoration of contact with the Great White Brotherhood. That we had lost the contact with the Great White Brotherhood. He came to restore that contact.

Ascended master concepts are very, very precise. They are not nebulous, you know. They are precise. They can be remembered and they can be studied. But they are at a very high plane, the etheric plane. The reason they become nebulous is that the effluvia in your own consciousness, your own aura, makes things that are highly vibrating look like they would look if you needed glasses and didn't have them on. You look across the way and you can't see anything.

So, defining the points is important. Maitreya came to restore the thread of contact with the Great White Brotherhood. And I had that worded especially because there were three points of contact. Does anybody remember the exact wording?

Student: He said it was a restoration of communion with the saints, and also with that we got the ministrations of angelic beings.

ECP: And wasn't restoration of power in there also?

Now the second one, then, has an initiation. An initiation is a conferment of light. Every master comes to confer light. He makes a lot of statements and says a lot of words in the process, but somewhere among those statements and those words he has a way of telling you what he is most concerned with, what is his greatest emphasis, and what he is doing for you.

Student: I think he mentioned that each person has a doorway, a certain doorway he has to walk through. He came to confer that wisdom, I guess, the knowledge that each of us has their own path. No one can do it for you. No one can . . .

ECP: No one can do *what* for you?

Student: Make you walk through the door.

ECP: *What* doorway?

Student: The doorway of consciousness.

ECP: *What* consciousness?

Student: The consciousness of God.

ECP: No, he named it!

Student: The divine consciousness of the Father.

ECP: No, he didn't say that. What did he say exactly?

Student: I think he said he came to show us the Christ Self when he says that I see the clarity of your Holy Christ Self and then you see your Father.

ECP: First of all, he describes how he's hovering over Mark—four feet behind, three feet above. Then he says that's how your Christ Self hovers over you. But the most important thing he is saying is that *you must make contact* with your personal Christ Self, your Holy Christ Self and your I AM Presence. *No one* can do it for you. *No* ascended master can do it for you. *You* have to do it!

But he gave us an assistance to do it, and the assistance that he gives us is the conferment, or the initiation. Do you have the statement of his assistance?

Student: It was the initiation of an increment of light to give us the determination to be that Christ consciousness.

ECP: I'll read it to you.

> **I AM the full expression of the radiance of God!**
> **I AM the full expression of the power and glory of God!**
> **I AM the full expression of the kingdom of God!**
> **For now I AM expanding the consciousness of light here, and I AM increasing the strength of the great stream of light that comes from the power of my office.**

The power of his office—Maitreya, Initiator, is increasing the great stream of light.

> I AM the Buddha, and therefore I enfold you today in the great "budding divinity" that shines over your form, that desires to change your form into those golden light rays that

shall make you outpicture that which God intends—not which the human intends, but that which the Father intended from the Beginning.

That's why someone over here said "Father."

Blessed ones, when the great laws of God are thoroughly understood by you, then the veil of mystery is removed, and the clarity with which you behold the face of your Holy Christ Self will determine how you will behold the face of your God Presence. And when you are able to see the face of your God Presence in its own fullness of glory, you will *be* that glory.

The initiation, then, was that transfer of "the power of my office," of a "great stream of light," and he denotes which level, which person of his office that he is transferring, because the very next sentence says, "I AM the Buddha, and therefore I enfold you today in the great 'budding divinity' that shines over your form." So his initiation is to give you the light of the Christ Self of you that pertains to the person of the Buddha—hence the crown chakra; the Buddha is always the crown chakra—shining over you.

As Maitreya is radiating over Mark Prophet, he is telling you now that he is shining over you as the Buddha, enfolding you "in the great 'budding divinity' that shines over your form," which of course is part of your Christ Self. So therefore, he says, "Open, therefore, your hearts today." *Therefore* means "as consequence of." As consequence of my coming, my standing over you, my transferring this light, I want you to open the door, open your hearts, "open the doorway to your own budding divinity."

Now the heart is the initiation of Lord Maitreya as well as the head. The Buddha, the balance of mind and heart, is the balance of Alpha and Omega. We think of the Buddha as the crown chakra and the Christ as the heart chakra, but you must of course realize that they each have equal attainment in both chakras. The point is that each one outpictures a different path so that those of a different leaning can follow that one. But if you're going to follow Jesus Christ, you're going to be following, in actuality, one who attained to the Buddha. And if you're going to follow Gautama Buddha, you will be following the Christed One.

A Thread of Contact to Everyone on Earth

As you know, Gautama Buddha holds the threefold flame of life for the evolutions of earth at Shamballa. Sanat Kumara came because the hearts of men were hardened. Their hearts were covered over, and they no longer gave adoration to the threefold flame of life. The earth was about to be destroyed because no one was giving adoration to the threefold flame. So Sanat Kumara came, the Ancient of Days, and he set up his retreat of the threefold flame, of the heart chakra, for the earth—Shamballa, the heart chakra of the earth.

And from the heart of the Buddha, from the heart of the Ancient of Days, Sanat Kumara sent a thread, and he directed that same thread of contact to everyone evolving upon earth. Because they gave no adoration to their heart, Sanat Kumara gave the adoration himself to the heart of God. And by his adoration, he transferred that adoration through the thread of contact. In other words, he transferred the flame, or you might say the oil, to keep the lamp burning.

So everyone's heart flame on earth today is sustained by the hierarch who holds the office of the Ancient of Days. The Ancient of Days took his leave of earth and transferred that office to Gautama Buddha on January 1, 1956. Sanat Kumara had maintained that office, of course, for thousands of years.

Sanat Kumara, the Ancient of Days, graduated. He became Regent of the World. And Gautama Buddha became the Lord of the World. And the next initiate under Gautama Buddha is Lord Maitreya. So Lord Maitreya is known as the Planetary Buddha, the Cosmic Christ. The initiation he is giving, then, is to increase your own attunement with your own Christ Self and I AM Presence so that you can open the heart and begin to keep the threefold flame of life, the budding divinity of yourself, an open door for all the children of God.

If you just meditate upon the concept of Gautama Buddha extending a thread from his heart to every heart on earth, and by that thread life is sustained, it's just very, very exciting as a concept. And so each time an individual begins to keep his own flame of life by his adoration, it's like a mother giving birth to a child. When the child is born, the umbilical cord is cut and the child then is acting on its own, independent of the mother's lifestream. So we're all on the umbilical cord of Gautama Buddha from heart to heart. And that is one of the services of the Brotherhood. And obviously without that service, there would not be life.

Why is that necessary? It is because people do not give enough adoration themselves to their I AM Presence and Christ Self. They do not give glory and praise daily to God by any name. And to daily keep that flame burning, praise must be given. Praise is the means of drawing energy from your causal body down to the heart chakra that provides the energy for it to burn.

The earth was to be canceled out because no one was giving adoration. There wasn't one person left giving adoration to the threefold flame. So Sanat Kumara said, "I will come; I will be that person. And I will make my adoration count for everyone on earth." So the first and most important initiation was to reestablish contact with the Great White Brotherhood, with the heavenly hosts.

The Second Initiation: Contact with Your I AM Presence and Christ Self

The second initiation was to establish contact with your I AM Presence and Christ Self. Who can tell me why it was more important to first establish contact with the Great White Brotherhood?

Student: The reason that we had restoration was so that the ascended masters could show us how to establish contact with their I AM Presence.

ECP: *How* to establish contact—that is a very important reason. They first established the contact to the Brotherhood so that we would be in contact with our teachers, who would show us how to make contact with our I AM Presence and Christ Self. What is the next reason?

Student: I think it's that we have to recognize the divinity in them before we can see it in ourselves.

ECP: That's an important reason, but it's not the one I want yet.

Student: I think it's to establish the guru-chela relationship, the teacher and the student.

ECP: Yes, we needed the guru-chela relationship, but *why* did we need it?

Student: Mother, because they had already attained it.

ECP: They had already attained it, that's true.

Student: So the only way we could see it is by seeing it in them.

Student: I think to make it possible for us to attain Christhood.

ECP: Yes, it is to make it possible. I'll make it simple and state it. It's not that I am trying to hold you in suspense; I am trying to help your own thinking process. The point is that at this particular conference—a hundred or more people were there, 150 people at the most—they were told and given the dispensation of the power of Maitreya's office, and they were bidden to make contact with their Christ Self and their I AM Presence. The question is, how many people who went to that conference, do you think, when they walked out of the room actually made the contact?

The reason that they gave us contact with the Great White Brotherhood first is that we were like people drowning in the astral sea. When somebody's drowning, you don't toss them a cake or a steak or a game or a radio. You toss them a line. So the Great White Brotherhood tossed us a line to save our souls. Then when they got us hauled in on the ship and all dried, then they began to teach us how they throw out a line and how they save our soul.

It's like giving a drowning man the theory on how you're going to save him but not saving him. And so the point is that if we had been given the other initiation, basically we would not have known how to do it. But it's not the know-how. It's the density and momentum of our own human consciousness.

Why We Have the Guru

The whole explanation as to why we have the guru is this: Up here is your great I AM Presence, here is your great Christ Self, and down here is you standing and invoking your Christ Self. But over thousands of years of building up layers of human creation, there is just rock, like mountains, between you and your Christ Self.

We record this density by showing an electronic belt in the lower portion of your aura, but there is a vast layer of density between the lower self and the Christ Self. And the more karma they have and the more dense and the more ego-centered people are, the more mountains they have between their heart flame and their Christ Self.

That means that the knowledge of God, the knowledge of Christ, has never been sufficient—not in thousands of years—for people to suddenly see Christ, to see God face-to-face, and to have the unimpeded flow of the light come forth. So the substance between the soul and the Christ Self takes work. It takes violet flame. It takes service. It takes balancing of karma. It takes meeting every bit of that energy. In the meantime, the soul has to survive. The threefold flame has to keep beating.

Now despite all of this substance, coming from your I AM Presence through your Christ Self there is this tiny, little thread, and that thread keeps enough energy going to maintain a biological existence. It sustains the physical vehicles so that people can be born and evolve and make choices to use energy, to study, and so forth. It's not an overabundance. The size of the crystal cord was reduced in the judgment. The crystal cord used to be the size of the tube of light. People had unlimited power, unlimited wisdom, unlimited love. When they began to abuse it, it was reduced.

When it was reduced down to that thread, that is when all we were able to do was to live a short life span and basically procreate and study a little bit and supposedly become masters in some field of endeavor (but very much surface masters) and then we go on our way. We really don't get to accomplish too much in a life span because of the reduction of the crystal cord. So we have embodied many, many more times than was necessary in the original divine plan. So with the dissolution of the earth, even this thread was going to be withdrawn because no one was giving adoration to even this much.

Here is the point of placing this heart in contact with the Great White Brotherhood. The hosts of heaven, the hosts of the LORD are assembled by the thousands and the millions.

When Maitreya reestablished the thread of contact, the restoration that we had in dictation number one, that restoration bypasses all of your human creation and puts your heart directly in contact with the Great White Brotherhood as many, many ascended masters and cosmic beings. It bypasses the layers of density of the human consciousness. You might say it bypasses it, goes around and up through your Christ Self and over to the ascended masters. So that's the point of the guru. The guru has become that God Presence and that God consciousness.

Whether the guru is ascended or unascended, he is supplying his momentum of God consciousness as a transfer of energy to sustain the chela on the path of finding his own God consciousness, which Lord Maitreya says in this dictation that no one else can ever do for you. So merely because you have a guru and that guru is holding the balance while you work through your human creation, that doesn't guarantee that you will get your own God consciousness. The only guarantee is your determination to use the light that is offered, to use the light that is given. It's the basic little proverb or maxim: you can lead a horse to water, but you can't make him drink. So they brought us to the water, and for a certain dispensation they have given us the opportunity to receive the light and to be themselves.

Sustaining the Transfer of Light

You notice when you are in a dictation how powerful the light is. Then you notice the increments of how it is diminished as you walk out of the room, and you realize that you are not sustaining the full intensity of the Goddess of Purity that was there when she came. You had the capacity to sustain and absorb it while in her presence because she was the fullness of this cosmic consciousness of purity and was transferring it in close proximity.

So that was an initiation. An initiation is a transfer of light or energy or consciousness—all three meaning the same thing. Sometimes the masters will tell you, for example, that for so many seconds we are sustaining the momentum of the atomic accelerator, which is a chair in Saint Germain's retreat,* and you sit in that chair for so many seconds or so many minutes and it accelerates your atomic energies for the ascension process.

That happened in one of these conferences. The ascended masters actually brought a focus of the ascension chair to the Dodge House Hotel in Washington, D.C.[8] The focus was placed over a chair, and it was to remain there for an hour. People were lined up to sit in the ascension chair. Everybody got a minute, and then they got up and the next person sat down. So that was an initiation, or another word is a dispensation.

We needed teachers to show us how. But even if they had shown us how, we wouldn't have been able to do it ourselves because of the momentum of karma. Now, there are easy parallels to this. You can see that many people can be shown how to do things, but they will not be able to do them by merely having been shown how.

Jesus was a great example. He did everything publicly. He gave a great deal of inner teaching to his disciples. But how many people walked out of that mission and that dispensation with the full attainment that he had? The reason that they couldn't appropriate it was because they hadn't balanced their karma. Karma is the great limiting condition as to how much light you can carry and hold.

You Cannot Outpicture the Christ Consciousness from the Human Level

I have seen a number of instances, which I can tell you about, of people who cry out for help: "Help me, help me, help me!"

---
*the Cave of Symbols

So you help them. You give them everything they need. You give them the teaching. You make them comfortable. You give them every possible opportunity and all the answers that they could possibly use. And yet they are not satisfied, or they are uncomfortable—they want to go back to their homes or back to their situations.

In fact, they'll want to go back to their entities. Their houses will be full of entities, and they'll be very homesick when they come to Summit University or come into a family of light, because their old, familiar things are not with them, their familiar landmarks, little, silly things like their favorite pots and pans or their favorite furniture or their favorite little patch in the garden —whatever it might be.

And so it's because they cannot transcend from that level to the level of the ascended masters' consciousness, that no matter what you give them, they will go back to where they were. Jesus said, "Can the leopard change his spots?"[9] And Maitreya says that you cannot do this yourself:

> I say to you today that never in all eternity can you outpicture the Christ consciousness by merely doing it in the human level. It must come from an invocation.

You cannot muster your Christ consciousness just by trying to do it at the human level with your human will or by human study or by working yourself up into emotional states.

Basically, religious people polarize in two directions. They polarize mentally, in which case they may be Theosophists or great students and know a great deal of studies. Or they polarize emotionally, and they may be in the charismatic movement. They should be polarizing to the mind of God or the heart of God, but they descend to their lower vehicles, to the mental body or the emotional body. And that basically divides religious trends in America today.

People who are mentally oriented think that people who are emotional somehow are quite simple and they tend to feel that they are uneducated. But many times emotions are an expression of the heart, and people who have a real heart flame have a real, direct route to God by their hearts. They may be untutored mentally and uneducated, but they have a real and a living flame. And those who have a mental polarization have to get to God not through their mental body but through the mind of God or the mind of Christ. I think that heart people make it more successfully than head people because the head is really a much greater stumbling block. You tend to get caught in the head and in the reason of the head.

So when you are asked this on your quiz, I want you to be able to explain to me that not only did we need to know how to make the contact with our Christ Self, but we needed those gurus to stand in for us, to hold the light, to hold the flame until we could sustain it on our own. To me, that is a very important point. It explains the entire need for the Great White Brotherhood. It explains the need for the guru-chela relationship.

The Withdrawal of the Master's Presence

The first conference I attended was this conference in 1961. I came to Washington, D.C., from Boston for this conference before I had actually moved to Washington. My training was to begin on August 28, 1961, under El Morya, and the course of that training went on for a number of years. Morya was a very stern guru, very stern and very concerned about completing the training during the expected life span of Mark and seeing to it that the transfer of the mantle of the messenger was made before he would take his leave of this earth—his life span was actually extended.

So in the course of having the very intense training, for some reason I was disobedient or whatever it might have been that I had done wrong as a chela. And my discipline was to be cut off from El Morya for twenty-four hours. He had established the thread of contact, the direct guru-chela relationship, and he cut it off for twenty-four hours. By that time I was into the full year of my training.

When you have the thread of contact with an ascended master and that ascended master is giving you his Electronic Presence and is in your aura as the guru, you reach a point where you don't know any other life. You don't have any realization of what it is like to be without God.

Now Lord Maitreya did this with Jesus when Jesus hung on the cross in the hour of the crucifixion. All kinds of people have tried to rationalize that Jesus never said those words, "My God, my God, why hast thou forsaken me?"[10] It was the initiation that Jesus was cut off, not only from Lord Maitreya, his guru, but he was cut off from his I AM Presence and Christ Self and required to sustain all of the light of God within his own heart. His heart was the only God that he had and knew, and the attainment of his heart was the requirement for his passing of the initiation of the crucifixion.

Morya did not cut me off from my I AM Presence and Christ Self, but he did cut the thread of contact with the guru for twenty-four hours. It's the greatest and most productive lesson I have ever learned, because until it was cut off, I had no idea what bliss I was in and how blessed I was to have this living ascended master totally one with my lifestream.

We call people who receive the *Pearls of Wisdom* and study the teachings generally *chelas*. And that term is used loosely in the sense of "student." The real root meaning of the word, as you learn in El Morya's book *The Chela and the Path,* is "slave." And the word *slave* means at the beck and call of the master, totally living for the master. Becoming accepted as a chela under any one of the gurus, the ascended masters, is a very high privilege, a very great privilege. It may come on day one of your encounter, or you may wait ten years. Dictations have been given by the masters concerning individuals who think that they are chelas and speak of how they enjoy the favor of the ascended masters' company, when the ascended masters have said that they simply are not chelas.

Chelaship Is Something You Work For

So chelaship is something that you work for and earn, and you get it because you've given your life to the Brotherhood and you're not simply a student of the teachings, using them now and then. Now that's between you and the ascended masters. It's a very personal and private experience. But I just want you to know that once it is given to you, it is something to be treasured because you are actually living in the consciousness of the full, total attainment of the office of the guru.

And this is what Maitreya gave in that dictation, "the power of my office." He gave it to the people at the moment he was speaking. It's like going into any healing chamber or any kind of a mechanical device that might be used to accelerate atomic action. For the time you are in the presence of the master, you are accelerated, and it's a help at the moment, but you go out of it. That is a pattern and a blueprint and an experience given to you so that you can imitate it, so that you can bring yourself to equal it, so that you can make your goal in life the attainment of that same light.

That is why the ascended masters speak to us. When they come and give their dictations, they are giving you a standard. They're setting a standard. They're saying that this is what light feels like. This is what the light of wisdom feels like. This is what Morya's power feels like. This is what love feels like. Now if you want that love, clear the chakra that it corresponds to. Go after it. Clear it with the violet flame. Exercise the heart and let your heart be the focal point for that release of that same energy.

The message of every ascended master as they stand before us is, "What I have become, you can be. The works that I do, you can do also."[11] That's the whole point of the Brotherhood. "We are the sons and daughters of God. We have overcome. We have attained. Here we are! Here we are in the flesh and blood that's in the plus and minus polarity of the Spirit. What we are in Spirit, you can be in Matter."

They are the greatest living testimony. They are the witness of the Christ in you. We were all called to witness as apostles of Jesus Christ. They have never stopped witnessing. They are witnessing to your Christ consciousness so that you will witness to the same. So I think that that is a very exciting moment in this Maitreya dictation.

The Gift of Contact with Your Holy Christ Self

The contact with one's own Christ Self and I AM Presence was the great, overwhelming message of our beloved Godfre. I am told by people who knew him and who attended his meetings that he would never conduct a meeting without giving the basic, preliminary teaching on the Chart of the I AM Presence. He was so concerned that individuals make contact with their mighty I AM Presence. He knew that was the key.

Someone said that the most important initiation in this

dictation was the gift of the power of the ten thousand-times-ten thousand. I would say that the gift of contact with your mighty I AM Presence and Christ Self is a greater gift. Without that gift, you can make little real use of the dispensation, because your decrees and the power of your decrees are determined by your contact.

You can attain a certain amount with no contact, because the Law acts, and if you don't have the direct, face-to-face contact with your Christ Self and I AM Presence, the decree takes care of it because it says, "In the name of the beloved mighty I AM Presence and Christ Self, I AM in me." It gives that in the preamble because you have to decree in their name and not in the name of your human will and not by your own human action or energy or determination. So in that sense, you've made the contact and that decree is multiplied by the power of the ten thousand-times-ten thousand. It definitely is.

But that decree is like a thimbleful compared to a lake or an ocean when you actually make the contact with your I AM Presence and your decree session is based upon that very personal contact, that very personal meditation, and that seeing of God face-to-face. It makes all the difference in the world when you have a conscious contact and a conscious vision of your I AM Presence and Christ Self. How do you get the contact? You give adoration. And the magnificent decrees that beloved Mark dictated for that contact are the "Adoration to God" (30.03) and "Introit to the Holy Christ Self" (30.02).

The Problem of Someone Who Had No Contact with Their Christ Self

I have counseled people who I saw had such concrete-hard heads and such an amount of emotionalism that I saw that they had no contact with their Christ Self. I have counseled them,

"There is nothing more important that you can do but to sit down and give this decree to your Holy Christ Self. This is the one thing above all that you need. It is your inner teacher; it is your personal guru. And I am the messenger of your personal guru. I am standing as a witness of your own Christ Self, standing in for your Christ Self until you have that contact." The ascended masters do not like to see you dependent on themselves, on me, or on anyone else, because while you are dependent, you are not making your own attainment.

I remember I could see the danger signs of a particular individual who was so polarized mentally and was so self-deceived that I assigned this decree to him in place of Astreas morning, noon, and night because I felt the impending loss of that soul. And sure enough, within three months he left. He never did make the contact, even though I gave him that decree. Basically he lost the thread of contact because he entered into a very intense criticism of me, the representative of his Christ Self, for giving him that assignment of having to do that decree so many times. That criticism led to a destructive analysis of my entire person, supposedly human and divine, and that destructivity itself destroyed his own relationship to his Christ Self.

So he went out on a path and looked at Gestalt and took the est weekend training[12] and all kinds of other things trying to find identity. But the motive was not pure. The real motive of that person in coming to me was first of all to get power without responsibility, without obedience to his own Christ Self, and secondly to seek a way out of his own karma, a very treacherous karma in which there were quite a number of deeds of betrayal against various ascended masters when they were previously in embodiment and against other sons and daughters of God.

And that burden of that karma was so heavy, the guilt of that karma was so heavy for him that, instead of going to God and confessing the Christ and confessing the sin and looking at the great gift of the violet flame and of the life of service to overcome it, he did not want the direct road to the Christ but wanted to retain his ego, circumvent the Christ and circumvent the karma. And that individual to this day is still trying to find a way to justify and cover over the gnawing feeling in the subconscious of his various betrayals of the Brotherhood.

The only way that he can compensate for it psychologically is to therefore continue to attack me and to join people organizing in the realm of deprogramming, actually going after our students and telling them all sorts of things that are untrue about the messengers. All of that is done to deny the personal Christ, deny the Path, deny the path of initiation, and ultimately to deny responsibility for one's karma.

The Fear of the Loss of the Ego

This is a very, very sad phenomenon, but it is seen in individuals who long, long ago denied their allegiance to God, imitated the Luciferians, denied the all-power of God and of his Christ within his sons and daughters, and went their separate ways, convincing themselves that they were fit to rule and direct the universe. So there are a lot of such people around, and they are heavily burdened psychologically because they don't even have a situation of grace, being in and a part of grace. That grace of God makes up for our sins. And so that's why daily confession to the Christ Self and daily invocation of the violet flame puts us in daily attunement.

There are people who do not bow, bend the knee, and confess the Christ in Jesus, in Maitreya, in themselves, in the chelas. You all have the Christ. Every child of God, every son and daughter of God has a Christ Self. However, there are people who are not only loath to recognize that Christhood, but they will spend their lifetime and many lifetimes viciously and vigorously denying that Person because that Person of the Christ is a threat to their whole buildup of the synthetic foundation that they have laid. And it gets to be (they think) too late in the game to go back, because their pride is committed to a certain way in which they are walking. To renounce that way and suddenly confess the Christ, they would have to deny the only ego that they know.

They greatly fear the loss of that ego. It is a tremendous fear. It is an anxiety beyond all anxieties, and it causes the deep depressions. It causes escapism. It causes splits in the personality. And it finally ends up in succeeding embodiments as being born insane. This is the anxiety of the fallen ones who have not accepted and confessed the Christ within themselves, within Jesus, or within whatever hierarch was there when they left off the Path, when they went and said, "I reject you, God. I rebel against you."

The reason anxiety is mounting in our culture today is that the hour of the judgment is coming, and these people have the sensation that there is an imminent descent of their returning karma. That's why it's written in the Bible that they will cry out to the mountains, "Fall on us."[13] That's the mountains of their karma, and they get so anxious that they want the physical mountains to cover them and hide them from the impending presence of the person of God, the person of the guru.

They fear the coming of the personal God. They can play with the law of energy. They can play with the universe, they can play with karma. But when someone comes along, an ascended master or a chela or a messenger of the ascended master who has the light, and when that person makes the call of the judgment and challenges them, then they know that their light and their darkness will be separated and they will have to give an accounting. That is the time we are in, and that is why you see so much mental and emotional disease, and physical disease as well.

Open the Doorway of Your Heart

So Maitreya is giving you contact with your I AM Presence and Christ Self in this dictation, giving you the power of his office to expand the flame in your heart and telling you to open the doorway of your heart. This is very sound advice because he knows that the hearts of men are filled with fear. That's what Jesus said about the end of the age: that the hearts of men will fail them for fear.[14] And he wants you to transmute the encrustations, the karma, the hardness of heart, the lack of forgiveness, the pride, the human ego—everything that sets itself against God the Father, God the Son, God the Holy Ghost, who are the Person in the threefold flame of your heart.

He wants you to start your initiations with your heart. He wants you to open the door to your heart because that's the open door to your direct and personal contact with your I AM Presence and Christ Self. So essentially Lord Maitreya teaches us the religion of love. And if we are not loving but we become brittle in fanaticism and in all kinds of doctrines of what to eat and what not to eat, and all kinds of things that become more important than love, then we've lost the religion of Jesus Christ; we've lost the religion of Lord Maitreya.

Love itself is the judgment. There is no love anywhere without the judgment, because people react to God's love. Pure love is something that many people cannot handle. They'll abuse it. They'll misqualify it as lust or sensuality or overeating or all kinds of habits. That's a misqualification of the light of love. They will amass to themselves entities and discarnates through alcoholism, nicotine, marijuana, the drug culture, or excessive uses of all kinds of substances. And those entities and demons, all of them are a substitute for the living guru.

Every Entity Is an Impostor of the Guru

People can have hundreds and thousands of entities. And every entity and every face of every entity is an impostor of the guru. And so long as people have entities within their temples in any quantities, they can't hold on to a contact with the gurus. Their entities will chase them out of the very presence of the gurus. They cannot stay; they simply cannot stay.

That's why you're listening to the lecture on entities.[15] Those entities have to be challenged, and they have to be cleared. It's a very important ritual in level one of Summit University. So just remember, every ugly tobacco-worm entity, every weepy entity, every entity that you can name is an impostor of your guru Lord Maitreya. And the poor people of the earth are simply plagued with these things.

If you ever want to see a depiction of an entity, you can see *The Lord of the Rings*.[16] You see this little creature that crawls on the ground. I got caught up going to that movie with the high school last week. I wanted to leave shortly after I got in, but it is a very good movie about the astral plane. It shows the hordes of the astral plane; it shows the beasts. You hear them grunting. They have no ability to communicate the word, but they grunt energy, grunts and groans that are unintelligible. They are attacking the lightbearers, basically.

It's a very noisy movie; it's very poorly done. It's all in red and black. I am not sure that it's really worth seeing just to get a look at the astral plane, but it is a very good rendering of the astral plane. There's a creature that's gray that looks like a human body without skin, just muscles. He's all gray, and he crawls around on the ground making all kinds of silly noises and speaking in a weird way. He is very typical of entities that hang around people, and it's very repulsive.

You know, it's an interesting thing that doctors will tell you about the body: the last thing to go on the body is the outer layer. You can look at people dying of cancer and all kinds of internal diseases, but the outside is not corrupt unless it's the last stages of a surface disease. The point is that nature really doesn't tell us what's going on internally. And the same thing is true of the astral body. Morya used to comment on all of the astral caricatures that are done in the newspapers of public figures, totally distorting and exaggerating their worst features. He said that if you could see their astral bodies, they are many, many times worse than the caricatures that are done of them. They are hideous.

And so the entities themselves are hideous. Tobacco entities are hideous creatures, and they are the impostors, and people are so comfortable in their presence that they actually prefer them to the presence of the guru Maitreya. It's amazing but it's true. So that's what you're up against when you go forth. When you go forth into the world to heal the world, to convert the world, you need more than a mental discussion. You need the power of the Holy Ghost to turn people around, to challenge their discarnates, to exorcise them, and to actually cause the soul to turn around and go in the opposite direction—like Jesus caused Saul to turn around and go in the opposite direction and be the apostle Paul.[17] It takes the power of conversion. That's why Jesus told the disciples to "tarry... in the city of Jerusalem, until ye be endued with power from on high."[18]

You Can Earn Chelaship with Lord Maitreya

"So I am giving you the power of my office." That is what Maitreya is giving to you. And that office can be yours in the sense that you can earn chelaship with Maitreya. You can become the chela of Lord Maitreya to the point where you and he are functioning as one person, one "pure son." "Pure son" is the meaning of *person*.

When Jesus walked the earth, he was the incarnation of his I AM Presence, his Christ Self, and Lord Maitreya. Lord Maitreya is the one who was giving the teaching. And the great wisdom that you find in chapters 12, 13, 14 and 15 of the Book of John, which Gabriel was commenting on in the *Pearls* that he dictated to me this morning, was that Jesus declared very clearly that he was a messenger. He said, "He that hath seen me hath seen the Father, and the words that I speak are not my own but the words of him that sent me. And God has given me the work and I speak as I am commanded by God, and these are not my words; they are his words."[19]

He made it very clear that his office was the office of the messenger. He was the messenger of "your God and my God."[20] He was the messenger of the I AM Presence, of the Christ Self, of Lord Maitreya; and through Lord Maitreya he was the messenger of everyone who had ever gone before him—all of the prophets, all of the saints, all of the ascended beings. And all of his teaching was the collective teaching of the Great White Brotherhood specifically dictated by Lord Maitreya through his I AM Presence and Christ Self.

Of course, that doesn't mean that a messenger is no more than an electric typewriter. A messenger has to become the Word. Jesus was the Word that he spoke; he was the living Word. He was the power that flowed through him. He was the Word. The Word is the Christ; the terms are synonymous—*Word, Logos, Christ.*

Jesus was the incarnation. And the Word that came through him was his own God consciousness and Christ consciousness of Lord Maitreya. In other words, Jesus was a complete participant in the teachings. He had proved the teaching, lived the teaching, become the teaching. He was its messenger—not only vocally but by vibration, by example, by attainment, by all of that. It's just amazing to think of the phenomenon of his presence, the presence of Jesus Christ being the Word that he spoke.

Since you are due for the Wednesday evening service, I am going to ask that this dictation be repeated for you in the morning so that you may tie into those initiations. And as you go to your service, do make it a point this evening in all the decrees you do to close your eyes and really give gratitude for the blessedness of your personal Holy Christ Self as your innermost Self and your innermost guru. And look forward to the day, as David did, when his soul would be totally integrated with that Christ Self.[21]

The wording of "We of the Great White Brotherhood, we of the light, would restore to man the power that removes shadow," the layers of density between the individual and the Holy Christ Self, "would restore to you the power of the communion of saints and the communion with the angelic hosts."

He used the word *power* twice. Power is another name for "God's energy," but it's a very specific sense of that energy. When the crystal cord was reduced, we lost power—just power to move around. We could no longer walk like giants. We walked like little Lilliputians—except that we all are alike in the same boat, so we don't look so little to each other. But you know, the masters are seven and eight feet tall and we're not, and that's because we lost the power. You might say we're a little shrunken race down here.

Comments on the Students Coughing

I have one more thing to tell you. The coughing that you're hearing is quite usual at Summit University. It's not conditioned by the place, the environment, or the season. It would like to make you feel that it's because you were in the cold that you caught a cold and you got this condition, but actually it is energy and it is emotional energy.

And the thing that you find, especially at first level, is that when you come into the presence of the light and of the ascended masters and your Christ Self, that light, like a big thousand-watt light bulb, exposes the dust in the corners of consciousness. The reaction is guilt, and coughing is a vibration of guilt.

When that guilt manifests and then you have the coughing, sometimes you get very resentful about the coughing, and you say, "Well, it's because of my long hours, or I am not used to this food, or I am fasting, or it's just this place and the way they run it. I am getting sick, and I am never sick." Conditions might be better, but you really are not sick because of conditions. You really are dealing with your own energy, and you need to take responsibility for it. You do need to take responsibility for your own energy.

Obviously, if you haven't done a lot of fasting, fasting will bring up toxins that may cause problems. I do want you to get help; I do want you to take whatever you need to take. And if you need a prescription, if you need antibiotics, you should be taking them. If you would like a homeopathic remedy, that's fine; but it has to work. We have an excellent and well-known homeopathist here, and you can try that remedy. But if after two weeks you're still not better, you do have a responsibility to your class and to yourself to be on the proper medication.

Be careful, then, of your food and of keeping a good balance. If you have a real problem condition and you're just going to eat fruit, you might get worse before you get better. And sometimes it's better to eat hot food, cooked food, and not try to cleanse everything out at once.

**Guilt Should Last Only as Long as
You Do Not Have Forgiveness**

But the guilt is the underlying cause of the coughing. Naturally, we've been running around thinking that we were not being watched by the gurus for tens of thousands of years. And we've all done many things that we regret. So you might as well face up to that and realize that guilt should only last so long as you do not have forgiveness. But God has given you an advocate with himself, who is the Christ.

So you confess your sins to your Christ Self and state your desire to do better, and then do better. And then you have nothing to feel guilty for, because that's why Jesus Christ was nailed to a cross, to bear your sins, to bear your karma. And you are finally coming of age now where you can say, "Jesus, look! I am alive. I am in contact. I've got my Christ Self. I've got the teaching. I can bear my own karma now. And what's more, I can take on the karma of the world." That's nothing to be guilty about. That's something to rejoice about, not something to be burdened by.

So throw all these entities and this substance into the flame. You do not have to be sick. But only you can do it, no matter what powers I have. Maitreya said to me today, "You might as well tell the students that not one of them is going to be healed by you of their coughing and their sniffles. They will have to take full responsibility—etherically, mentally, emotionally, and physically."

Don't neglect the physical part. When you're not well, you need special care. You do need to dress warmly, and you do need to get extra sleep and eat intelligently, and take medicine if you have to. So with that, we'll send you to the healing service, and you can all heal yourselves by invocation to God.

> *In the name of the I AM THAT I AM, I call forth the light of Lord Maitreya to accelerate the contact of the mighty I AM Presence and the Christ Self. I call for the opening of the door of the heart, the opening of the threefold flame of life. I demand that acceleration now. I demand that acceleration now. I demand that acceleration now. The light of God never fails and the beloved mighty I AM Presence is that light.*
>
> *O soul of light, rise now to the level of your heart chamber and be bathed in the infinite sacred fire of love from your own Christ Self, from beloved Lord Maitreya, beloved Jesus, and the I AM Presence. Blaze blue lightning from the heart of God in the Great Central Sun! Blaze blue lightning! Bind all entities of guilt! Bind all entities of emotional substance! Bind all entities of these colds and coughs! Burn through the ray of Morya! Burn through! Burn into the cause and core of it! Blaze the light of Oromasis and Diana! Burn through all viruses! Burn through all substance of anti-Christ within the cells of the temples! Blaze the light of Maitreya! Blaze the light of Maitreya! Blaze the light of Maitreya!*
>
> *In the name of the living God, I accept it done this hour in full power, Amen.*

Would you repeat that last line. [Students repeat with the messenger:]

> *In the name of the living God, I accept it done this hour in full power, Amen.*

The entire effect of the call depends on your acceptance. Acceptance is a condition of the emotions. It begins in the emotions. The emotional body has resistance. The mind does also. The mind has its points of resistance, but the attitude of acceptance is something that you can train your four lower bodies to have. It's a *be-attitude* of accepting God, an uncomplicated attitude, a childlike attitude: God is, I AM God, I AM whole. That's the attitude of acceptance.

God bless you.

January 17, 1979

CHAPTER THREE

The Goal of Chelaship

Light of the magnificent will of God within each heart, rise now and take dominion within the mind of these beloved souls. Beloved Lord Maitreya, we come together now for the infusion of the mind with the mind of Christ, that the soul might make the transition in this life from the mental body to the Higher Mental Body of the personal Christ Self.

I invoke the initiations of beloved Lord Maitreya for the infilling of the mind with the love of the Holy Ghost, for the instilling of the mind with such stupendous love of the person of the Son as to imitate that Son and to become that Son light.

O mind of God, O will of God, by the light of Alpha, send the rod of the Great Initiator for the acceleration of these chalices that they might become the fullness of thyself, regulated in and by the heart, O living Word. In the name of thy chela Jesus Christ, in the name of the Father, the Son, the Holy Ghost, and of the Cosmic Virgin, Amen.

This is my favorite spot on the earth. The spot is the point of the adoration of the Magi, because when I come, I come to adore the birth of the Christ within you. And that is a very exciting mission of the three wise men.

They came in the full awareness of beloved Lord Maitreya. They came fully tutored by him in the knowledge of the chela Jesus Christ and his incarnation. I emphasize the term the *chela* Jesus Christ because Jesus desires that you should sense yourself entering the path that he walked.

Now and then as I have walked this path in this life, Jesus has stood by me and said the most comforting words, "Now you know how I felt when I was at that point on the Path." And as I would read in the Bible and see where Jesus was when he had those initiations, I would have such an enriching experience to understand that what the Bible recorded and what he really felt and what he was passing through were two very different versions of the same event.

I am in wonder in the contemplation of the guru-chela relationship. I have found in communion with Lord Maitreya and in receiving the *Pearls of Wisdom* of beloved Gabriel,[1] that there is such a vast teaching that God so lovingly desires to give to us so that we will understand the privileges and the joys of chelaship and what it means. So the *Pearls* that are being published now contain absolute gems of God consciousness on chelaship. And they come in such a spherical release that one cannot think of them in a linear fashion.

When we go to a university, most subjects are taught on a timeline of the historical development of the subject, the sequence in which things occur, the simple to the complex. Basically there is an order and it is linear. That is the way we are taught to write, and that is the way we are taught to think. It is an unbendable system, and it makes the mind unbendable. And so in the guru-chela relationship, spontaneity and responsiveness to the Holy Ghost is what makes life joyous and worth living.

Even an Electron Has Free Will

Now, you can have a system to your life, and it's very important. The regulation of order and system is seen throughout a cosmos. There are established guidelines and within those guidelines, freedom. There is nowhere where this is more apparent than in the observation of an atom. An atom has precise components in the nucleus. It has a precise weight. It always functions exactly in the same way. It will always have the same properties. When combined with other atoms, it will always produce the same molecule, the same substance—absolutely dependable law. And yet within that atom is a random electron whose course around the center has never been traced and never been established. We do not know what the pattern of the electron's journey around its nucleus is. That is what is most exciting about free will—that God would not create even an electron without free will.

Now supposing that he has an order that is so vast that even computers cannot figure it out, and that one day we will determine that there is a set course. The point is that the freedom of the soul within the disciplined environment is the most opportune combination that God has conceived. It's an absolute law of Alpha giving birth to an Omega that operates within that law and yet is free to exercise ingenuity, creativity, application to the Cosmic Christ, application to God Almighty, application to the Holy Ghost, within an established order.

It's like having rules to a game. It's like playing with children the various games that are made for children these days. You read the directions and you have the rules and everybody has to play by the rules. There are no exceptions, and you can't cheat. It's a very important experience that children understand that you enter life, life is a game, it has its rules. And yet there is such vast freedom to innovate, to win or lose within the game of life, that one does not sense that one is in bondage to a mathematical formula.

Sometimes we feel freedom because the complexity of the order is so great that we would have to evolve almost to become the thing itself, as the Creator outside of the sphere that the Creator has established, in order to finally and ultimately appreciate the great intricacy of the limits that are placed upon that freedom.

In other words, when you look at the stars, and you realize that we are all subject to astrology, that there are thousands, millions of stars—there are actually only a very few that we can see, surprisingly, but those that we cannot see are there—the vastness of that configuration affects all of us. Now, if we were the Great Astrologer that God is, we would see all of those stars and we would see the precision timing of ourselves operating within the midst of those stars. Some people have said that if we really knew the law of energy, we would realize that every movement of our finger and every movement of our brain cells is governed by astrology.

Your Will Side by Side with God's Will

So the freedom within order is not a freedom that ignorance is bliss, but it's that the order is so vast that within it there always is free will. There really is free will. And what does free will finally come down to? It is the free will to elect to fulfill God's divine plan. It's the freedom to elect to follow the inner blueprint.

The balance of understanding your will side by side with God's will is terribly important on the path of chelaship. Some people feel that all they have to do is say, "Not my will but thine be done," put themselves in neutral gear, and wait. This becomes a misunderstanding of the surrender to the divine will. Will is a very active person of God the Father. God has a definite will, a definite will of action.

I have found that the will of God can be known if we really have the courage to know that will. I have never found it difficult. I have found that the place where I find out what God's will is, is when I find out what God's greatest need is, what humanity's greatest need is, and in the midst of those two factors, what is my greatest ability now developed in my outer consciousness, my greatest ability right now, to meet God's greatest need and to meet humanity's greatest need?

You need to learn how to think logically. God has a will. It's a total plan. Now, you at the optimum attainment of your Christ consciousness would be capable of fulfilling your optimum service.

The Cross of Alpha and Omega

In the mandalas that computers draw where they connect all the points on a circle, you see these beautiful thoughtforms. Well, the teaching is that wherever two lines cross, every crossing of a line is always Alpha and Omega. Even if it's at a sharp angle, it's still Alpha and Omega, two crossed lines. And when I say it's Alpha and Omega, I mean it is two energies, two polarities of energy, the positive and the negative polarity.

So wherever two lines cross, that is the point of the burst of the Christ consciousness. That's the point of the burst of energy like the stars in the heavens. The lines of Alpha and Omega have to meet in order for there to be a Person of the Christ in expression. So Alpha and Omega have met where you are, and the result is that you are a Person of God. You are a Christed one. You are the focal point for the realization of the Christ consciousness.

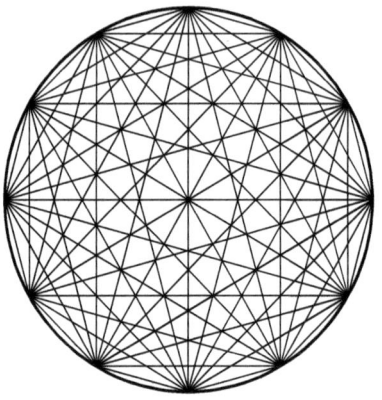

A mandala is formed by connecting twelve points on a circle to each other.

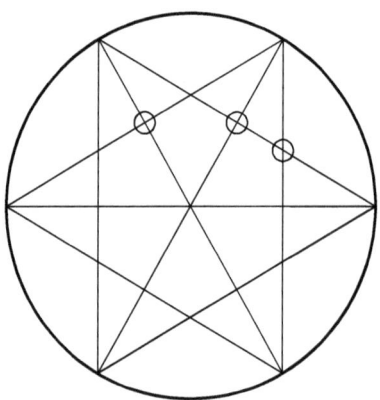

Each point where lines intersect forms a cross.

Intersecting Lines in a Mandala
FIGURE 1

Now, that Christ consciousness in physical expression is latent. It has not fully manifested itself to your fullest dominion because it is blocked by your karma and by the warps and the out-of-alignment nature of the four lower bodies and the chakras. So you all know that when you line up a sieve with another sieve with another sieve and you have one hundred of them, unless they're perfectly aligned, the water will not fall through but you will begin to block the flow.

So that is the definition of the absence of self-mastery. The absence of self-mastery is the state of being out of alignment with the inner blueprint, hence, not being a transparency for the light to flow.

What It Means to Be in Alignment

Now, being in alignment would mean that you are at that literal point where Alpha meets Omega on the cross. Jesus hung on that cross so that you would have the vision, the visualization that in order to become the Christ you must go to the nexus of the cross. And when you go to the nexus of the cross, the light is so intense—it's the all-power of God; it's the all-energy of God; wherever those two meet, there is the Great Central Sun energy—and to stand at that point, to be at that point means to be willing to be crucified by the anti-light, by all of the out-of-alignment energies of the earth, which are now very uncomfortable in the presence of true alignment.

It's like people's taste buds being destroyed by bad food, their ears being destroyed by bad music, their eyes being destroyed by distorted images, so that now they're uncomfortable with true beauty, with true classical music. It's very irritating; classical music is grating to people who are used to rock music. People who are on bad diets do not like pure food. They can't taste it, it has no flavor, it's upsetting to their digestion, et cetera, et cetera. So that out-of-alignment state is an anti-light state because it does not emit light.

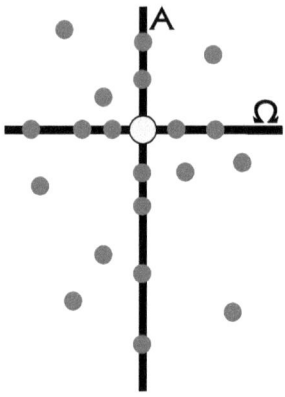

The Cross of Alpha and Omega
People position themselves at
many different places in relation to the cross
other than the nexus where Alpha and Omega meet.
FIGURE 2

Now, people do not want to go to the nexus, so they find alternatives. They position themselves somewhere on the cross or off the cross. You can see that there are a lot of places to be: you can be somewhere along one of the lines of the cross, or completely off and not on either Alpha or Omega. And you can spend your embodiments kind of looking at that place at the center of the cross and backing off, looking at that place and backing off.

I've seen this; you've seen it. You see people who could take a moral stand, who could take a stand for truth, and they don't take that stand. They back away. They go into a corner. You don't hear from them anymore. They know what's right, but they're not going to be heard on that point of what is right.

You are somewhere in relation to that cross, and the full-fledged crucifixion will reveal to you that you have definitely made it to the center. Fulfilling the will of God at your optimum capacity, you have to be at that point of the cross. So when people say, "I don't know what to do with my life. What should I do? Should I go here? Should I go there? How shall I serve you?" they can only perform the will of God to the level of their capacity. And capacity is determined: Where are you? Where are you in relationship to the nexus of your own origin? Your origin is the nexus of Alpha and Omega, where those two lines meet.

The Guru Doesn't Tell You What the Will of God Is

It's not the messenger or your guru who is going to tell you what is the will of God for you. It is you who are going to tell your I AM Presence and your Christ Self, "I am determined to get as close as I can to the nexus of my Reality, where Father and Mother are one, and as close as I can get—considering the configuration (the astrology) of my karma, of my density, of my out-of-alignment state—there will I serve until that service becomes the means of a transmutation that can thereby accelerate me closer to the nexus of my cross."

No matter how much you want to be at the center of that cross, God will not let you come to that cross unless you are ready, because unless you are ready, you will be consumed by that fire. It will cancel out your identity. So you can try to take heaven by force, but you can't take heaven by force.[2] The black magicians attempt to steal God's energy—and they do—but ultimately they are canceled out by it. It's just a slow process. But it does occur; they pay the penalty for their misuse of energy.

So I can see your ultimate, glorious destiny of who you are, what you are, and what your intended service is. But I cannot say to you, if you do not have the outer manifestation, "This is your assignment. Go and do it." It would be very discouraging.

It would be very poor psychology to tell someone who is now ready for the second grade, "Your destiny is to go and be a physics professor. Now go do it." So you would expect to prepare at the level of the human consciousness. You need to expect to go through cycles of preparation in the divine consciousness.

Integration of the Alpha Self with the Omega Self

So this problem of the will of God seems to hit chelas at first level of Summit University very hard. Without having developed their own attainment in this plane, the mental plane, with what resources we've had in this life, what mental training we get, what upbringing we get, what moral training, what spiritual training—if in your life you have not developed a strong will, if you are not successful in a sacred labor, if you don't have something you can do, something you've mastered in the world, then proportionately you have less to surrender when you come to the altar.

A person who is skilled, who comes to the masters educated, having lived twenty years, having been successful, having accomplished, having met and mastered many different sorts of challenges and crises, having a definite idea of who he is and what he wants to do, knowing I AM WHO I AM—"I want to serve, I can offer you this talent, I'm ready to speak for the masters, I'm ready to work in this or that office because I have the complete talent"—that person has a highly developed, let us say, an outer ego, and that would be a very large ego.

So when he surrenders that block of substance upon the altar of God and says, "Here I am, Lord; send me,"[3] then what happens is that a corresponding portion of the Christ Self can be exchanged, and day by day this outer attainment goes through the alchemical process of being exchanged for its inner counterpart.

It's like the Omega Self now integrating with and being totally infused with and assimilated by the Alpha Self, until the Omega Self takes on the beauty, the crystallization of the Alpha Self. So the Alpha and the Omega Self need to be realized.

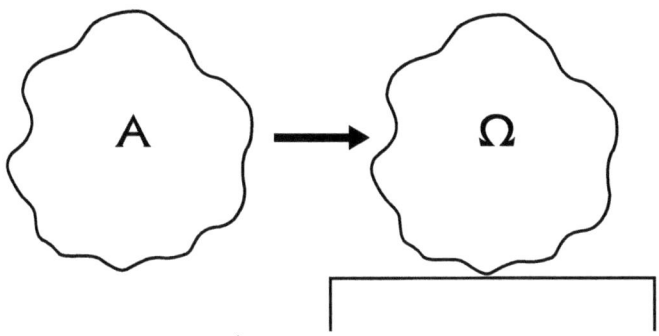

When a person places a large externalized attainment of the Omega Self on the altar, the exchange from the Christ Self, the Alpha Self, can be a correspondingly larger portion.

FIGURE 3A

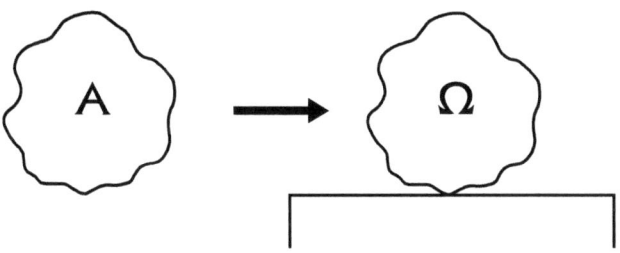

A person who lays a smaller externalized attainment on the altar will receive a correspondingly smaller portion of the Alpha Self in this exchange.

FIGURE 3B

The Alpha Self and the Omega Self
FIGURE 3

The Ascended Masters Are Specialists

Now, if you are just out of high school but you have done well and you have from previous lifetimes a momentum of independence and identity and development, you still may have this outer self, but it may not be this large. It may be smaller because in this life you haven't outpictured the mastery one gains by meeting the adversities of life. But whatever you have, you are only going to be able to get back from God the equivalent. You could balance all of your karma, believe it or not, but that would not suddenly give you the full attainment of a cosmic being who had worked for eons at inner levels for his God consciousness.

And so this is why there are people in embodiment who have more attainment than some ascended masters. Did you know that? You can ascend with the balance of 51 percent of your karma. You could balance the 51 percent of your karma by being a maid. You could go and be the most balanced person, full of light, full of devotion. You could be a maid cleaning the houses of whomever, whether you're serving in a priest's parish or a rabbi's office or one of the buildings downtown. You could be having such devotion to the Hail Mary and to God and giving so much energy that by your simple service of carrying a torch of freedom you could make your ascension.

Now, the person who would ascend with 51 percent of that karma balanced could be side by side with a person who had developed to the point of being a genius in previous lives, had become a mathematician, used mathematics to the glory of God, instructed many people, had many original scientific inventions, and in his spare time at home would have given all of his devotion to the keeping of the flame through dynamic decrees and prayers.

They each balance 51 percent of their karma and they each

ascend. They are unequal. They are not suddenly equalized. Those two individual ascended masters each have their own unique flame, each have their own unique causal body. But "One star differeth from another in glory."[4] That star is the causal body.

At the hour of the ascension, you can go to school. I'm sure that that maid would be right there in the retreats of the chohans learning the mastery of Pythagoras, learning this and that and the next thing. I've known of ascended masters who, the day they ascended, went and took voice lessons so they could sing better. So, suddenly you aren't becoming a cosmic being who knows how to do everything, which is very interesting because if the disciplines that you pursue on earth are truly gained by your Christ consciousness, you simply continue with those disciplines.

The ascended master Kuthumi has a great attainment in the field of psychology.[5] That doesn't mean to say that most ascended masters wouldn't understand more than you and I understand about psychology and that they wouldn't have a great understanding. But the ascended master Kuthumi is a specialist. Other ascended masters will consult him in the areas of human psychology or the psychology of other planets, which would differ and vary. So there are specialists, and you have been taught this. This is why some beings in heaven are chohans and some are archangels and some are doing this and some are doing that.

Psychological Problems Create a Small Self-Awareness

When it comes to the will of God, you find that many people with very severe psychological problems—people who have a very low self-image, people who have split personalities —will come to the Great White Brotherhood and surrender very quickly. But their self-awareness, compared to these other people, is very small. So they'll say, "Here I am. I surrender."

And that is as much of their self-awareness as they have gained. That's the amount of the Christ Self that they have *concretized* ("made concrete"), that they have *crystallized* (another word), that they have brought down into this plane, into this heart, into these chakras, that is functioning now within them as the Real Person, however inadequately, let's say not totally perfectly, but through the mental body, through the emotional body, the etheric, and the physical. Now that small portion is really all they have to give. That's their Omega awareness. And so when they surrender it, they will start integrating with that much of Alpha's self-awareness, that much of their I AM Presence.

When people with severe psychological problems come to the Brotherhood, they have a very small portion to offer. They may easily surrender this, but the portion of the Alpha Self that they can receive in exchange is correspondingly limited.

FIGURE 3C

So there is very little will in that Omega Self. Now, we have people with psychological problems, and as long as they are not violent, as long as they keep the guru-chela relationship, as long as they do not challenge the guru, they can continue to walk the Path.

The Rejection of the Authority Figure

However, many people with psychological problems will challenge the guru. They will get the complex of being omnipotent, where they have to be omnipotent over the therapist or everyone around them or anyone who is in a position of authority to them. And so they have a very difficult time in an authority situation. They will swallow the guru whole. It's like downing a fish in one gulp. And so the fish as the guru sits in their stomach, this whole fish, and it's totally undigested. There's no assimilation. There's no putting on by the reasoning, thinking, feeling process, step-by-step the assimilation, the chewing, the digesting, the thinking through; but all of a sudden, "Ah, I have found my guru. Now my worries are over."

And so they will live through the guru. They will take on the identity of the guru. These are the kind of people you have running around the false teachers. They are flattered. They are taken care of. Their needs are met. They are robot-like. They enjoy an authority situation where they're told to do this, they're told to do that, and they don't have to think.

But sooner or later that undigested fish is going to come back out whole. That's the moment of the rejection of the authority figure. And that's the moment when the individual says, "I know everything you know, and I'm better than you are, and I can do it better." So now they completely release that fish. It comes back out the same way it went in, and that becomes the point of the breaking of the relationship.

I can see that coming a mile away, and I know that that individual is not ready for the Path. And he really should not be in any association with me whatsoever, because it's really dangerous to his soul development.

But if there are people who have a basic understanding in the therapy that I would give them that they have these problems, and they will settle down and give a service—and service will be the means to the transmutation of the misqualified energy of rebellion that created the psychological problems—and if they will generally function within the disciplines of the Great

White Brotherhood, they are always welcome—as long as there's not a state of violence, as long as there's not a state of constant, day-by-day questioning the system, questioning the order, or questioning any specific direction they're given. They wouldn't last with an employer either in that state of mind. You simply cannot function within an organization when you are that kind of a person.

Healing Psychology in the Guru-Chela Relationship

So when I have such people whom I understand to have such problems, I will give them an assignment that involves physical work. Physical work is therapy, whether it's taking care of the grounds or doing other things. The motion of the body, the rhythmic, ordered motion of the body begins the rhythmic, ordered motion of the mind, the emotional body, the etheric body. And the daily rhythm of it begins the integration of the microcosm, of this whole complex solar system that man is. And combining that with the decrees, the community of the Holy Spirit with Lord Maitreya in its midst gives the optimum opportunity for people with psychological problems to work through those problems.

If a person has serious, deep psychological problems, it may take five, six, or eight years of therapy, up to five sessions a week, to get at the bottom of some of these more serious problems. These may be normal people, functioning in our society, may be successful, having jobs and basically getting on, but they have deep-seated splits, and only by that length of therapy can they actually come to a resolution. I have compared that with the path of initiation under the gurus, and I consider that the healing of psychological problems is far greater in the guru-chela relationship. It's the far greater solution.

The Interchange with a Therapist Will Not in Itself Lead to Healing

What's happening in the field of psychology and psychotherapy is that the psychotherapist becomes the guru. He sits in the seat of the guru. He is the authority figure. The person is putting out all of his human creation on the table, and that is being gone through day by day. But the therapist, not having the light or the flame of the ascended masters, does not have the means to transmute it.

You have established a figure-eight process of interchange between the therapist and the patient, but what's happening is that the psychotherapist is in the process of giving his human awareness, his identity, which supposedly he has resolved, to the patient. And it's an interchange where the patient takes on the greater human strength of the therapist, which supposedly would be the means to the transmutation of his lesser human strength or his lesser will or his lesser integration of identity. So it isn't really healing.

If the individual is going to be healed, it will have to be through an attunement with his own Real Person, his own Christ Self, or through the attunement of the therapist to his own Christ Self, because there is no healing except through the light of God. And therefore, unless either the patient or the therapist is the instrument of the light of God, nothing is going to actually happen except the rearrangement of energy, the rearrangement of molecules. It hasn't gone through the sacred fire of the Holy Ghost—and the only permanent change is by the sacred fire of the Holy Ghost.

You can get more comfortable by rearranging energy, just like it feels good to rearrange the furniture in your living room or to redecorate or to get a whole new color scheme—or to get rid of this wife and get another wife or to get yourself into another community or to move here or to take a trip. We rearrange energy in this world to get away from our human creation. People pollute the cities, and when they're all polluted, people go to the suburbs. And when they pollute them, they have to go somewhere else. You go to new developments and the vibrations are better than in the city only because the people haven't been there long enough for the akashic records to accumulate.

So this rearrangement of energy, supposedly producing enormous results, has gone over into the psychic field in all kinds of things—everything from Rolfing of the body, to the taking of drugs, to est,[6] to all kinds of systems that have been evolved. And all they are doing is creating conditions in the consciousness where energy moves around. So you get relief here; you get relief there. And we know that orthodox medicine often does the same. You take a pain pill, and it kills the pain. It hasn't really healed the problem, but you get a little bit more comfortable.

The Masters Need Students Trained as Counsellors

So psychotherapy is a very important field. We're preparing to release beloved Kuthumi, Lanto, and Meru's book, *Understanding Yourself*.[7] It's a marvelous series of *Pearls*, those eighteen *Pearls* on that very subject. The ascended masters need students under Kuthumi, who himself serves under Lord Maitreya, to serve as counselors to people. But that counseling needs to be understood in the light of being an adjunct to the guru-chela relationship.

Ultimately, the person who is not willing to be disciplined under his Christ Self is only coming to the therapist to have his energy rearranged for a greater state of human comfortability. I don't think that a disciple or an initiate on the path of the Great White Brotherhood who is really serious should spend his life as a psychiatrist or a psychologist treating people who are not committed to God, have not confessed the Christ, and are not willing to be disciplined under their own Christ Self.

I recognize that in the world as it is today, there need to be compromises. If you are in the field of psychology, you need to keep in the field, especially when you can work with young people. But one should open oneself up to the challenge of getting into a position of counseling people who can be brought into a basic commitment to (whatever you want to call it) their Real Person, and where there is a willingness to surrender the unreal person.

The Swapping of Identities

When you hear people who are talking about cults and programming and all of the people in our society who have flocked to Sun Myung Moon or the Hare Krishna movement or various places, it is in many, many cases this very problem of very low self-image. Gabriel is talking about this also in one of his *Pearls*.[8] The personality of the leader has so much more of either the plus or the minus of relative good and evil—either they're more daring to do good or they're more daring to do evil than the person coming to them. And so it's a swapping of identities. The individual with a very small self then is exhilarated in the fact that now he has gained an identity because he is near an important person.

It's the same theory with fans of leaders in the entertainment industry. You identify with the movie stars, and you gain a greater self-awareness. So those are the kinds of people who also go to the so-called cults. But they're also in the churches. Jesus said, "They that be whole need not a physician, but they that are sick."[9] And so when you are in this field, you expect to deal with those who know that they are not whole or who don't know that they're not whole.

Now, we're not whole until we ascend. So you get a combination of the very wise who come to the feet of the ascended masters, who probably have a great deal more wholeness than a lot of people in the world who think they are whole, but they are wise enough to know that they need a guru. They have enough wholeness in themselves that they can appreciate a greater wholeness.

A person who cannot appreciate an Elijah or an Elisha or a Gautama Buddha or a Mother Mary—a person who has no ability to realize that here is a God-man, here is a God-woman; I want to get near that person because I recognize that I am incomplete by comparison—a person who doesn't have that capacity cannot see the value of a guru-chela relationship and would not be the wise individual who would recognize the advantage of being associated with the Great White Brotherhood.

The Obligation to Care for the Poor in Spirit

So those people who have enough clarity of vision to see an ascended master and know that they can be more of who they are with that ascended master, those people make the best chelas. Those are your shepherds and those are your leaders. Then you have the people who have very little self-awareness. But they know that they are sick, also. They know that they are sinners. And so they, too, come to the feet of the gurus. So you will find them, and you will find that these are the ones who are more easily entrapped by the false gurus. But they are the people that the community needs to care for as long as they are not in a state of rebellion.

And so every community, every level of the human condition, has its obligation to care for the poor in spirit. Jesus saw that the sinners and the sick had a greater awareness of their incompleteness than those who were whole—than the Pharisees, the Sadducees, who had wealth, power, learning, education, and yet were very fragile in terms of having any spiritual reality.

And so we deal with the question of the will of God. The size of your externalized Omega Self represents in you that portion of your consciousness that has determined by the will of God to be something Real, to be God, to be a Real Person, to be your Real Self. However much identity of God you have right now, you've probably spent the last quarter-of-a-million years getting it and losing what you got and getting some more and losing it. You know, it's that game of life we play.

So, many times I will hear the ascended masters rebuke someone who is in a particular service in the organization because they did not perform the service well. And I've heard the masters say, "You've had ten thousand years to get ready for this job, and if you're not ready, it's too bad." And that's just about the way that Serapis Bey and Morya feel about people. If people have been fooling around all these centuries when it was time to get ready, well, you are what you are. You're going to have to live with what you are. You're going to have to accept a job and a service under the gurus commensurate with your Christ consciousness—not necessarily commensurate with your education or what you have been able to accomplish in the outer world.

The Christ Perceives the Need

So that is where we start. And as I was mentioning on Sunday, there's the initiation of being stripped of the garments that you have not gained by attainment.[10] And so this Omega Self is the core of what you are and what you can offer on the altar. And that represents your will. That's how you have exercised your will, your determination to be God. Starting with that point, that is where you will position yourself in a distance from where your inner matrix and your inner being are the two lines that cross, Alpha and Omega. And you'll have to work your way closer and closer.

The best way to work closer and closer, as I say, is to analyze what is God's greatest need, what is humanity's greatest need, and what is your greatest outer attainment right now to help fulfill that need. That is basically the way the logic of my life has been. The perception of a need is the perception of the Christ. Your Christ Self is aware of absolute Good (God) and aware of you and your human person. Your Christ Self is *always* aware of your needs and *always* ready to supply them if you will invoke in prayer that need.

A need is an absence of wholeness. *Need, lack, want*—those are words used in the Bible, and they signify a certain percentage of your circle of wholeness. A certain piece of the pie is missing. Let's say it's 22 percent here that is absolutely missing. That's your need. That's your want. That's your lack. There's a piece out over here. There's a piece out over here, and there's a wide one over here.

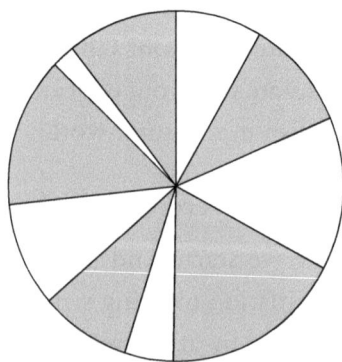

The Circle of Wholeness
Each portion of the circle that is missing represents a need.
FIGURE 4

So, you can look at your wants or your lacks, and that is what Jesus meant when he said, "Blessed are the poor in spirit."[11] The poor, the impoverished ones, are the ones who have the lack or the want of Spirit consciousness. And those absences represent wedges of karma, wedges of density in those four lower bodies.

So, blessed is he that seeth his brother's need and supplieth it.[12] When you see that you have outer spiritual attainment that your brother does not have, you supply, you make up for it. You help on that committee. You help in that situation. And you find that your brother has a talent that you do not have that he is supplying for you.

The Process of Integration

That's what makes the community of the Holy Spirit so exciting. People come. They have an attainment concretized. They lay that on the altar. They begin the integration process where that attainment now becomes accelerated and passes through the flame. And so it becomes a real Alpha energy of the I AM Presence that they're carrying in this vessel. And from that point of that will and that determination to be God, day by day they are increasing. Day by day we study to be more of God. We decree to be more of God. And we're in action in our sacred labor, which is teaching us things about ourselves, things about what we're not so good at and how we have to improve.

The process is the attainment of wholeness. So you see, if you give up what little or great capacity you are in the Omega Self and put yourself in neutral gear, you're likely to have a setback where now you are somewhere in the middle, where you haven't put on the corresponding grace of the Christ mind but you have left behind what you had formerly attained. You have to be careful not to do that. You have to be careful not to throw out who you are without having become who you really are, without going through the very logical progression of integration.

Integration is the key word. That is what initiation is all about. It's a process of integration. So when we bring fruits meet for repentance,[13] we're bringing all of the karma of our good works, all of our good momentum, but we know that it's not good enough because there's only one good and that is God. There's only one good, and that's the absolute Good of God.[14] And so we want our human goodness as well as our human badness to go through the alchemy and become the balance of Alpha and Omega. That, then, will be the Real Person and the Christ Person that will make it now, whereas the person that came to the altar won't make it.

Chelaship in Community Is Another Level of Acceleration

What I'm saying here is that you may be the finest this or that. You may be the most professional person, the most successful person. You may have excelled everyone in your field in whatever talent you have brought here, but you will find that chelaship in an ascended master community is another level of acceleration. And the finest specialist, the finest this or that, will find that his human attainment or his human goodness will not be adequate to the next level of performance. I've seen it again and again. It's just the most amazing thing. But people who have the best skills and the best human consciousness that the world could bring together have to have that cup broken and the new chalice of the Christ Self exchanged for it.

This is why Jesus explained that many times it's easier for a sinner than it is for the righteous to come into God's kingdom, because the person who is righteous, the person who is accomplished humanly does not have such a great need for his Christ Self, for that upper vehicle, as the person who is not. And so the people who are less clever and have less attainment sense their utter dependency upon the Christ mind, and they can more easily gravitate toward it. But for a person who has learned to be totally dependent on his mental body and has created a very independent, accomplished, successful, wealthy career existence within that mental body, it is very threatening to him to give it up, to surrender it—plus the fact that he has a certain amount of pride in that accomplishment, and his desire level is much lower to give it up.

So when I have seen these marvelous geniuses who will come along the way and do things so well that they don't need the ascended masters, I have told them that "I pity you that you do not have my condition, which is that I don't have such brilliance. I don't have such outer attainment." So it's very obvious to me that when anything great happens where I am, that it is God who is doing it. And that is the great gift that God has given to me. He has not created me to be one of these individuals who has all of this worldly attainment, all of this capacity, so he feels that he can actually deal with an ascended master as a coequal and put that ascended master down and disagree with him when he thinks that the master's wrong.

The Luciferians Have a Very Large Self-Awareness of the Lower Self

That's what the Luciferians do. They are very brilliant people, extremely brilliant people. And unfortunately the children of God in America are extremely impressed with the Luciferians. They are their idols in every field. And they think that the Luciferians are just too marvelous for words, and that they obviously should be given preeminence because they are such marvelous beings and have such great, great talent and success and wealth and so forth.

Such are the individuals who have a very large self-awareness in the Omega, but the self-awareness is entirely in the mental body and entirely uncommitted to the Christ Self. So they will be very imposing personalities. They walk into a room, the room fills with their aura. They're part of the angelic kingdom, part of the fallen angels. They had large auras to start with because they have huge desire bodies because they are instruments of God's feeling and God's virtue. And so that's why they can take over a stage, and that's why they become the idols of movie fans. That's why they become rock stars. And that's why you will see them gaining power in political and economic fields as well. They have a commanding presence, but that presence is entirely the development of the carnal mind that has not bent its knee and confessed the Christ.

On the other hand, when an ascended master or an ascended master's chela who has that light enters a room, it is also a very great presence. But it's a delicate quality of light, which the sensitive will appreciate. When that light becomes the power of the prophets of Israel, the fallen ones know it also. They're very much aware of that presence and that light, and they tremble before it. They fear it. Even if they're on the other side of the earth and they don't even know the person, the fallen ones will feel that light in embodiment and they will begin to tremble.

The Will of God Depends on Your Will

As I come to you today with a message on the will of God, I'm very anxious that you should be able to assess that the will of God depends on your will. When people say to me, "What is the will of God for me?" I say two things: "What can you do, and what is your will?" What can you do? really means, What is your will? How have you used the will that's in you to become the Christ so that the Christ could be the instrument of the Holy Spirit in action?

How much Holy Spirit you've got is shown by what your skills are. What can you do? It's amazing, isn't it? But if you can't do anything, you haven't progressed from the point of being a son of God to being the activator of good through his Holy Ghost.

So then when you decide what is your will, when your desire really comes out—"Well, you know, I'd like to go back and get my degree, or I'd like to maybe help in a teaching center"— I say, "Well, then, that is what you should do. That's the level of your will. That's the level of your commitment."

Within that context, I'll counsel you. I can only counsel you in the context of your own will. So draw back inside of yourself. Don't expect God to come down and tell you his will. He told you his will a quarter-of-a-million or a million or two million years ago when you left the Great Central Sun. You know what that will is. You've experimented with that will, and evidently have a certain weariness with the experimentation. So you've come to the Great White Brotherhood now to learn how to extricate yourself from the snarl of string that you've wound around yourself in this tangled ball of karma. So we all sit in this room in that similar dilemma.

When I have come to the Path and I have had to make choices, I have never seen since I was a tiny child that if my desire body was tied in purity to my heart and my heart was tied in purity to my mind, I have never seen where when I prayed, "God, show me your will," that it has not been revealed to me: What was that will? What was the highest challenge for me? What was the greatest good I could do to meet God's greatest need and humanity's greatest need?

God Has Needs in the Earth

God has many needs in the earth today. He has many, many needs. He has a need to be championed.

Sixty thousand people saw God's need yesterday and assembled in Washington, D.C., to demonstrate for pro-life, the sixth anniversary of the Supreme Court decision *(Roe v. Wade)*. There were sixty thousand people shouting, "We will not compromise! We will have an amendment that forbids abortion in the United States of America."

It was a tremendous demonstration in Washington. It was on about the sixth page of the *L.A. Times* in a tiny little article with no picture. Jesse Helms spoke and he made the statement, "We will not compromise." And the head of the whole pro-life movement was approached by those of the abortion movement, "Let's get together and talk and resolve our differences and work together." And her answer was, "We will not compromise. We will not talk with people who are killing babies. We will stop those who are killing babies."

And the *L.A. Times* wrote it from such a biased standpoint. They wrote it from the basis that six years ago the Supreme Court gave women the right to determine what shall be done with their bodies during the first three months of pregnancy. The *Times* did not state it as six years ago the Supreme Court made the decision that a woman was free to decide to murder her child. That would be the way the pro-lifers would word it. And the other way is that woman had the freedom to do what she wanted to with her body. That's the way the abortionists, or anti-lifers, would word it.

Now, we have freedom of the press in this country. And freedom of the press means that you can own and operate your own newspaper, and you can publish in it whatever you want to publish. I feel that freedom of the press must include a responsibility to the public to present unbiased news and to serve all of the public who are subscribing to your newspaper and to equally present all sides of the question. The *L.A. Times* does not do that, and I feel that it's an outrageous thing. And I think that in our newspapers today we should see the equal coverage.

The Issue of Abortion

In the abortion book that we are writing now, we have given equal coverage to every view that has been presented by everyone on the spectrum of pro- and anti-abortion, and all people in all fields of religion who present their views—why they are for abortion and why they are against it—because I have the *absolute* conviction that when you see all of the arguments lined up, truth will always come out being superior.

You don't need to hide arguments. You don't need to distort the facts and figures to convince the people to vote for you or your way. If you give the people all the information in a careful analysis of all sides of the picture, then you will still have people aligned on two sides, but you will have exposed the truth and you will have exposed the tares and the wheat. You'll see a direct alignment.

You see, many people who are pro-abortion accept the idea that human life exists at conception. They are not arguing on the basis that it's not life. They are ready to murder one life for the sake of the freedom of another life. That is their rationale. And they don't like to have to come out to say that in debate, so they don't debate very often. And when they do, it's just an emotional harangue of energy to control an audience with the Luciferian position that murder is right and that freedom can be won through murder. And that is the basic concept of the Luciferians' takeover of every system of worlds and every planet.

We Are Keepers of the Flame of Divine Life

Now, what I'm pointing out about those sixty thousand demonstrators in Washington is that they saw that God has a need on earth. It's very clear to them that life is being aborted. Whether they will make the conclusion that that life is God or not, somewhere in their soul's being, somewhere in their consciousness, they have the inner knowing. And they know, as one of our congressmen who is pro-life made the statement, that we can say we didn't know what was going on in the concentration camps of Nazi Germany—we didn't know. But he said that when the tally is taken—about six million babies have been murdered since 1973—we will not be able to say that we didn't know. We will *not* be able to say that we didn't know. In the speech that this congressman gave, his concluding sentence was, "We are all keepers of the flame." And he went on to say that we are keepers of the flame of divine life.

The people who are pro-life come from every religion and every walk of life, and they have many different reasons for being against abortion. That happens to be the result of their upbringing and their human education. But they were all there in Washington, and they determined to make a show. And they did make a show, even if the newspapers who are pro-abortion were not willing to publish what was going on.

I've never been concerned about the newspapers, myself. I have the absolute conviction that the souls of the people have a Holy Spirit communication in this Armageddon. But I am saying that God had a need, humanity had a need, and sixty thousand people decided that their optimum capacity to meet that need was to be in Washington and to make their voice count—sixty thousand people chanting, "We will not compromise!"

To me that is such a tremendous release of real keepers of the flame because it starts the turning of the tide of the compromise that has gone on by our president and our leaders with people in foreign nations with our foreign policy, with our domestic policy, with truth everywhere where truth is, and with that terrible, despicable vibration of "Let's get together and talk and make a compromise."

Parallel Actions in the White-Fire Core and the World

I think it's *just tremendous* that we have such people today in America. And we are backing them with our decrees. The rising up of people who are of God and people who are of truth in the Omega plane, in the Matter sphere in America, is a parallel line with the founding of The Summit Lighthouse in 1958. Proportionate to our growth, proportionate to our decrees and invoking of the flame of life, proportionate to the dynamic decrees and the dispensations of the Karmic Board, has been the rise of a consciousness of righteousness in this country. And the correlation is absolutely there on the inner.

You can see it as I see it, and I study the charts at the Royal Teton Retreat at night. Many of you are in those classes that Lanello and I conduct at night, and we study these trends because they show us what our work is accomplishing, and we know it.

We see very clearly that without this Alpha backing of the white-fire core, those who are in the Omega plane, the Matter plane, would not have the inner support, the inner energy. So we support these people even though many of them do not support us and in their outer minds think we are not representative of the light. But that is not important. They will come to that resolution.

What Is Your Greatest Ability to Fulfill the Greatest Need?

As I was saying, seeing God's greatest need, humanity's greatest need, what is your greatest ability to fulfill it? When I made the decision to become a chela and to be trained as a messenger, there wasn't much to indicate that this was going to be a great career. There were three people in the organization in Washington—Mark and two women who were helping him.

There was nothing in the outer world that was of any concern to me. I had been to the UN. I had been to college. I was into political science and economics as my major. And it was very obvious to me that God had a need, humanity had a need, and I could fill it at many levels. I could become a diplomat. I could be sent somewhere and do this or that. I could teach. I could do all kinds of things that would help some people, and I could justify myself and I could say I was doing a good work. But it wasn't the ultimate key that would turn the lock into humanity's Christ consciousness. It was not the ultimate solution to the problem.

I wasn't ready to do what I'm doing now. I wasn't ready to run an organization. I wasn't ready to lecture before thousands of people. I wasn't ready to challenge the darkness pitting itself against Ghana and Liberia.[15] I wasn't ready to suddenly get up and know that my broadcast out of Liberia was going to five nations by radio, challenging the communists who were all listening to me, listening to me right in the room, listening to me wherever their radios were turned on. I felt them the whole night. I paced the floor the whole night after I gave that talk. I felt that enemy.

I couldn't have done that when I first became a chela. But there was something I knew I could do. I could submit myself to the training and I could be the right arm of the prophet, of Mark Prophet. I could hold up his arm.[16] I could help him.

I could help get him the things that he needed.

So I did everything I knew how to do. I did whatever my outer capacity was. In exchange for what I gave upon the altar, God gave me himself. And I'm still assimilating. I'm still integrating with that Great Being. I'm still learning every day. I'm still becoming more of the Great God of the universe. And the process will never cease from the hour of your ascension on. There's always the great self-transcendence, the law of self-transcendence where you become God and yet you're always becoming more of God. So there's no ultimate attainment.

The Four Lower Bodies Are the Four Horsemen

As you look at your life, you will have to realize that you have four horses that you're driving—your four lower bodies. And that horse of your desire body is always going to want to go in the opposite direction to your Christ mind. Many of you have disciplined your desire bodies for many lifetimes to be the subject of your Christ Self. Your Christ Self is the driver of these four horsemen of your own Apocalypse. You're driving those four horsemen, and they represent the four lower bodies. And they're capable of wreaking havoc in your microcosm, bringing death and famine and plague and destruction.

So your horses, your four lower bodies, are going to pull against your Christ Self. Your Christ Self is your guru, and the soul is the one who decides whether or not to enter into and be a part of that Christ Self in order to control the four lower bodies. So the soul is what is making the decision to be the chela of the Christ Self. And proportionate to the soul's union with that Christ Self, it will position itself nearer to the nexus. And that's where you will be once you have taken this twelve-week Summit University training.

Why is it a twelve-week training? Because you are given the options and given the teaching and given the whys and wherefores. You are reminded of what you've been told in the inner retreats. You're reminded of what you went forth from Alpha and Omega to do. And basically in a concentrated manner, you cannot be given more until you make some choices. Until you position yourself for your service, God cannot position himself vis-à-vis yourself.

Decide Where You Will Position Yourself

See, when you take your position, God is going to take his position. And he'll interact with you wherever you go, wherever you place yourself. And you shouldn't feel inferior to someone else. You should feel, "This is the most I can be. This is the most I can understand to be. This is the real desire of what I want to do, so I'm going to do it. I'm going to have the courage to be what I am. I'm going to position myself."

The thing you also have to realize is that in spirals of greater and greater surrender, you can position yourself closer, even with less attainment. You can come sick. You can come with a psychological problem. You can come without attainment. You can come into the community or into a teaching center or into a very key position in your home community, in public service as well as in service to the Brotherhood in that community. You can come into position without the full outer attainment.

So within this community there are people going to school, spending a lot of time at night school furthering their individual careers while they're serving in the daytime. But their individual careers are given to the service of the Brotherhood, so they're taking more training to do what they have come to do, better. And so the ascended masters are very much for the continuing education of chelas where that education will enhance chelaship and not detract from it.

The Highest Choice Always Exceeds Your Present Attainment

I could give you all kinds of examples along the years and along my path of having to make the choice to do the most that I could do for God's greatest need. But I would like you to know that the highest choice always exceeds your present attainment.

God had a need for a printing press when we began. Humanity had a need for the teaching. There was no printing press or printer. I'd never seen a press and I wasn't a printer. But I looked around the room. I saw Mark. He wasn't going to run the printing press, because who was going to take the dictations? I saw Christel Anderson, who was almost eighty, and I said, "She's not going to run the printing press." And then I saw Mary Spelzhaus, who was on in years and had problems in her body and was also not going to run the printing press. So there was only one person left to look at. It was me, and so I said, "I'll run the printing press."

So that has happened hundreds and hundreds of times. All kinds of things that I don't know how to do, I will take logical, human footsteps. I will do the research, I'll go to the library, I'll read up on it, I'll study. I'll study the best I know how to do so that God has somebody who's awake, alert, alive, and aware. And then I'll say, "OK, here I am. I'll go and do the best I know how to do because there's no one else to fill that job."

And that is the greatest position to be in because there's that dependency. With all that preparation, you know that God has to do it through you. You just know. You still can't do it yourself. You could be humanly preparing for fifty years, but what the situation calls for is not only the son of man but the Son of God.

Jesus was the son of man. The only begotten Son of God was the Christ Self of him. The son of man is not sufficient to the task. The Son of God must interact with you.

The Greatest Genius Is Humility

And it's a funny thing. After you do these things, because the Holy Spirit works through you, the observer looking at you thinks it's just like rolling off a log, you know, that you just do it with such facility that obviously you could do it because you were the expert. But that's not true at all. God is the expert. The Holy Ghost is the expert. And the only expertise that you could ever possibly have claim to is the absolute genius of humility. The greatest genius in the world is the understanding of what humility is, of getting yourself out of the way and understanding how you actually click into that God being that you are, and it acts through you.

So even those of you who are new have probably already seen me do things that I don't know how to do. And you probably don't realize that I didn't know how to do them. Going stumping was something I didn't know how to do, and dealing with crowds that are aggressive and attacking and physically attacking. I've never done it before in this life, and I don't recall having much to do with it in recent embodiments. I didn't actually deal with it. God dealt with it. I just put myself in the position, and God himself did what he did.

So there's that trust. There's that guru-chela relationship. And there's the spontaneity, the freedom of the electron. There's the excitement of being in a free relationship with God, of feeling creative, of figuring out how you're going to meet God's need and going up to his door and knocking on it and saying, "Here I am and I've got a plan and I'd like you to look at this plan and see how you think it'll work"—doing exciting things, working with God, being a co-creator with him, and knowing that because God is your consciousness, that God appreciates your input. God appreciates your advice and counsel and how you think things ought to be down here—how you think school ought to be run, how you think Montessori International should be improved, and what you think is the best way to create a correspondence in the community of the Holy Spirit to the inner etheric community, the inner temples that we've come from.

Your Word Is Important to God

There's that sense of importance, the sense that your word is important to God. The way that you deal with the chain of events is very, very important to Alpha and Omega. I mean, the ascended masters get excited when sixty thousand people give a decree: "We will not compromise!" It's a dynamic decree. Where did they learn to give dynamic decrees? It's in the ethers. It's rolling across America.

Before the fifties, people didn't get together in crowds and chant. Mark and I remember the day when Soviet spies came into our meeting in Washington, D.C., and heard us decreeing. And then we started hearing crowds chanting in the communist countries and by left-wing groups in America. But the right-wing groups soon followed, and all of a sudden the spoken Word is becoming much more used today.

People are outspoken. They write good letters to the editors. They tell people what they think, they'll march, they'll demonstrate, they'll write signs. I don't remember seeing a lot of that going on in the fifties. I don't remember seeing that in the first half of this century in the United States, not nearly to the extent that we're watching it today. People are a lot closer to their Christ mind. They're very much being aligned.

Our Purpose to Provide Information and Enlightenment to All New Age Groups

The purpose of the chela under Maitreya in this organization, the purpose of the collective chelaship of this organization, is to provide information and enlightenment and education to all New Age groups on what the real issues are. There is a psychic fair that is being held in Pasadena now. It's called ICC (International Cooperation Council), and it's all kinds of New Age groups.[17] We always have a booth there, and we showed our slide shows there this weekend. A staff member gave a talk, and people were very interested.

But there are a lot of people there who are in a New Age consciousness who haven't the vaguest idea of what they're talking about. Somebody got up to give a lecture on psychotronics with no facts or figures. He just said, "Psychotronics—it's a terrible thing," and shook his head.

We were there with a completely packaged, 180-minute lecture on psychotronics, which was researched and well documented. It's not something somebody else couldn't have done—research the whole field and make a proper presentation. The added ingredient that makes our presentation unique is the obvious input of the Holy Spirit and the teachings of the Great White Brotherhood.

So there we were with an album for anybody who wanted to know about psychotronics. Well, it was twelve dollars and fifty cents. Now, twelve-fifty is a lot of money for some people to put out, so the obvious need is for the lecture to be in print. So getting that word out becomes a very, very high calling, a tremendous calling of people who are chelas and are looking for the will of God.

The getting out of that word is *terribly* important. And you would be amazed how few people we get out of a given quarter of Summit University who are willing to edit, write, or print, or do any of the things along the lines of getting out the teaching. From the time it gets out of my mouth till the time it gets in your lap as a book, there are many challenging jobs, which can be learned.

Now, there are some people who volunteer and don't have the skills, so then they have to be trained. But the appreciation level of people for that printed word, when it comes down to going and helping do it, is surprisingly shallow. People are always ready to eat the bread, but they're not so ready to sow the wheat and go through the process. So it's an obvious service. It's so obvious in the world today that does anyone need to get up and shout about it? The ascended masters have mentioned it many times in their dictations, about this crying need for publications.

There were people at the fair who were talking about community life according to the system of communist China. And the principles they were teaching were very much on the basis of the original Founding Fathers and the basic Republic of the United States, but they had no awareness of the correlation. They hadn't done their research. They were New Age people with a New Age ideology, and they were in the New Age movement.

What was the other subject they were so woefully ignorant on? Oh, we're running out of energy—the usual New Age people having their booth on "We're running out of energy."

When asked, "Well, what are your figures? What are your statistics?" they had none.

"It's just generally accepted," they said, "that we're running out of energy." So as soon as they're challenged, they have nothing that they can give as the facts and figures. And they get quite disturbed that they are being challenged. They try to make you look very stupid because obviously, "This is the latest finding and this is what everybody believes, and where have you been?"

And so we have right there, ready to publish, the entire *Touch of Shiva* conference in a paperback book. We just don't have the hands to typeset it and get it out. We have the infinite capacity to illustrate such materials—for instance, the collection of graphs and charts so that that book can be a set of two hundred slides that could illustrate it—so a person like you could take the printed book, could take the tapes, could take the slides—that's the ultimate combination, having the spoken Word, the written word, and the illustrated word all together—and out you go with your suitcase, and you're ready to give a talk.

But, oops! You're not ready. You never learned to give a public talk before in your life. So you go to the Ashram of the World Mother for three months after you come to Summit University, and you go on the training program, and you start learning to speak in public and to give talks to groups around Los Angeles. You get some training in the Ashram, and you get some training maybe at UCLA or at a Toastmasters club, and you learn how to speak.

The New Age Groups Need You, the Chela

Well, that to me is exciting. And I feel that New Age groups, groups that seem to all congregate through the local health food store—you get all the people that kind of have a little more awareness than anybody else in the community when you go to the health food store—groups that are tied up with various Indian yogis, et cetera, they need you, the chela, not the guru. They don't need the guru; they don't need me. I'm quite an unacceptable commodity. I'm much too much the authority figure. I'm much too threatening.

But they need the chela who is a chela like they are chelas (or like they would like to think that they are chelas) to come along and say, "Have you heard?" And in a very relaxed situation with maybe ten or twenty, thirty people, more or less, sit down and be presented the whole concept of Marx, the Satanist, or of Jesus Christ, the great guru of the free enterprise system, of psychotronics, or of refuting the Club of Rome as we did at this class, or of any other subject that we would research.[18] So the effective person in the Matter sphere going out of Camelot is the person who has been saturated with the Alpha sphere and then can go out as an extension of the white-fire core.

The Need to Keep the Flame in the White-Fire Core

Some of you did not see the play of the children about Camelot, which was performed last July. The most exciting thing about that play was the part where the vision comes of the Holy Grail. One sees the Holy Grail—Galahad. And all of the knights suddenly say that they want to go out in search of this Holy Grail.

Morya (King Arthur) rebukes them and tells them, "If you leave, Camelot will be destroyed. It is not your dharma. The one who has seen the Grail is the one who has the initiation to go out and find it. The rest of you must keep the flame here in the Alpha white-fire core."

They disobeyed, they went out, Camelot was destroyed, and here we are again. So, what is that? It's the temptation to go out and be a teacher before you have become a student. And Saint Germain dictated again and again through the Ballards, through the I AM movement that everybody wants to become a teacher, but how many people want to become students? How many people realize that they must go through their human creation, they must have a period of chelaship?

So that is what we're offering. We're offering chelaship, and we're offering education supplemented by training in night courses at the local universities, whatever they may be. There are lots of students who, when we finally sit down and figure out what their dharma is and what the will of God is for them, have to go back to school. There's just no question about it. They must go and complete their education.

And this is one of the things you'll read about from the people who are analyzing cults. They say that these cults are against education. These cults are against the individual developing himself, and so they are stealing tomorrow's leaders by assembling this glassy-eyed group of people who are just following the leader. Most of those glassy-eyed people are people of a very small identity pattern who are willing to exchange it for the guru's identity because he has a powerful aura. He's got that fallen-angel aura where he is so commanding.

One of our students came out of Satchidananda's group[19] and gave him the tape album *The Rhythm of Shiva,* because he was allowing the students to play rock and jazz music. As soon as Satchidananda heard the dictation by Shiva[20] (this is hearsay; I'm only repeating what a student told me), he announced to his community, "There will be no more rock music and no more jazz played."

What was the point here? The point was that he knew in his heart it was wrong, but he was afraid he'd lose students if he made the edict. So he heard somebody speak the truth. Somebody had the courage to say it—somebody who was American, and somebody who was successful in the line of being a guru. So he took courage and he made the edict. So I sent him the tape album of *The Science of Rhythm*[21] for Christmas, and he acknowledged it and was very sweet.

But the point here is that you have an Indian teacher—and there are many of them in the United States today, some who are well known and some who are not—they come under the old dispensation, and they lead people around in a consciousness of meditation on God, but they are not diligent in studying the Matter plane, the Matter disciplines. And so their followers have no idea that we're not running out of energy, that rock music is bad, that Communism is an enormous threat—all of the things that you are taught.

Now, there are nine gifts of the Holy Spirit. One of those gifts is the gift of knowledge and one of them is the gift of wisdom. The gift of wisdom is the gift of the knowledge of the plane of Spirit, of heaven, and all of its teaching and all of its laws and its hierarchies and its light. That's the gift of wisdom. The gift of knowledge is the gift of being able to penetrate the Matter plane and to know what's happening in it and to be able to analyze it. It's the knowledge of the actualities. Actualities are what are concrete here in Matter.

The Humility to Meet God's Need

So the dharma, the will of God for you, is to become a chela and find out what is the greatest thing you can do to meet God's need and humanity's need. We have somebody sitting here in the front row who decided that his greatest ability to meet God's need and humanity's need was to poster for us. He's put out hundreds of thousands of posters all over the United States. You had better stand up so everybody can see who I'm talking about.

It's a real point of humility. There's somebody in the back who went with him. That's the team right there. He's got a master's degree in marketing, and you don't have a degree, do you? Have you been to any college?

Student: Yes, I went to college two years.

ECP: They saw God's need to contact humanity and humanity's need to contact God. They made a very practical decision. "We will go ahead of you, Mother. We will poster all these cities." They came to all the cities on the stump tour. And because those posters went up, some of you are here today. That's an extremely practical answer to an extremely practical need.

Yet how many people would go out and poster? It's hard. It's lonely. And you get the first brunt of the opposition within every community to the coming of the light. You live in all kinds of different places. You don't know if you're going to get a shower today or not. You're not sure what you're going to eat, and there are all kinds of contingencies that are totally unknown.

But it's very simple, isn't it? It's not a grandiose feat of doing something enormous and feeling successful. It's an unknown and an unsung accomplishment. It's like the lady master Nada, who had tremendous talent but sublimated that talent to keep the flame for all of her talented brothers and sisters who wouldn't have made it unless she kept the focus in the Alpha plane.

You need to be very disciplined when you choose this solution, because when you see that you can do any one of fifty different things and do them well, or even ten things or three things, then it starts narrowing down. And you have to ask the question, "Yes, I could serve in the government. Yes, I could have a career. Yes, I could do that. But fifty other people could do that."

But only one of those fifty people, namely me, could run that printing press to publish the *Pearls,* because the person who runs the printing press to publish the *Pearls* has to have qualifications that those other fifty people do not have. They have to be a chela. They have to have a God consciousness. They have to be able to sustain a flame at the Spirit level, or the Alpha level of Camelot. They have to be able to deal with all the astral projections to that project.

So then you start doing the job that nobody else can do. If God has a need and no one else is going to feed him, then you have to feed him. You have to sit down and cook a pot of porridge and feed it to Siddhartha, who is hungry. And if he doesn't eat, he can't meditate under the Bo tree for forty-nine days and gain enlightenment.

So if there's no cook in the kitchen who is a chela, Summit University won't keep going because the chelas have to eat. And that kitchen area, for instance, has been a place that we have not so many volunteers for. The people who do volunteer are the utmost devotees working the longest hours. Some of them don't get off an hour in seven days to do their laundry. And the Montessori students took pity on them and volunteered to put in time in the kitchen last year because of that situation.

It's an amazing thing. When you love God enough to do the job that nobody else is willing to do, you get the greatest training in chelaship. It's very exciting. You make the greatest progress on the Path. You get the greatest compensation of light. You transmute the most. But you probably get the least amount of the world's recognition.

The Goal of Chelaship

This talk is not given to you with the idea of trying to enlist you in an outer way of serving here. I'm talking to you about chelaship, which is the most precious gift that God has given to me in all of my lifetimes. And I feel the Brotherhood releasing teachings on chelaship from every level and every area. I came to you this morning to deliver to you one great single truth, one great single distillation of my observation of chelas, and that is where I have come to in this talk. I'm ready to give it to you.

The goal of your chelaship is to see the guru, the ascended master, face-to-face. And the principle that we have taught you is that you don't get in that proximity to the guru face-to-face until you can show that you receive the representative that the guru sends in the name of the guru and that through the interaction with that person, namely the messenger, you prove yourself capable of holding your harmony and holding your God consciousness so that when you come face-to-face with the ascended master, you will not make the karma of sinning against an ascended master.

So all of the teachers we have in our life—our parents initially represent the guru to us, Alpha and Omega; our teachers in school; the people we work for; life itself, karma is the guru; experiences, circumstances—all of these are the personal or the impersonal teacher. The impersonal teacher is a train wreck that you're in the middle of. It's an impersonal teacher teaching you a lesson—many lessons.

Your soul always gets the lesson. Your soul is always aware of what karma, of what previous incarnation is being worked out. But the outer mind doesn't have that awareness, so sometimes it rebels against the impersonal teacher. The outer mind doesn't even recognize it, calls it an accident or circumstance or bad luck or astrology, or blames it on circumstances that are supernatural (superstition, in other words). So we have the impersonal and the personal teacher.

We work our way through all of these until we have some glimmer of hope that we're actually approaching the door to the retreat. And that glimmer comes the first time we meet someone who knows something about the teachings of the Great White Brotherhood. We find a book or we find a chela, and the chela takes us to another chela, and so we get closer and closer.

Find Out What Is Important to Your Boss

Well, as I am the instrument for the ascended masters' diligent preparation of their chelas to be ready to stand in the masters' presence and to accelerate the chela's God consciousness, I have a very good bird's-eye view of what the masters expect, of the standards that they set, and of what is important to them.

Now, one of the things that I learned early when I began to work on various jobs through high school and college and after college was that the best way to get ahead in any job is to learn to think the way your boss thinks. If you're pigheaded and meatheaded, and if you're determined to show your boss how to think, you're likely not to be employed very much longer.

If you are so stubborn that you are going to do *your* thing within the framework of the organization and you are not identifying with your boss, you don't learn anything. He's the boss because he knows more than you do. He's learned to handle a business, handle money, market a product, or whatever he's doing, so you have something to learn from him. But some people think that they have more to teach their boss than they have to learn. And so they go from job to job because they can't get along with the person who's over them.

It's a very important step in getting closer to your guru. If you don't try it out in the human scene, if you don't learn to work with people, and if you don't learn a systematic order of hierarchy in the human kingdom, you'll never get admitted to the divine kingdom to find out how it works there.

Now there comes a place when you fulfill yourself as an employee and you're being paid to do a job and you may so totally disagree with the policy, the attitude, the morality, or the climate of your job that you may resign in protest. That's another matter. That involves the integrity of your soul. But if you are in basic agreement and can work under an individual, the way to get ahead, the way to accelerate, is to learn what is important to that person.

If punctuality is top on their list, you be punctual. Don't make it your value that it's not important if you're late or not late. If it's important to your boss, it's important to you. If being clean and neat and properly dressed is important, then it's important to you. If your boss is very casual and wears casual clothes, then it doesn't matter. But people have their areas of what is important. If you violate that area, you have set yourself further and further away from that individual.

Now, it may be totally unimportant to you whether you arrive at nine o'clock or three minutes after. It may be ridiculous to you to even be concerned about it. But I've worked for people to whom it was the ultimate. If you weren't on time or ahead of time, you couldn't do anything else right the whole day. Whereas you know your supreme value in sixteen other areas, that seems to be the situation. The other thing is dress. Dress is very important to a lot of people. And then there are all the other qualities that go to make up a good employee and a good job.

What's true in the world is exactly true of the ascended masters. It's a funny thing. I have been teaching and giving the teaching to chelas for years. And somehow you get the vibration and you get the chela who is so in love with himself and so appreciative of himself, so liking himself that he very easily will excuse himself on those very points that are of ultimate importance to the Great White Brotherhood.

And so even when corrected on a point of disobedience or a lack of efficiency in work, he will continue to place his own set of priorities on the situation and think to himself, "Well, it really wasn't important that I didn't do that right. It didn't really matter"—right when the guru, the ascended master speaking through me to that person, is making the obvious point that "this is of the *ultimate* importance, and if you do not correct this particular point you can go no step further." So then you see that it becomes a question of self-evaluation vis-à-vis the Self-evaluation of the guru.

Initiation Begins with El Morya

There are two people in the guru-chela relationship. There's you and the guru. So you have two selves to evaluate. There is the guru and there is the chela.

Who is the guru? The guru is Morya, and the chela is you. The guru is Morya because, first of all, he's the chohan of the first ray, and you can't get past the first ray until you get past Morya. And the order of initiation in the seven rays, which is the path of your Christhood, is from the first ray to the seventh ray. So when you are initiated by the chohans, you are initiated in the order of the rays. You always start with El Morya. If you can't get past El Morya, you never get on to Lanto, Paul the Venetian, Serapis Bey, Hilarion, Lady Master Nada, or Saint Germain.

Now, Saint Germain may be the goal of many of you. I'd like you to know that Saint Germain had been the goal of my life and of many incarnations. Saint Germain is a cosmic being. He takes the office of Chohan of the Seventh Ray like a world-famous surgeon would take a position on the board of directors of a local hospital for a dollar a year. Saint Germain takes a chohanship as something that is beneath him in attainment.

He's very busy. He's got a lot of worlds that are in his hands that are in the midst of Armageddon, not simply the planet Earth. He's got a lot to do. He's got a lot of people to see. There's no reason why he should sit down and talk with you when you haven't passed the first initiations of the lord of the first ray, who is known to be the one who gives you the tests of obedience and chelaship that are the requirements of every ray. So that's the point of hierarchy.

I was pursuing Saint Germain. I've had a number of embodiments when I was very close to Saint Germain personally. But nevertheless, when it came time for me to work for Saint Germain, El Morya was the guru who took me on, gave me the initiations, gave me the chelaship, and then said, "*Now* you are ready to be received by Saint Germain." And so when El Morya was all through training me and all through dealing with me and the human consciousness' reaction to the light, then Saint Germain came and ordained me as a messenger and gave me the mantle of that office in a very sacred ceremony in Holy Tree House.

Getting to Know El Morya

When I met Morya in Boston and when I knew him in Washington, D.C., being trained by him, I found out that I was meeting a very extraordinary personality in God, who had extraordinary standards, who had certain things that he would never compromise, certain standards. I found out that many teachers that I'd had in this life had those very same standards. I had been in the family of El Morya in his previous incarnations, so I had come to learn those standards by living with him. Much of it was ingrained in my soul.

But getting to know El Morya is the whole key to being accepted as a chela. There are things that El Morya will absolutely not tolerate, and they always seem to be small. But if you look in his eye, you will see the magnifying glass and the projector that can project that small detail on the screen of a cosmos and show you that if you leave that flaw in the diamond, when the diamond expands, the flaw will mar your whole cosmic consciousness. It would be the unraveling of an entire chain of chelaship.

I can give you a lot of little examples of this. I can remember a most outstanding statement that El Morya made. I don't remember specifically what the occasion was, what the particular incident was, but the statement was, "If I cannot accept the giver, I cannot accept the gift." And the translation of that is that you shouldn't accept a gift that comes from a giver whose consciousness you cannot accept.

Well, I have observed Mark be obedient to that rule over the years in small ways and in big ways. I've seen Mark turn down millions of dollars because the person offering the money was attempting to control him and manipulate not only the messenger but the message as well.

A Lesson about the Consciousness of El Morya

I had an occasion this Christmas with someone who'd been to Summit University Level I, to Level II, and to the Los Angeles Teaching Center, where I had to dismiss him because of dishonesty. There he stole from the collection plate, stole from the treasury of the teaching center. He never told anyone about it, and six months later, after many calls made by the members, he mentioned the fact that he'd borrowed the money and was now returning it. He in fact had not borrowed the money, of course. He had taken the money, but he was able to rearrange it in his mind. The dishonesty of this person coupled with the disobedience caused me to dismiss him from the teaching center.

I have a real heart for this person. I know he has a problem. He has psychological problems, and the problem is in the area of self-deception. He's self-deceived and so easily deceives others.

He is very easily in a situation where he'll make money and cheat the government, not pay taxes, not report his income, not keep his books, and things of that nature, and which I've counseled him about. I've even counseled him to take some therapy in counseling with one of our psychologists.

This Christmas he came with the best purity of his heart that he could muster, given his situation, and came with a gift for me and for each of my family members—very nice gifts, very thoughtful gifts. Well, the very next day after these were delivered, my son was misplaced on the campus, couldn't be found anywhere. It was during the conference. And when I'm on the platform and I don't know where my children are, I'm concerned.

The campus had been combed, and there this individual was attending the conference and his van was in the parking lot. One of the people looking for my son said to this man, "Have you seen him?"

This man knew that my son was in his van, but he told the person, "No, I haven't seen him." So we went on looking for my son. What he did was, he turned around and told my son that people were looking for him. And of course, my son was where he should not have been and knew he was. So the person was covering up for him with the same deception that he would cover up for himself—covering up for the carnal mind's little rebellions instead of being loyal to the Christ and being willing to expose, even though it might hurt.

I called him in when I found out where my son was. My son was in his van. I called him and I said, "Did you know he was in your van?" He knew my son was there. And then he told me himself that he had told this person, "No." Now this is after about *four years* of my personal interaction with this person *stressing* this particular point of chelaship, and two whole sessions of Summit University with the explanation that you cannot get the Holy Ghost if you don't have personal integrity; you cannot lie to the messenger. You see, he's never identified with the guru, Morya or me, with what's important to me.

"Well," he said, "I wasn't lying to you. I was lying to so-and-so."

And I said, "That so-and-so is a chela. The chela *is* the messenger. The chela *is* the next person down in the chain of hierarchy. When you talk to a chela, you talk to the messenger. When you talk to the messenger, you talk to the ascended master."

Morya says, "If the messenger be an *ant,* heed him!" That's my favorite statement of El Morya. You *heed* the word of truth no matter who is the mouthpiece. If you don't receive the chela in the name of the messenger, you're never going to get to the messenger. If you don't receive the messenger in the name of the ascended master, you will never get to the ascended master. Jesus said, "He that receiveth a prophet in the name of a prophet shall receive a prophet's reward." "And he that seeth me seeth him that sent me." The person who knows the son knows the father.[22]

So I wrote a letter to this individual in answer to his letter to me, which came with the Christmas gifts, expressing that no matter what it would take, he desired chelaship. I wrote a letter with that statement of El Morya, "If I cannot accept the giver, I cannot accept the gift," returned all of the Christmas presents, and said, "You cannot flatter the messenger with gifts and yet lie to the messenger."

Now that to me is a great lesson about the consciousness of El Morya. And when I learn something about El Morya, I learn something about God. I learn something about the will of God to which he is dedicated.

Well, my son said to me, "But so-and-so is my friend. I'll insult him if I return this gift to him." So we had a long discussion about "Who are you insulting?" You're insulting the Christ Self of the person by accepting the gift and allowing him to do this. And you're the better friend to the soul by doing something that apparently hurts at the moment.

I explained to my son that I knew that I was the only friend that this boy has who would go to the trouble of giving my life for him and exposing him at the same time, exposing his human consciousness. I'm holding him in the hollow of my hand. I'm holding him up. I'm giving him my love. I'm supporting him with my total life, right while I am chastising him, right while I am throwing a bolt of blue lightning at something that's a very personal part of him.

That's a very shattering experience, to give these gifts to the messenger and family and have them returned. It's a very shattering experience. But I'm not leaving him alone outside of the circle of God to be shattered the way the world will do, because the world is not going to tolerate or accept him. The world is not going to keep him in a job. A wife is not going to keep him. Nobody is going to accept this individual, because of his psychological and self-deception problems.

I haven't said, "I reject you." I've said, "I reject these dark threads in your garment, and I'm going to help you carefully extract these threads while we keep the garment intact. I will support you while I reject the human vibration and accept the Christ consciousness and receive your soul." Now, that is the great office of the guru that El Morya gives to us. That is the support and the love that people need.

The action that I took is the most loving action that could have been taken, because it was championing reality. It was saying to him, "No matter what you've done, I love *you*. I don't need these gifts in order to love you. And my love is not lessened because you've lied to me. So whether you do good to me or you do evil to me, I still love you the same. But I love you because I want your soul to ultimately become one with God."

Now this is what is going on in the guru-chela relationship within the community. The master will take the trouble to deliver that light to his chelas, but he will always keep the chelas in his arms. He will always love the chelas in the process. The world is much more cruel. The world doesn't give you a second chance. The world throws you out. There are a lot of lonely people in the world because people didn't take the trouble to explain to them what were their problems, what were their shortcomings.

Most of people's problems, and this problem of deception, are long, long developed as a defense of the human ego. The human ego feels that in order to be accepted, it has to have wealth and money. Well, it can't get it legitimately so it gets it illegitimately. It does it illegally. So dishonesty is a defense of an ego.

What the guru will show you is that he'll take you the way you are, so you don't have to be someone else. You don't have to lie about yourself. You don't have to cheat and steal. You don't have to enter into all of this. Lying is an ingrained habit and it is not overcome easily. But it is totally unacceptable to that guru —totally unacceptable. And how long he'll stand by you for you to overcome it, no one knows. You never know.

The Timeline of Opportunity

The most amazing thing about chelaship is that a person could have been lying for the last ten thousand years. A person could have had great teachers in many embodiments illustrating the great example of truth. We have a lot of heroes in our history and in our literature who exemplify virtue and show us that virtue wins out. That's the basic underlying morality of the Western movie and all kinds of other fairy tales and scriptures that we're given.

For ten thousand years a person may have had this habit of lying and never made the decision to stop. So he might get with the ascended masters and with the gurus on this timeline of his existences. He's come into embodiment here, here, here, here, here, here. Finally he gets to this place over here where he's in embodiment, and there he gets this opportunity—he meets El Morya, he reads his book, he has the opportunity.

I can't tell you if that person's opportunity will be up in one month, one year, five years, or if he's got the whole lifetime to overcome it. That is the individual's karma. It's his karmic clock and it's his relationship with the inner gurus. But if the individual refuses to put on and become the consciousness of the guru, when the time is up, the guru will drop him. The break will occur and he will be removed from the Great White Brotherhood for that embodiment.

There was a very startling dictation that I remember in Colorado Springs where an ascended master stated that whoever rejected that dictation would not be contacted by the Great White Brotherhood for a hundred years, which means into the next lifetime.[23] It was a very astounding piece of energy, to say the least, to hear that. And it happened, I believe, as a consequence of a long series of events of people mocking the ascended masters and mocking the messenger Mark.

What I'm saying here is that you never play games with the gurus and you don't tempt God. I was riding in a car with Mark Prophet in the streets of Washington, D.C. He was discussing with me a question, a matter to which I had to commit myself and my life. And I was meditating upon it, and I wasn't giving the instantaneous response. He flicked on the radio. It was a legitimate radio, so help me God. It was a radio! He flicked it on, and "Pomp and Circumstance" started playing. And Morya said through Mark to me, "You have till this piece is over to make up your mind."

That really was amazing to me. I can tell you, when you start seeing the wonders and the miracles of the ascended masters and how they perform them and how they act, and you've never seen them before, you really are quite amazed at the Brotherhood. The Brotherhood is very, very real.

The point was that when you get that close to El Morya and you get that great an opportunity to be a messenger for him, they expect that there shall be nothing wanting in your consciousness. And the point was that I had made such decisions thousands of times before. It was not a request that was beyond my attainment. It was *because* of my attainment that I was expected to be able to give a commitment in the period of time that the piece was played.

And this is a law you will find explained in Hinduism, that the more advanced you are on the Path, the more severe is the initiation. The people with less attainment are given a much wider latitude than people with more attainment. It also works that way with the fallen ones, who've been around thousands of years.

The Top Priority on Morya's List

Now I'm about to tell you what I feel is absolutely the top priority on El Morya's list. We see a group of chelas whose hearts are devoted and who have a very intense love. The heart is like a furnace of fire. Have you ever seen pictures of Mother Mary where there's a burning heart that symbolizes the sacred heart? I always find those pictures amazing because it really looks like the heart is a cauldron of unlimited fire.

That's how love feels. Love energy within you is like an unlimited resource. And people who are loving are just loving all around. They're beautiful people. The channeling of that love into the highest action, the most needed action, takes the discipline of the will of God and the wisdom of God.

A vat of love is only as good as the supporting arms of blue and yellow, the real energy that enables you to wisely invest your resources. This vat of love is like a gigantic bank account. Love is like all of the natural resources in the heart of the earth. It's pure energy of the Holy Ghost. You can multiply it and increase it, and it can bring forth the Christ consciousness over and over again. Or it can be quite impractical. So we see beautiful people come to the feet of the ascended masters. Their hearts are pure; their hearts are full of love.

But here is the area of weakness. It may be weakness because of our generation, because of the effect of drugs on the mind, because of a mechanical educational system, but it is a weakness. It's a weakness that we must overcome because it is so much a priority to El Morya.

El Morya is a Mercurian. The quality of the Mercurian is communication. Mercurians are communicators of the Word. You are a mandala of Mercurians. Whether you're from Venus or Jupiter or wherever else you may be from, some other system of worlds, you're a Mercurian right now. You have to think like your boss, and your boss is a Mercurian. And he's going to communicate the Word to this earth and her evolutions because that's the requirement of the hour and that's why he was hired for the job—because he has aeons of experience as a communicator of the Word. And there is nothing more *vital* that this planet needs right now than the communication of the Word.

The Communication of the Word Is the Need

The Word gets communicated through seven chakras. The throat chakra communicates it as the spoken Word, but the other chakras communicate the Word (capital *W*, the Logos) as healing, as love, as enlightenment, as vision for every project that's going on, as the flame of God-government, as freedom out of the soul. So you can see seven portholes in your being, and out of every one must come the mastery of the communication of the Word or the transfer of the Word to people, to institutions, to wherever you are, to the subconscious of the planet, to the superconscious Being. Morya's an expert in communicating the Word.

The communication of the Word is the problem. And specifically in the chela, it is receiving the instruction of the ascended master and carrying it out in the spirit and the letter of his intent —carrying it out with his spirit, with his flame, but also exactly and precisely in the way in which he has expressed it.

When I was in high school, I had the great good fortune of having an English teacher who was a woman who would talk and lecture, and suddenly in the middle of that she would stop and point to someone and say, "Repeat what I just said." And they would have to repeat the whole sentence.

Some people would always be able to repeat it verbatim, and other people couldn't repeat it at all. I've done that a number of times in teaching class. Whatever training I've had, whatever teachers I've had, whatever I've done at inner levels, this is a preparation that I have received: a very careful listening, a very careful assimilation of what was said, a careful notation of the exact words, and then the implementation of that direction into action.

That particular fundamental point will enable you to excel anywhere—in education or in a job or in the professions. I feel that people are successful proportionate to their ability to take in, assimilate, and then act on what they have taken in and assimilated. I think the most successful people in the world are those who can accurately take in information. It goes through the computer of their creativity, their Christ consciousness, or their mind, and it comes out as the implementation of a plan or of a direction or of an education.

Now, it involves the ability to think, because El Morya or any other guru does not stand by you twenty-four hours a day, "Now go to bed, now take a shower, now brush your teeth, now get up, now take your vitamins, now drink your green drink, now do this, now do that, go here, go there." There are some people who walk around trying to hear every little thing that God would be telling them to do next, when God expects you to run your life.

The Law and Its Interpretation

So, the translation of the letter and spirit of the guru involves the understanding of law itself. What is law based on? Law is based on, first of all, a set of absolute principles, and they are wide principles, and they govern life. And from those wide principles we have the interpretations of the law and its breakdown for many human situations. For instance, the Ten Commandments were given, then they were broken down into all kinds of rules and disciplines that Moses set forth. The two commandments of Jesus Christ—they can govern our whole life.[24] The Constitution of the United States—it's a brief document, but out of it comes the breakdown of everything else that we do.

Law is a set of absolute rules, and then under those absolute rules there will be interpretations such as those given by the Supreme Court or those who occupy the seat of authority of the Christ. And then comes this whole long list of things that come under the word *precedent*. A precedent is set in a Supreme Court decision, and then all other decisions must reflect that precedent unless the precedent itself is going to be overturned. So we're always looking for a precedent.

Going from the principle "Thou shalt not kill"[25] and then interpreting it in all given human situations, that is a process of the Logos. Remember, *logos* means "logic." It means "reason." So logic and reason are the clue to the understanding of who is the Son of God. "The Son" in Greek is acknowledged as "the Word." And the Greek word for "Word" is *logos,* and logos means "reason" or "logic."

So when you meditate upon the mind of Christ outpictured in El Morya or outpictured in Paul the Venetian or Lanto, the mind of Christ is the basic mind of the universal Person of God, the Second Person of the Trinity. But that mind in El Morya is manifesting *uniquely* in the way in which he has mastered that mind. El Morya's Christ mind is different from Saint Germain's Christ mind, as your Christ Self is different from my Christ Self. They're not cookie-cutter Christ minds. They weren't all just punched out.

There is a universal Logos. It's the Second Person of the Trinity. You identify with that mind, and you begin to develop it according to your devotion to God, whether it's love or wisdom or science or truth or healing. Whatever your expertise is, that's the way in which you develop the use of your Christ mind. In other words, it's the way you program a computer. It's how you use a computer. Computers are different by the fact of their programming and their use.

So you all have access to the universal mind of God. But you might all just have one little chip of that mind, and how you work with it is how you will reveal that mind to others. Jesus revealed to us the Christ mind in a very personal way. But most Christians today cannot see any similarity between the Christ mind of Jesus and the Christ mind of Saint Germain, because Saint Germain developed that Christ mind as an alchemist, as Francis Bacon, as a writer, as a scientist, as a playwright. To them there's just no comparison, but there's every comparison in the world because the Logos, the origin, is the same.

From Principle to Application

Now, in the Christ consciousness, then, you take a given set of teachings of the ascended masters or a given set of requirements within the community, and through the logic of your Christ mind, you don't have to be told fifty steps to take. You know what they are because you go through a logical, geometric progression from an original principle to its application on how you mow a lawn or how you clip the roses or how you make the soup. You won't have to be told. You may have to be told a recipe. You may have to learn from the gardener at what point on the stem you cut that rose. But there's a basic underlying principle that is the extension of the guru's consciousness that will enable you to do that.

So what do you find? El Morya began many years ago in Colorado Springs to have every staff member carry a notebook and a pencil because it was very clear that they could not keep an oral tradition. The sacred scriptures of India are handed down by an oral tradition. Before the age of radio and television and mass media and mass communication and our senses being bombarded by so many words, so many books, so much thinking that's pre-distilled, and so much information that does not require us to retain it because it's all available—before that age, people had much greater facility in the memory body.

The etheric body worked for people. So they memorized vast, vast tomes and works of scripture, and they've been handed down verbatim century after century with never a change, so developed was the memory body.

Our memory bodies have atrophied in this century. I was never more astounded than when I went to see Williamsburg in Virginia after the July Fourth conference in Washington, D.C. I had never been there before, and I took the family there. And when I entered the houses of these people who lived there, who were the statesmen, who were the people who fought in the House of Burgesses and whatever other bodies they were in, and who were the ones who really carried the truth for our independence—when I stood in their homes and I stood in their bedrooms and in their kitchens and in their drawing rooms, and I listened and I contacted the akashic records, what was most amazing to me was the fact that there was such a purity of consciousness.

There was no bombardment of rock music, of TV, of radio. There was not the puncturing of the astral plane, which we have had progressively in this century. The bottomless pit and the astral plane have been punctured and are spilling over into the mental and physical planes. That is happening. This is one of the great tragedies of our age. This happens through the drug culture. It happens through rock music. And our society has gone crazy because the astral hell itself has become a living hell in the earth.

When you lived on the earth two hundred years ago, the astral plane was sealed. You could live concretely in your physical body, clearly in your mental body, and have access to the etheric body. Today it's in another equation.

Another thing that made up such clarity of consciousness was the purity of their food. There were no chemicals. There were no plastics. There was no automobile exhaust. The atmosphere was clear. Brains were clear. And because they had the clarity of their cellular structure and the cells of the brain, they had a greater transfer of light from their Christ mind. Those people who laid the foundation of this nation were initiates of the Great White Brotherhood.

It was like night and day stepping in and out of that place, that one particular house where I remember I was so shocked by the purity of the forcefield. Even with all the crowds that had come there visiting, it still never lost the pure record of what it had been. Then when we left and we went out into the world and wherever we went, restaurants and places, again the intense pollution was there.

So you can see why we need the violet flame. We have that condition of consciousness today and the atrophying of the etheric body and the lack of creativity in our school systems, where people are fed information and told to feed it back without it spiraling through the figure-eight flow in the heart, without original understanding coming to take place, without original integration. School should be a guru-chela relationship. And with the guru and the chela there is an integration. Even though the chela is required to give absolute obedience, whatever he becomes, he becomes through a process whereby he is putting on thoughtfully, by free will, taking on the attainment of his master.

The Need for Obedience

And the master says, "The quickest way that you can have this attainment is to do what I tell you," which is exactly what you would find if we had the system of apprenticeship in the guilds in this country today. If you become an apprentice to be a printer or a carpenter or a candlemaker, you watch the master of the craft or of the trade. You learn under him. You be quiet and you do what he says and you do what he does. You learn by working with him, and you learn the quickest if you will completely parallel what he is doing, because he is the master. And the one who wants to become the great pianist will listen to him play and then imitate his style, imitate his performance as well as study the technique under him.

But we come to the guru-chela relationship, and we hear all of this outrage because of the false gurus and their enslavement and their imprisonment of souls. And so we are suspect of the authoritarian figure who says, "Do what I tell you to do and don't deviate." The difference between the false guru and the true guru is that the false guru is the tyrant because he embodies the carnal mind. The real guru has become the Christ, has paid an enormous price in becoming that Christ, like Jesus hanging on the cross. And the guru says, "I will give you my Christ consciousness and spare you what I have gone through to get what I am. I will give you my momentum and my attainment. The one price I ask is obedience, because if you don't do what I tell you, you will not be in alignment with my being."

So learning to be obedient and learning to take a given set of instructions and carrying them out from beginning to end—seemingly simple, insignificant, and unimportant—becomes of the ultimate importance because on it hangs the thread of whether or not you can get into that relationship of integration.

Saint Germain made a statement in the I AM movement, which I can't quote verbatim, but it was to the effect that if you will just give me anyone—it doesn't matter who they are; anybody off the street—and if they will give me obedience for so many years, I can revolutionize their consciousness and bring them to the point of the ascension. All he asked for was obedience.

So obedience has to do with being willing to be realigned with your personal inner blueprint, which the guru sees and knows and understands and which he already has become through his own Christ Self.

Striving to Hear the Voice of God

I have spoken on different occasions about the period of five years when I was searching for Saint Germain and when I had to go through college and get to Boston and finally come to the place where it was time for me to meet El Morya and Saint Germain and the messenger. And for one reason or another I had come to the realization that I should try to be ultimately attuned to my inner Christ Self—whom I didn't know by that name, I simply talked with God and God talked to me.

And so when I heard the voice of God and God would instruct me or give me things to do, it was such a relationship of friendship that I would answer God. God would talk to me, and I would talk to God, and I would reason with God. And when God would tell me something to do that was totally not understandable, I would ask questions why.

On a couple of occasions, because I couldn't see why I should do something, I didn't do it. And I found out that it was ultimately a case of life and death and that I should have been obedient. So I came up with my little motto that I wrote all over my college books, which was "Obey immediately." I would read that as I would walk to class. I had never heard of Mother Mary's path at that point. I hadn't had a conversion to Mother Mary. I didn't know the meaning of the term *the state of listening grace,* but that's what I was doing.

I walked around all the time with my ears straining to hear the voice of God, always in that point of reaching for the highest attunement. I would not have even used the term highest attunement at that time, but I was straining to hear the next thing that God would tell me to do so that I could quickly do it because I knew that obedience to whatever he told me would lead to the next thing that he would tell me. And the faster I would do that, the closer I would get to the goal of finding Saint Germain, because ultimately through that contact and through that obedience I would reach the goal.

So there was a long series of events of God talking to me. Perhaps it was my I AM Presence, perhaps it was my Christ Self, and perhaps it was Saint Germain or El Morya, but it did go on for years. And ultimately I was obedient enough to get to the place where the contact was made. I don't really know where that came from except the inner guru.

Have you heard the lecture that I gave after Mark's ascension where I go through all of this? It was a sermon I delivered within a week or two following his ascension because I was almost aghast, in a state of shock, over the concept that had I not been obedient from the first to the last, we wouldn't be where we were.[26] As he made his ascension, my life passed before me the same way they say that it passes before someone when they're about to drown, that all of a sudden everything they've ever done through their life passes before them. I think it's a prelude to standing before the Karmic Board.

Mark ascended and a part of me ascended with him, and I saw my whole life. And I realized that everything that had ever happened that was good had hinged on a point of obedience—my coming, my chelaship, every point of that chelaship, many crossroads in that chelaship to obey or not to obey, moving the organization [from Virginia to Colorado Springs], doing what we were told, holding the conferences, traveling around the world, having the children, working with the chelas. Everything that we'd ever done reached a climax in the moment of Lanello's ascension.

I realize it today because I go through it every single day with staff members. It's that point of contact with those who happen to be around me, that the more they are able to receive of the Word and translate that Word into definite, precise action, the faster they accelerate as chelas, the more useful they become to the Brotherhood, the closer they come to their ascension, the closer they come to inner fulfillment.

Now, the only reason for that requirement of the Law is to increase your attainment. It's not something that inures to the benefit of the guru or the Great White Brotherhood. It is given because it is the key to your light. So when I look upon this in my own life, I see that every point of obedience has resulted in a greater God consciousness in my lifestream. I am the total benefactor of having given obedience. I am the one who has reaped blessings and joys and abundance and light and bliss beyond measure.

The Rebuke of the Guru

Yet, I have seen people who watched my chelaship under Mark, older people who would not give up their pride or whatever else they had, their criticism. And I can remember one particular woman saying, "I would never let him talk to me like that," when Mark would be rebuking me or whatever he might be doing. If he felt like rebuking me in front of an audience, he would rebuke me in front of an audience, you know. And I can remember that after these two sisters were around for a number of years, they left and went back to their old hometown, where they have sat and kind of vegetated, wishing they had never gone back, for the last five or six years, I guess.

I think I've actually heard that from a lot of people. I've heard that from people who one by one drifted away from Mark because of what they interpreted as the harshness of his treatment or his voice or his attitude or whatever that might be, because of the energy that he would exert to break a crystallized pattern in a person's consciousness. And where he saw that it was the development of a human character trait that was causing a chela's downfall, he would go after it like an enraged lion. He would literally attack that forcefield, that point of energy.

How many of you have ever had foot reflexology done on your feet? Well, there are what are called crystals that accumulate in your feet, and you come to work on those places and they're very painful. And unless you press hard and break them up, you don't get rid of them. We have crystals—crystallizations in our desire bodies and in our mental bodies—and it takes an extra release of energy, which is often conveyed by a more intense level of voice. The voice gets louder, it might get faster, and there will be a lightning that will come through it. And that lightning does not always come through a soft whisper.

Gautama Buddha has the total capacity to deliver the lightning of the mind of God in a very, very quiet tone. What is lacking in that is the receptivity of the chela. The chela does not interpret a very soft and quiet voice as the lightning. It takes something to totally jar the consciousness out of the socket, the mold, the rut that it's in.

You read about the greatest gurus of the Far East having these absolutely impossible personalities that would keep everybody else away but the most determined chelas. I think Mark was like that in spite of himself, because Mark was a very sweet, soft, and tenderhearted person. And so I think the ascended master gurus would use him in that way, and it was definitely the medicine required by the chelas.

It was the medicine I required—no question about it—even though I had a tremendous distaste for men with loud voices who would yell at me. I'd made the determination before I ever met Mark that no man was ever going to yell and shout at me.

I've seen people fail their chelaship because they could not take the energy that is the white fire and that is referred to in the path of Buddhism as the energy of the wrathful deities. The face of the Buddha delivering the white light is like the face of an enraged lion—the growling and the roaring of the lion.

In all of the years that I have been the recipient of that ultimate expression of love, that intense love that cares enough to exert itself, I have never felt a vibration of discord. Mark was uniquely the guru who could deliver the word of chastening and the rebuke to totally strip you of your human consciousness and leave you feeling totally loved in the process—whereas the false gurus and the human tyrants will direct their venom and their anger and flatten you to the ground but not provide any way for you to come back up. You're totally condemned, you're totally belittled, and you're totally destroyed. But the ascended masters know that the human consciousness will respond in no other way. The carnal mind will not be challenged in any other way, and the soul will not be jarred to come up higher unless it receives that light.

The delivery of that light and that Word is absolutely necessary to all of us. So the person who is going to be a chela by reading the books and the publications is the chela who doesn't want the personal confrontation. The chela who doesn't want to do anything for fear that he might do something wrong is the chela who fears the rebuke of the guru. "Thou art neither hot nor cold; therefore I will spue thee out of my mouth."²⁷

Being hot or cold means making a decision and doing it and knowing that if it is wrong, you're going to get that sacred fire and you're going to hear it from the guru, and saying that it doesn't matter: "I'm going to make this decision and I'm going to act because I'm basing my action on the absolute Law, the interpretation of that Law, the precedent of that Law that I have seen through the person of God in all of his saints, in all of the teachers, and in the messengers."

Balance Your Threefold Flame

I have seen the best chelas in this organization, who are at the board level and the department-head level, make hundreds of decisions that they had to make in their departments without me and come back and say to me, "I made that decision because I knew it was the decision you and Mark would have made." That is precisely the right consciousness.

They went through the logic of the Christ mind. They entered the Christ mind of their bosses (the messengers) in whom they trusted were reflective of the Christ mind of the ascended masters. They had learned that Christ mind by observing: How do the messengers respond to given situations? What do they allow and what do they not allow? It only comes from experience, because the messengers are setting a standard. If they set it low, everybody will act low. If they set it high, everybody will reach for the highest.

So there are things that you really don't know until you live with someone of the Brotherhood, and you've probably all lived around someone of the Brotherhood in some previous lifetime. You all have certain standards inside of you. You definitely have standards. And they were set in you because you were near a person who was tied to the Great White Brotherhood, and it has left its mark upon you. So you are an accumulation of being around the gurus for a long time.

This message, to me, is very important, and it's a prelude to a message that Lord Maitreya will be delivering to you, which he has promised to give as a dictation before long. It is the practical application of the Law. Going to Summit University doesn't make you a chela of Maitreya or anyone else. It gives you the tools of the trade. Just like going and getting all your carpenter's tools doesn't make you a carpenter, but without the tools you can't be a carpenter. So you get all the tools, but the only way you can be a chela is to be a chela in action.

Action is the key. And action is the sign of the Son who comes down from the Father, who is the agent of the Father, and who becomes through that agency the agent of the Holy Ghost. The Son and the Holy Ghost are the active manifestations of the Father—one as wisdom, one as love; one as plus, one as minus polarity in the great sphere of being.

Now, you know that the requirement of Christhood is the threefold flame balanced: Father, Son, Holy Spirit. Being Father is having the Law. You came to Summit University to say, "OK, what is the Law? What are the laws of God? We've gotten mixed up. We've gotten confused. We don't know which way to go."

The Son is the wisdom of that Law. And *wisdom* means that through the Law you take "wise dominion" over the earth. *Wisdom* is *wis*e *dom*inion. Dominion implies action. It means running a good ranch or running a good household or running yourself well—wise dominion. So you see, it already implies action.

The Holy Ghost is the infusion of that wise dominion with the ultimate love. And the Holy Ghost gives you twin flames, cloven tongues. A cloven tongue is a tongue with two forks. So a cloven tongue of fire is a fire that has two flames. And those two flames are the flames of Alpha and Omega, the wholeness of God. That's why it's called the *Whole-I-Spirit* [Holy Spirit]. So the Holy Ghost gives to you the balance of Alpha and Omega and finally endows your wise dominion with a multiplication factor of Alpha and Omega: the miracles, the gifts, the graces of the Holy Ghost.

So to be a chela, you have to be on the path of balancing that threefold flame. And Father principle is the power to create. Power and law are the same quality; the Law is the inherent power. So without being the Father, without knowing the Law, you can't take wise dominion and you can't be love in action.

Morya is the Father principle on the blue ray, so that's where it all starts. He is a lawyer. He was a great lawyer in his time. He understood the law of Church and State. He balanced the two in his embodiments as Thomas à Becket and Thomas More, and he set a tremendous example. All of that he bequeaths to us, and I feel that the heart of love and energy cannot function at full efficiency without the Law and the wisdom. It just becomes that raw energy of devotion.

Devotional people will sit and decree all day. They will work hard for you, but they're not necessarily leaders. They don't know how to tell ten other people what to do to get a job done, so they always need a shepherd—until that day when they become the shepherd by learning the wisdom and the Law and the integrating of the whole and thereby being able to lead not ten people, but ten thousand people or ten million people.

So the way you get to be a carpenter is to work under carpenters. And now you're being given the tools and the instruction, but I would leave you with the wrong impression if I allowed you to feel that just taking the teaching was the equivalent of chelaship. Chelaship is direct interaction with the guru.

The Single Seed of Your Christ Consciousness

I was saying to someone the other day, the purpose of the founding of The Summit Lighthouse was to publish the teachings of the ascended masters. That was its only purpose—it had no other purpose—so stated in its bylaws. That's why El Morya founded the organization. So I said to this person, "Do you know why we have Summit University, Montessori International, a print shop, this whole community, and all of the various projects that we're doing? Do you know why all of that is added unto it?" The reason is chelaship. The guru always provides his chelas with a situation where they can interact with him through service.

The only way the individual can put on the consciousness of El Morya is to get involved with him in action in a day-to-day working with him. And the number of people who want to be chelas far exceeds the people who can publish the teachings. Those who actually write and publish and print the books are a very small percentage of the organization. The rest of the people may not have the talent or the ability to be in that publishing arm, so Morya creates other jobs. And the more people with the more talent who come, the more jobs he will create—all kinds of departments that don't even exist, that would be adjuncts to departments in the world, even a full-blown university.

And Morya has this tremendous concept of every department being a cell. And this cell is the shape of an octagon. I believe beehives are hexagons, are they not? Well, the cell that I see is an octagon, and I see these octagons side by side. And that turning of energy in an octagon is a cosmic thing. The four above and the four below represent the four planes in Spirit and in Matter. Morya said an amazing thing. He said to us the other day, "Whatever is your dharma, whatever your sacred labor is (and that's interconnected with your karma), you have the responsibility of bringing to the community everything that is necessary for you to fulfill that dharma."

Some people's dharma is quite vast, and unless they establish a situation where they can fulfill it, they will not complete their divine plan. For instance, we were talking about the fact that some people feel an absolute calling to make movies of the organization, the chelas, the messenger, the dictations, the lectures, and so forth, and then take these movies all around the world. And they feel that calling and that dedication, and they think about nothing else night and day. And whenever I meet with them, they are always on fire about making these movies.

Well, two of them got together the other day and they all of a sudden realized that if they didn't make it happen, it wouldn't happen, because they were the ones who were on fire with the Holy Ghost over the project. And it was then that El Morya gave me the teaching. He said, "When you went to Pasadena, Jesus set down the ground rule for every individual on the staff: Every man shall bear his own economic burden," which comes from the biblical statement "Every man shall bear his own burden."[28] That burden means the burden of his karma. Each one carries his own bundle of karma. It's the only way community or church will work.

So the interpretation of that statement was that anybody who wants to be a chela of El Morya and of the Great White Brotherhood who comes to the organization must meet his own expenses, must pay for his own food and pay for his own living. It's ever been the requirement of anybody who's ever gone to any guru anywhere, East and West. Why? Because the chela resents the guru who gives him something for nothing. The chela wants to know that he's earned what he's got, because it gives him a sense of independence. You hate the person who does it for you. It's inbred. There's no way of getting around it. That hatred may be subconscious, but it will always be there.

The wisest parents are those who help their children get and do for themselves. And those are the children who have the greatest love and respect for their parents. So that was the basic point of the guru's reason. And the obvious point is that if you're offering free room and board, you get all kinds of people who want free room and board and you water down the discipline and the excellence of the quality of people.[29]

If you offer high-paying salaries, you could get all kinds of people into the organization. I hear that all the time when I am stumping. "How much do you pay? I can do this and that." And then we hear, you know, "Can I move in? Can I just come and live at Camelot?" And so there are the people who will come for a big salary, and there are people who will come to freeload. But the masters want the people who will come to give their service and who will pay the highest price for chelaship, who will give themselves in service and understand that that is their acceptable offering.

So in *this* situation of fulfilling one's dharma, one's calling, Morya said, again, that every chela must bring to the setting whatever is required for him to fulfill his dharma. Hundreds of thousands of dollars are necessary to set up a proper moviemaking department, so that's a pretty high challenge to a bunch of people who are on fire night and day to make films, isn't it? And the people whose dharma it is to print, the same thing.

Well, how do they get that money? All kinds of ways, whether it's personal inheritance or personal funds, or whether you come without anything and you work until your input in the community has produced the income. The person who's grinding away at the printing press is helping to sell the books, and the books will return the funds that can increase that department. So service itself is a means to enhance the department that serves your own dharma.

We each have a divine plan. It was definitely my dharma to do what I am doing. And in order to do what I am doing, I needed this entire organization and every department in it and everything it's got today and all of its buildings and this campus. Look at all I needed to fulfill my divine plan, which God has supplied. And what did he require of me? He required that I give my life and everything that I had. So what I had at the time I came was not very much. But it was because it was *all* that it counted for all and that it was able to be increased to the level of the necessity. So whatever you need to fulfill your divine plan, you can through your causal body render the service that will cause and allow the supply to multiply for you to fulfill the divine plan.

It may be your divine plan to write music and to bring New Age music to the world. Well, you can see that most of the people in our music department have other duties that are considered more important, mainly because there's no one else to do their other duties. So if it's your divine plan and divine calling to bring the music of the spheres to the world, you can see that you have to bring the light. You have to attract the supply by the magnet of your Christ flame. You multiply the mandala by attracting souls from the four corners of the earth who are of a like vibration. And you would be amazed how that octagon of the department that you are called upon to raise up will multiply by the single seed of your Christ consciousness.

Ultimate Creativity Under the Gurus

And that's the ultimate creativity under the gurus. It's like obedience to your divine plan—which they're showing you what it is through this interaction—gives you exactly what you want, which is the full and total expression of the creative freedom of your soul to bring forth ultimately your dharma, your sacred labor. And that's the key to your ascension.

The most exciting moment that you can look forward to in your embodiment is when you have gone through the initiations beginning with El Morya through the seven rays—and that's called the Christic path of Christhood—and then you go through the initiations of the five secret rays—the Buddhic path of the white-fire core of Alpha and Omega—the seven and the five, whose integration is through the thirteenth, the Christ consciousness or the mind of God. The seven and the five are the twelve; the thirteenth is the center.

You go through and you pass those tests—and it's amazing how quickly you can pass those initiations—and you reach a level where you're still full of life and vigor and vitality. You still have years ahead of you, but you sense that you've reached a place where you have an abundant and an exhilarating freedom to create within the octagon, to create within the great geometry of God.

Devotion Can Become a Magnet
for the Balancing of the Threefold Flame

But there is the period of actually resetting the bones that have grown crooked. It's like breaking them and resetting them. This can be a very painful experience when your carnal mind and its human habit patterns have to be broken down by this lightning of the ascended masters. You ought to consider yourself fortunate to have ever been around anyone in the world who was more loyal to the truth than he was to your human personality. Mostly those are the teachers we resent at the time and later in life appreciate the most—we realize how much they did for us.

So my understanding of chelas is that the heart flame of love that has the devotion can become the magnet for the balance of the threefold flame, hence the balance of the Cosmic Christ, when it is diligent in the disciplines of the very first steps of the path of the chohan of the first ray, El Morya. If there's a point of the Law and a teaching that is important to the guru, it has to be important to you, and you have to make it your own. It's all a question of values—*self-e-value-ation*. What is the value you place on the Self of El Morya?

When I was in embodiment and very close to Thomas More, I had a very, very hard time understanding why he had to go and get himself beheaded. It took me years in this life to come to that understanding. I can understand the obvious facts that he was standing for a principle. But when the person is very close to you and you love him very dearly, it becomes another matter. And I can remember in this life being El Morya's chela, of having to learn that.

I don't think I ever really understood the totality of that experience until I stood in the cell that he was in, in the Tower of London a year ago in January. I meshed with his mind, and I saw that an age was built upon the firmness of his will. It was a *very* exciting moment—just cherishing the fact that one can have a teacher of such attainment, just realizing that one can come that close, just realizing that a man like Thomas More could accept us as his chelas and give us the accumulation of his devotion to Jesus Christ.

There has not been a peer to Thomas More in the whole history of England. There has been no one who has ever come near him—except Francis Bacon. I think that I'm a better person because I have placed supreme value on what's important to El Morya. I've become a better person for God. And El Morya has given us Camelot so that those who want to can come closer and closer to his aura, which he gives freely. I deem Camelot the ultimate gift of the Brotherhood—something physical and in the earth that's not a mystery school on the etheric plane.

Take in the Body and Blood of the Brotherhood

So I would like you to listen with a new determination to the dictations and the lectures. I know that there's only so much that your minds can absorb. But I'd like you to understand that you are absorbing not just points of the Law. You are absorbing an elixir, a sweet distillation. You're drinking the blood and eating the flesh of the Brotherhood.

And when it comes down to active participation in the building of community, whether it's here or at home or wherever your obligations take you in life, you may not remember the point of the Law, because it already has been digested, just like you no longer taste yesterday's meal but you're going on the energy. It's in your body. But the decisions you make and the way you live your life will be because your whole body is vibrating with the totality of the message.

It's amazing the way it works. If you're going to bake the cake, you measure carefully the ingredients. And that's where you are now. You're measuring carefully the ingredients of the points and the teachings of the Brotherhood. You're taking good notes, copious notes. You're studying those notes. But when all is said and done and you're on the battlefield of life, those ingredients will have become the cake. The cake will have been baked. You will have eaten the cake; you will have become the cake.

And you will do the right thing without going through your notes to see what was said on a certain date. You'll do the right thing because all of the Law and all of the logic and all of the geometry and all of the precedents have come down to you having become the Word. You have now become the Christ through this guru-chela relationship. And in becoming the Christ, you have instantaneous access to the computer of the mind of God and you take right action in the moment, on the spot, without thought or deliberation. You have become the Law.

The definition of *guru* is "the one who has become the Law." He is the embodiment of the Law. Because the Law is impersonal, you have to follow the gurus around to see what makes them tick. You have to study the lives of the saints. You have to read their writings. You have to see what Morya did. You can follow somebody like Mark around and see the way he would act in situations, totally in an unorthodox manner. What does *unorthodox* mean? It means not according to the traditions of the scribes and the legalists, who have their human interpretations and their human statements, but totally spontaneously according to the law of God.

Training from Mark

Mark taught me to do things that I would never have thought of doing because I was already too educated. I was already too East Coast and too European in my upbringing—too much conscious of what one did and what one did not do in conversation or in public. And all of a sudden he would do something totally outrageous in public or in a group of people, and everybody around would just absolutely fall apart. People would polarize, for him or against him. And that would be the test, and that would be the release of the Holy Spirit. And he'd walk away. He would never be concerned about who thought what of him or what impression he left. His only concern was to bear the standard of truth.

I've seen him absolutely never reveal himself, carry a low profile, and never say a peep or a boo in a situation. And in other situations he would totally challenge injustice. He was very wise the way he did it. The wisdom was beyond what one could perceive. He knew when to be vocal and when to be silent, when to speak and when not to speak. But his motive was never for how he himself would look. His motive was to get to the core of the issue and to save a soul who he knew would rise higher because Mark would make a sacrifice of what other people thought of him for doing it.

There are, fortunately, quite a number of people on this campus who had years of training from Mark. And those who had the best training from him are the best chelas, and those best chelas are department heads. In the order of the organization, they act under Lanello and me to transfer the initiations to those in their departments. And so there is a direct lineage here of those who still know exactly what Mark would do in a given situation. And what Mark would do, I can assure you, is what Jesus would have done or Saint Germain or El Morya.

The further you get away from a tradition of a teacher, the more watered down is the interpretation, until today most people who call themselves Christians haven't the basic idea of what the personality of Jesus was really about. And they never really do quote the right quotes to illustrate what they're doing, showing that they completely bypass the very heart of what he was.

Laying the Foundation for Great Avatars to Come

So it is an exciting path. And I would like to remind you of something—those of you who are devotees of Jesus—that you are sitting in a classroom today studying under Jesus' teacher, the teacher of your own Saviour. To me that's extremely exciting. And the fact that Maitreya could come is the fact of your own presence. Your presence makes possible the coming of the gurus. And we see that as we multiply our body, multiply our God consciousness, how much more we will open the door for the physical, tangible manifestation of the ascended masters to the people of earth.

I've always considered that what I'm doing is just laying the foundation for the great avatars to come and the great beings who are just over the horizon of this century. And I think that what those who come after us will do will be immensely exciting to watch. But I'm seeing what you have done and what your numbers, tens of thousands around the world, have done and it has already changed the face of the earth—the anchoring of the ascended master gurus. I can't stop talking about it because it's the very *antahkarana* of the earth.

Do you have any questions?

What Is an Antahkarana?

Student: What's an antahkarana?

ECP: An antahkarana is a web of light. You can visualize it as a four-dimensional spider's web in very intricate lines. It's lines of force. And it's the very grid on which a cosmos is hung. It's like the skeletal grid. Every planet has its antahkarana. It's made up of light, and it is the light energy of the guru-chela relationship. It's all those lines that I drew this morning. Wherever you sustain the nexus of Alpha and Omega, that cross, you are now holding up the web that holds up the earth. You are now at that point of the release of light that guarantees that that place is secure and now you have become an electrode for that particular energy.

The reason America is falling apart is that there are not enough people standing at the nexus of the cross of Alpha and Omega to hold their focus of light. So this or that industry, this or that labor union, this or that government, when all the souls of light are not there, goes down the drain because nobody is an orifice, nobody is an opening for the anchoring of the light of the nexus. When you think of Jesus, one person on the cross, one person who elected to do that, sustained the light for two thousand years of the antahkarana of Western civilization. And the imitation of his path and works has been the undergirding of it, and the abandonment of his path and works is the undoing of it.

Finding Your Twin Flame

Student: You spoke during the conference and said that part of the reason for finding your twin flame is to make that two-by-two program work, that we should find our twin flames and go out into the world two by two. I was talking to someone from England who was here at the conference who said that if you were born in another country, that your twin flame is probably there or that your I AM Presence keys into that place. I wonder if you would explain that, or is that just some hearsay?

ECP: You mean that if you were born somewhere else, your twin flame was also born there?

Student: Yes, is it possible? I have no understanding of why I came here, except I did and everything just unfolded itself. I'm here right now in this place, but if what he said were true, I would have to go back to England to find my twin flame.

ECP: That's not true at all. That's just not true.

In the case of twin flames, even if you never meet your twin flame on the physical plane in this life, you can fulfill the function of the two-by-two program with your twin flame. That was the whole point of the dispensation of *Twin Flames in Love*. And that was that the initiation tying you to your twin flame at inner levels enables you to serve right where you are as a counterpart of your twin flame wherever he may be. Finding your twin flame is really the least thing that should be on your mind.

The explanation of the dispensation is that you go two by two because you've been initiated by the Brotherhood and received the blessing of the Karmic Board through the conferences held, which they gave then, so that you are reunited with your twin flame as an arc of light at inner levels. And so at inner levels you are now part of a whole, and it may take you this lifetime to balance the karma to bring you into the same situation.

There are twin flames in this organization who are not married to each other, who are married to other people, and they're perfectly content and perfectly happy. And so it's not necessarily important, even if you know your twin flame, to be married.[30]

Was Jesus a Messenger?

Student: You described Jesus as a messenger on one occasion. Did he walk and talk with Maitreya in the same way that you walk and talk with the masters?

ECP: Oh yes. Many of Jesus' teachings were dictations. And many of his teachings he learned in the retreats and was giving them as I would give a lecture. But much of what he said was the dictations of Maitreya or the distillation of his I AM Presence and Christ Self.

Jesus was the Christ. When you are the Christ, your Christ

mind is one with every other Christ mind. So if I'm speaking a teaching to you, it may have the vibration of sixteen ascended masters from whose Christ consciousness it was distilled, any one of whom, standing before you, would give you the same teaching.

So you do have to see life and God as one. And there is no need to break it down and say, "Well, when Jesus gave that Beatitude, so-and-so was speaking, and when he gave that one...."

One with Maitreya is one with God universally. Jesus was one with the Father, the I AM Presence. He was the Son. He had the fullness of the Holy Ghost. He had access to the entire Spirit of the Great White Brotherhood. And the entire Spirit of the Great White Brotherhood is the entire *Holy Spirit* of the Great White Brotherhood.

The Descent of the Holy Spirit

When Jesus said, "If I go not away, the Comforter will not come,"[31] he meant, "I have to ascend so that the mantle of *my* Holy Spirit can come upon *you*." And that's what every ascended master bequeaths to his chelas. The ascension is the means whereby the Holy Ghost descends upon the devotees.

When Lanello ascended, his Holy Ghost descended. And his Holy Ghost is the momentum of his causal body, of his good works, of his sacred labor, of his power. Jesus gave the mantle of his Spirit, his Holy Spirit on the day of Pentecost.[32] And that's why he told them to wait in Jerusalem until they would get that power.[33] When Lanello ascended, he gave everyone in this organization, beginning with me, his mantle. So I wear his mantle, and I am the open door for the continuing impartation to you of his Holy Spirit.

This is something that Christians have never understood. When the Holy Spirit comes, Jesus described that Holy Spirit as the Comforter who would come "and bring all things to your remembrance, whatsoever I have said unto you."[34] The Holy Ghost is a person. When the Holy Ghost comes upon anyone, the coming of the Holy Ghost is the coming of an ascended master, and that ascended master imparts to someone in embodiment his Spirit—*his* Holy Spirit—in other words, his accumulation of the light of the Third Person of the Trinity.

So when the Holy Ghost came upon the disciples, it was the Person of the Holy Ghost through Jesus, his attainment on the Third Person of the Trinity. That's why he said, "If I go not, the Comforter will not come. I have to ascend if you're going to get the Holy Ghost." That's what Lanello said to us: "I have to take my ascension for you to receive the Holy Ghost." It's the requirement of the Law that every community of the Holy Spirit, if it's going to multiply, have one individual in it who goes through the thirty-three initiations and will go through the crucifixion, the resurrection, and the ascension.

We have that community; we have that requirement. The Lamb has walked among us, and the Lamb has made that sacrifice. So we have access not only to *his* Holy Ghost, but because he is one with every part of God, we have through him access to the *entire* Holy Spirit of the Great White Brotherhood.

So when you name all the masters in the preamble of a decree, they are releasing a certain increment of their Holy Ghost to you. And the Holy Ghost comes upon you and miracles happen. You're being transmuted, you're being transformed, you're being enlightened, you're being cleansed, purified, forgiveness of sin. Miracles come into your life because the decree energy that tumbles down is the light of the Holy Spirit.

The Holy Spirit Is a Personal Presence

Here is to me such a great point of the lost teaching. Speaking in tongues, a gift of the Holy Ghost, is the manifestation of an archangel or an ascended master speaking through that person. When people force the Holy Spirit (and the whole emotional trip that sometimes occurs in the charismatic movement), then they get demons and discarnates speaking through them because they have demanded that God come to them but they have not purified themselves first. They haven't met the requirements of chelaship first.

They haven't first been disciples of the personal Christ Jesus in order to inherit his mantle of the Holy Spirit. So they bypass the guru but they want the power of the Holy Ghost. And when you do that kind of praying long enough and you don't do it legitimately through the real person of Jesus Christ, you open yourself up. You sit there waiting for it to come, and you open yourself up to the astral forces.

The real gift of the Holy Spirit is the great mystery that people have never understood. Every time God appears to man—to all of his prophets, to Adam and Eve, to the people of the Far East—whenever God manifests, he manifests as a personal presence, and that personal presence is a member of the celestial order of hierarchy.

So the teaching of the Great White Brotherhood is utterly and totally consistent with what the prophets and the people of the Old and New Testament knew. They had that one-to-one contact with the ascended masters. They walked and talked with angels. Angels were a common occurrence. When somebody said an angel of the LORD appeared to me in a dream and told me to do so-and-so, everybody listened and did it. Those were initiates of the Great White Brotherhood.

Now you talk about it, and they say it's a cult. It's the same old gang out there. It's the same old Pharisees and Sadducees. It's the same bunch. They never would recognize the personification of God in the heavenly hosts. So there is nothing new about this whole understanding, but you've got to get clear: the Father, the Son, and the Holy Ghost—that Trinity comes personally.

Your First Dictation

Student: Mother, I understand that the first live dictation that you hear holds somewhat of a key for you in your divine plan. Is that correct?

ECP: I think that is true, but I don't want you to be superstitious about it. I think that's very true. I've said it. I've told you that you should use that as a point of one of the many clocks that you might like to keep, if you like to keep cosmic clocks about events in your life.[35]

I consider it a very sacred experience because it has to indicate that that is the moment when God is giving you personally an opportunity to receive him in this life. I felt that my first dictation was just the final coming together where I had been obedient enough and served enough, and finally God's grace came upon me and allowed me to stand face-to-face with Archangel Michael and to hear him speak in this life. And I know there's a very important reason why it was Archangel Michael and no one else.

Maitreya's Guru

Student: Does Maitreya have a guru or is he sort of the ultimate?

ECP: Oh no. There's no ultimate. Everyone has a guru. Maitreya studied with Gautama Buddha under Sanat Kumara.

They were in the same class together. They've been brothers a long time.

Conscious Awareness of Initiations

Student: I was wondering that if somebody is obedient to the Law and obedient in service, is it necessary to have a conscious awareness of passing initiations like the Buddhic initiations or the Christic initiations?

ECP: I think that many times you're conscious of them. Many times your aura is so filled with virtue and light that doing the right thing hardly seems an initiation at all. You have such a blazing momentum going that you don't think of it as passing a test. There's nothing else to do and you keep going.

Student: That's what I experienced. That's what keeps the faith of moving on.

ECP: Good. I'm glad you are experiencing that. Every once in a while it becomes quite obvious that you had a choice to make and you made the right choice, and because of it you see an instantaneous blessing and reward and light. And what happens next is proof that you did the right thing, and you're awfully glad that in that period of being surrounded by darkness that you seized the one beam of light and took it and went on.

The Two-by-Two Program

Student: What is your vision of the two-by-two program?

ECP: My vision of the two-by-two program is being taught night and day at the Ashram of the World Mother right now. The dictation of Zadkiel from the end of last quarter stated that that is where he and Lord Maitreya and the Brotherhood wanted everybody to go who was on their way to a teaching center or even some people who would come on the staff—a minimum of three months in the Ashram in this program.

They have to cover their room and board—that's their obligation to the guru—and then all of the rest of their time is spent in training, in sessions, and going out. And they're going out door to door. They're learning to lead groups, to start groups. They're all on fire from Zadkiel's quarter, a very fiery bunch of souls.

Some of them returned to second level (who are here now) and some went right to the Ashram and others had other things to do. Many of them are on the staff here. But the Brotherhood doesn't want to send people to teaching centers who haven't first been a part of the white-fire core and learned a lot of things.

So you are welcome to go there following this quarter to get the specifics of how to go into a town where there's not a soul who is a student and how to contact people, start a meeting, give a lecture, do a follow-up, start holding weekly meetings getting people interested in the teachings, and so on.

The 144,000

Student: I wonder if you would comment on the idea of the 144,000 and the twelve tribes and if there is any relationship between those souls and, say, the success of Gautama's ten-year plan.[36]

ECP: Well, if there were none of the 144,000 who responded, the ten-year plan wouldn't happen. I consider them to be key, and I'm very heartened about some of the high souls of light who are coming to the fore in our country today. I think it takes a nucleus in the white-fire core of Camelot and that that nucleus can hold a lot of light for hundreds of thousands of people doing a good job around the world. I wonder what else you'd like me to comment about.

Student: I don't understand exactly the 144,000 as an alchemical number. Do those people have to realize who they are before a victory can be achieved?

ECP: Well, what percentage has to realize who they are before the victory comes, I don't know, but they're the ones who *should* realize who they are. They're the ones who should be the fruit of our service. They're the ones who should respond, who *can,* who have the ability to respond to the witness of the messengers and of the Brotherhood.

When you think about the earth, it's a very small percentage. And it should not be difficult within a century for that many souls to have fulfilled their divine plan and to be either in earth as the shepherds or to be ascended.

Mission Amethyst Jewel

Student: I'd like to know about the practical aspects of Mission Amethyst Jewel.[37] What are the actual things that you are hoping can be brought about?

ECP: Teaching centers in key cities maintaining the standard of the guru-chela relationship, hence being electrodes for the anchoring of the light of the Brotherhood. Mission Amethyst Jewel is you becoming the amethyst jewel, and then clusters of you becoming the greater jewel of the teaching centers.

The Meaning of the Masters' Names

Student: Why did Mark choose a new name after his ascension? Is there a meaning to it, and how was it chosen?

ECP: The *l-a-n* comes from "Lancelot," and the *l-o* comes from "Longfellow." He used that as his pen name. You'll find that in the early Keepers of the Flame Lessons. Whenever he would write a poem and sometimes when he would write a letter, he would sign it "Lanello." So when he ascended, I felt that he'd already given us the name that he would be called.

The reason is that he really isn't Mark. He really is the sum of every embodiment he's ever been, Mark being, let's say, the highest manifestation of all other embodiments. But Lanello is everyone else he's ever been. Lanello is the full expression of all of the talents and virtues that he's ever had. And so if we call him Mark, we only get the vibration of that one embodiment.

When the masters take a name, that name has an inner key that unlocks their total causal body to their chelas, or at least it unlocks in their causal bodies that which the Law allows them to make accessible to us. That is the whole key in an ascended master name.

The name Yahweh or I AM THAT I AM is what God gave to his people. And when it is pronounced, it unlocks that amount of energy of the Godhead that is lawful for the children of Israel to have. It's not the total power of God that suddenly floods the earth, but it is a sufficiency of light equal to every challenge that one could meet on this earth. If it were the total power of God, if we spoke the name, the earth would blow up.

Saint Germain means "Holy Brother." *El Morya* is a name given to us. *Hercules* is a name given to us. These beings have names that they would never utter. It says it is not lawful for a man to utter certain revelations.[38] It's not lawful for the ascended masters to give you the total key to their God consciousness. If they did, it would be like Merlin giving Lady Vivien the key to all that he knew. And what did she do? She put him under the earth and locked him up. The carnal mind would enslave the master.

So there we would be also if Hercules gave us a name that would be a long formula of words probably a mile long, which would be like the key to his computer. If he gave that to us, we could enslave Hercules. It would be like giving us the formula for being.

So the masters give us a name that unlocks that which they are allowed to transfer to their chelas. You call upon the name of the Lord, you call upon the name Jesus Christ, and you get that action of his causal body that he is allowed to give his disciples given the earth's level of evolution.

Student: Would Jesus have another name than Jesus on the ascended side?

ECP: I'm sure that there isn't an ascended master to whom God does not refer by names and vibrations that we have never heard.

As long as we are on the subject of names, I used to go with Mark wherever he went, and one day I was riding in the car with him and I said to him, "What is my inner name?"

He pronounced this long name that I didn't write down. So I don't happen to know what that name was, but it was obviously an inner key to an inner being, which was pronounced once on the earth. It was pronounced by Mark. And that's the name that is mentioned in the Book of Revelation that you are given that "no man knoweth saving he that receiveth it" from the Father.[39]

Languages of Angels and Fallen Angels

It was a very strange name, and it was a very strange sound. It was like Mark would sound when he was speaking in the tongues of various angels. Various angelic bands, archangel bands have different tongues. It's amazing to accustom your ear to these tongues, and it's just as difficult as it is to accustom the outer ear to other foreign languages. But they are beautiful tongues, and their outstanding quality is that they always emit light.

When the fallen angels speak, they always speak a perversion of those tongues. They speak a colloquial slang and a *very* perverted form of it. And those languages of the fallen angels you can find in Anton LaVey's *Satanic Bible*. He's got a total perversion of the angelic tongues in there. And their names are perversions of God names. Everything is a perversion.

When you have the ear of the Holy Spirit and you go into these churches and you hear the speaking in tongues, you right away know because your ear is hurt when you hear the language distorted. The Word of God gets distorted and it hurts. You feel a pain in your ear because when you have a perverted tongue, a perverted language, the vowels and the consonants—whatever those various formations may be called by the angels—are like they're bent, like you'd see an *O* all squished.

So when those languages are spoken, the energy coming out of the mouth of those speaking it, who are the rebellious ones, immediately has a rebellious vibration. It's like squishing hexagons and octagons and triangles, and they're all distorted.

There are languages spoken on the earth today that are laggard languages. They come from the planets that were destroyed. They're spoken by people who have rebelled, and they are terrible to listen to. As I've traveled abroad, and as Mark and I would listen to the speaking of these languages, we could hear the vibrations of the original rebellion and the leaders of the people that caused the distortion of the original angelic tongue of which that language is a perversion.

English is a language on earth that is closest to a pure angelic tongue. And the ascended masters can use this language to convey their teachings because it still has the purest symbolism. English, Hebrew, and Sanskrit are key languages. Greek is a key language.

Greek is key for the basic reason that the New Testament was written in Greek. The Old Testament was written in Hebrew. But Hebrew itself, the original speaking of Hebrew, is very close to an angelic tongue. Sanskrit is an angelic tongue.

If you're a linguist, as I used to love languages in high school and college, those are the languages you want to study. Those are the languages in which are hidden the greatest truths of the prophets. It's not necessarily practical, but it's a meditation on the Word. Sanskrit is a meditation on the Word. Just understanding Sanskrit gives you a greater understanding of God. And that's true of the English language. When you know the meaning of words, you're closer to *the Word*. And the more limited your vocabulary, the less ability you have to communicate the Word.

Look at the absolute attainment of Francis Bacon in the Shakespearean plays. The fact is that they're in meter and that they are a code, and the code reveals the entire life of Francis Bacon, a man who has such a mastery of language that he can write a story that hangs together, poetry that hangs together, and the whole thing in itself is a code and is telling something entirely different if you have the key to decipher the code.[40] It's just exciting. But that shows that the capacity of the language in itself, that the language is so close to the pure form of its angelic origin that it still has that immense geometry, such that you can read it from all these different angles, and all these different angles still produce a singular message.

Are There Other Messengers?

Student: You talked about the false gurus, and I've also heard you say that the masters do work through other people, or there are other focuses of the light on this planet. Do you know what they are? Or is there any reason why it's not a good idea to know who they are?

ECP: I don't know another messenger of the Great White Brotherhood in embodiment today.

Student: Didn't you say once that the masters have sponsored other organizations?

ECP: They sponsor people in the way of giving them a blessing or giving them a certain allotment of energy because they may be constructive. The masters help a lot of people.

Student: So for the whole world, this organization is the only way to get at this?

ECP: I don't like to make such absolute statements, because I'm not here to say that. I have to be what I am. I'm a messenger and I'm giving the teachings of Saint Germain. And I don't know of anyone else who is alive today who's actively sponsored by the Great White Brotherhood to give these dictations. I'm not barring the fact that there could be someone else.

El Morya once told me through Mark, when Mark and El Morya and I were discussing this, that the sponsorship of the mouthpiece of the Brotherhood includes the notification of that mouthpiece of the Brotherhood of any other mouthpiece of the Brotherhood that is functioning in that particular office.

The messenger is an office. That doesn't mean to say that there are not other gurus, or gurus in the sense of teachers in India, or people who carry a certain light, a certain energy of the Brotherhood, just as there are many different offices in corporations. So there may be people serving who have great value to students. But I just cannot tell you that there is another messenger who holds the office of the messenger.

Student: I really wasn't referring just to the messenger but just in general. You know, it's hard to believe that there's only one focus anywhere on the whole earth. How can it reach everybody?

ECP: Well, it's not supposed to reach everybody. It's supposed to reach those people for whom it is intended. There are not that many people in the world today who are ready to be chelas of the Great White Brotherhood. No ascended master organization was ever designed to become a mass movement of the people. It's a storehouse of light and energy that keeps the earth going. It's a battery of light, and its truths filter down in various fields of human endeavor. They become the foundations and the principles of a lot of things that happen after them.

Pythagoras' school at Crotona has had an unending application, as did Saint Francis' order. And all these great mystics sponsored by the Brotherhood, their works have had far greater effect than just their immediate circle, and ours does, too. But the Brotherhood does not really have that great of a welcome or a receptivity. The climate of receptivity on earth to the real presence of the ascended masters is very small, and most people feel very threatened by the ascended masters and their teaching.

Student: I think my question is that there's so much stress on saving the world and getting out there and getting the teachings out.

ECP: No, it's not on saving the world. We are not stressing saving the world. We're stressing finding the lightbearers who are lost in the astral plane. In terms of saving the world, that is, saving the souls of everybody on this planet, that's not our job. Our job is to save the people who themselves can hold the light for the earth so that the other evolutions of the earth themselves can also have the choice in future embodiments to take up the Path. Nobody is anticipating that in the next decade or the next hundred years, everyone on the planet is going to be converted to the ascended masters' teachings.

Kuthumi even said that in Theosophy. He said that this teaching is not for the masses. First of all, it's for the children of Israel, the 144,000. They're the ones who have the memory of it, who already contain the teaching, who came with the Ancient of Days. Once they are found, *they* are called to translate that teaching to the rest of humanity.

That's the same pattern of Jesus' mission. He came for a certain nucleus who were called the Jews. He came to preach to the lost tribes of the House of Israel.[41] And at a certain point the teaching was then vouchsafed to everyone who would accept him as their saviour and confess the name of God, I AM THAT I AM.[42]

And so at a certain point, because some have elected to become the teaching, it is made possible for anyone on the planet to accept and take it.

Do You Have to See Your Guru Face-to-Face?

Student: Does everyone in order to make their ascension have to meet their guru face-to-face? Pope John, did he have a guru?

ECP: His guru was Jesus Christ, and he communed with him all of his life and no doubt saw him on his passing. So I would say that you don't have to see your guru physically, in physical embodiment. You can make your ascension with what you have. With what we have here, we can make it.

Inner Temple Mysteries

Student: Would it be a violation of the Law, for example in our dealings with a politician that we're speaking with who has made several wrong decisions on the abortion issue, to face-to-face tell them that you call down the judgment of Almighty God upon them?

ECP: I think there are a lot of ways to skin a cat, and that's the wrong way to go about it in our movement. You can go into your closet at home and call down the judgment of Almighty God on that individual, and the judgment will take place, and you will have spared yourself the wrath and the reaction of that person.

If you keep doing that publicly, you'll immediately be labeled a kook. You'll not be able to get a job, not be able to have any standing in your community, not be able to have your voice count where an intelligent voice is needed, for instance, within the pro-life movement.

These are inner temple mysteries, and you don't repeat them to the world. I think that the greatest thing we enjoy is our anonymity. We are anonymous, and yet we are instruments of the light. So I think confronting people would be in very bad taste, and I don't think Saint Germain would approve.

What you're doing is depriving Saint Germain of yourself, effectively, because once you start operating like that, the masters can't use you anymore. And so you do your decrees at home, and you function in your community as a normal person. And when you work in political parties or in the pro-life movement, you don't have to quote the Brotherhood or quote me to speak the truth or to have a good idea.

Truth is not true because Morya said it. Truth is true because it's true. You don't have to go around quoting anybody to make a good point. Make a good and valid point because you've studied, because you've put together a good set of instructions, and because it's logical, because it's the Logos, because it applies to what they are doing, and because it's the next step that's humanly right within their situation. And help them where they can see, at the level of their own sight, at the level of their own ability to understand.

The Roles of the Three Kingdoms

Student: You mentioned earlier that angels and the angelic evolutions are responsible for the emotional body of God, and I'm wondering if mankind has a role in another quadrant.

ECP: The sons and daughters of God are the extensions of the Second Person of the Trinity. They're the ones who take wise dominion over the earth.[43] And they do so because they are backed by the power of the Elohim and the elemental kingdom, who represent the power, the first ray, and because they are supported by the angelic hosts, who represent the Holy Ghost. So there are three kingdoms, and they are expressions of the eternal Trinity. The builders of form, from the Elohim to the electron, serve as extensions of God's power and his law—Father. Sons and daughters of God serve as extensions of the mind of Christ. And all angelic orders and hosts of light serve as the energy of the Holy Ghost.

Plans for Publishing

Student: I remember Oromasis' dictation from *The Touch of Shiva,* and something was mentioned about publishing some kind of publication on elementals. To me the elemental kingdom seems to be the least understood. We know the least about them, and yet I'm very interested in them.

ECP: I think that the elementals are very exciting because they are so helpful. I mean, you always want somebody to do a job for you, and they're standing there ready to do it. Elementals are fantastic beings. The seventh chapter of *Climb the Highest Mountain* is on the elementals, and I envision the publishing of their collective dictations.

I tell you, there is no limit to what can be produced. I went before the Karmic Board and I made the call at the altar concerning all that we needed to implement God's plan, and Morya talked about coming with his portfolio of the Darjeeling Council.

After Sunday's dictation, I met with our board for eight solid hours on how to implement the Darjeeling Council's proposals. There is electronic equipment and computer equipment for typesetting that is far in advance of what we now have. What we now have is a Compugraphic machine that sets type. It does not have the ability to edit type, to integrate other type. If there's ever a change of a comma, it has to be reset and relined up. So it takes a lot of man hours, a lot of manpower. We're investigating the systems this week, and I'm determined that the building of Camelot is the building of our publishing arm because it's our lifeline.

I'm determined that we shall have this equipment, and the only way we can have it is to lease it, because we don't have the funds it takes to purchase it. But leases are fine. You just have to see to it that you increase your income on a monthly basis to take care of the lease payments, because if you keep on leasing things, you budget yourself right out of existence. So whatever the monthly cost of the lease of the equipment and the machinery, I have to know that I can produce that many more books that I can publish and get marketed and into the bookstores that will bring in that additional amount of money every single month right now so I can make my payments.

It's not just figuring out how to get the equipment. It's figuring out how everything else will happen. And that figuring out includes the most basic necessity of figuring out who the personnel will be, who are the qualified people who can operate the machines at their maximum efficiency. Advances in technology are just marvelous for the organization, but they're only as marvelous as the people operating them.

And so I can tell you that right now there's a book on elementals, there's the book of all of Jesus' dictations he's ever given,[44] there's a book of Maitreya's dictations,[45] there's all the back volumes of *Pearls,* which are ten in number. And for all of these, all that's holding them up is that equipment and the people to run it.

I have the basic people to run that equipment. And the people who are doing the lineup today will actually be able to do many more books in the same time because they will have less lineup time. But I do need people to prepare the manuscripts to go to the people who will punch the tapes that will go through the computer and that will print out the pages that then can be worked on.

So right at the present moment, I have more material edited ready to publish than I have the people or the equipment to publish it. And those are the problems I'm working on. I believe that we can publish twenty, thirty books this year with the proper people and the proper equipment. And I know that they will sell, and therefore I'm confident that if I can see the end from the beginning, if I can see the published book in the bookstores—in other words, if my marketing, my advertising, my book salesmen, my people who are going two by two, my teaching centers, my study groups, if all of that is being supportive of the books—if I can see all that, I can project that I can handle a budget for the purchase of that equipment and still not detract from Victory in the Holy City,[46] from the building of Camelot, and the other needs that we have. This is most vital to me.

Mother's First Encounter with Elementals

I want to tell you a story about my first encounter with elementals. I was in Boston in my apartment, and I was reading the first dictations that I had ever read and they happened to be by the beings of the elements. They were manuscripts of Virgo and Pelleur and the others, and in them they gave decrees that you could give to these elementals and they would come in and they would balance the conditions of the earth. And I thought, "Boy, this is absolutely fantastic. Here these beings are speaking, and you can give these calls, and if you make the call, all these changes will happen."

I would get so excited. I would read these dictations, and then I would shout these decrees at the top of my lungs. And maybe I would give them three or four times, and I would zonk out! I would fall fast asleep because so much light would be released from them, and my bodies were not used to that light. And then I might wake up fifteen minutes later, and I'd do the whole process all over again.

The impact of the light, when you really are excited and you love God and you have that initial sense of the excitement of contacting the beings of light, evokes a real, tremendous response. The masters are so grateful every time a new chela opens his mouth and gives his first call. And the elementals are like that. They give a tremendous release.

Every Book Brings in a New Group of People

And so, the book is there; the transcripts are there. We need people who value the experience of the books they've read and have the English talent to come in and punctuate and paragraph and check the transcripts, listen carefully that every word that was spoken is there in print. It's tedious work—I wouldn't call it tedious, I would call it detailed work. For some people who are not used to it, it becomes tedious. But it's a specialty, and we need the people who can do it or who can do anything on down the line—the setting of the type, either punching the keyboard or lining it up. There's manual work. There's the printing itself, there's darkroom work, there's the illustrations, there's artwork. And so you don't have to be an editor to be part of this assembly line.

But to me it is exciting because every book is an electrode of light, and every book has its mark. And you are absolutely right. The book on the elementals has a flare and a flame for a certain group of people on the earth who haven't been contacted. Some of them are elementals in embodiment. Every book brings in a whole new group of people. It creates its own mandala; it has its own antahkarana, its own inner key, its own vibration. And it goes out and it's like a signal. It's like a tone.

You know how with certain animals, you can blow a soundless whistle and they all come? Well, there's a certain tone that goes out from the vibration of a certain master's causal body when it becomes concrete. And the tone goes out and it goes out through the books, and I watch it. It goes out through the bookstores, and everybody who is of that vibration suddenly looks up. They're suddenly aware, and then they've got to go and find the source of the tone.

They're just like sheep coming home at the call of the shepherd. They go all over the place. They look here; they look there. They can't find the thing that they're looking for but they're following this tone. And they finally find that book, and they go home and read it. And here they are. How many of you have had that experience?

I've been very happy to be with you this morning. You're just the joy of my life.

January 23, 1979

CHAPTER FOUR

The Initiation of the Solar Radiance

You feel like the Twin Cities, like Alpha and Omega, twin flames of the Buddha. Lanello was very much a part of the Buddha seminar that we held in San Francisco.[1] We played some of his tapes, and Lanello was one of the five Buddhas who spoke there. Recognizing Lanello as the Buddha is a very joyous moment for me. As you know, the theme of the Buddha and the Mother runs through a number of our teachings.

A very interesting thing happened. Gene Vosseler will tell you the story. You may notice that he wears a pendant around his neck, and it's a pendant of the Buddha. Well, he had that pendant made, and the man who made it said that the pendant would not go any other way, that that face would be the face that it is. And if you look at it carefully, it looks very much like Lanello. It's kind of an elongated face of the Buddha. So whenever I look at that pendant, I think that Lanello is winking at me through every statue of the Buddha.

It's a secret ray, one of the five secret rays, and all of the secret rays are in the heart of the Buddha. And so Buddha in meditation

Gene Vosseler's Buddha Pendant
FIGURE 1

with his eyes closed is very mysterious. His eyes closed means that he has a secret. The symbolism of eyes closed is that there is something that he is not telling you, he's not communicating. And it's the depth of the secret rays.

I am very excited about getting into Lord Maitreya's dictations because I do believe that the very key to his coming in this age is in these dictations. Of the ones that I have played for you, the first one that I played, 1960, I had never heard. The other dictations by Maitreya I heard when they were given, and I haven't heard them since.

The fifth dictation given by Lord Maitreya was on December 29, 1962. It is very brief. It's given in the middle of a long dictation by Saint Germain, and there's a tremendous introduction to Lord Maitreya. Saint Germain says:

> I am here tonight to bring you freedom! But one greater than I is here, one whose footsteps I sought to walk in before my ascension. I bring you now a few words from beloved Lord Maitreya, the Cosmic Christ.

4 · The Initiation of the Solar Radiance

LORD MAITREYA
December 29, 1962

The Initiation of the Solar Radiance

Beloved Saint Germain, beloved friends of the heart of God, the great outpouring cosmic light of your divine identity enfolds you now in the radiance of the Eternal One. This light is raising you in a vibratory action that leads you upward in consciousness to the Great Central Sun.

The Great Central Sun can be thought of as a shepherd, as the Great Shepherd of the sheep. And all human beings who hear the voice of the great heart of God speaking from out the Great Central Sun—beloved Alpha and Omega—will know that peace of God which we, as ascended beings, share at a common table whereby we partake of the bread that came down from heaven[2]—the bread that, as mighty light rays, poured out from the sacred altars of God and brought forth the sun in splendor, shining both as a physical sun in the universe, and in the Universe behind the universe, and as a spiritual sun within the very heart of the being of God.

The rays of light from the Great Central Sun pouring forth to the sun of this system of worlds kindled the radiance of the Solar Logos. And the radiance of the Solar Logos sent forth its mighty light rays to this earth and kindled the radiance of beloved Virgo, the Mother Earth principle, activating the light rays within that great being.

And the solar radiance, then, of the Great Central Sun descended also from the Great Central Sun to the sun of this system of worlds—to beloved Helios and Vesta—and activated your own lifestreams, so that you are truly, in essence, a sunbeam, a ray of light, from out the Great Central Sun. I would like the students tonight to cherish this idea.

So long as you think of yourselves, beloved ones, as clay, as density, as a conglomeration of human effluvia, you are not enjoying the supreme radiance of light. Well, think of your bodies tonight, beloved ones, as light. Think of yourselves as light, as a sunbeam from out the Great Central Sun.

I, Maitreya, would initiate many of you tonight into the solar radiance in the solar chambers. If you will only devote your heart's attention tonight, as you pass into sleep, to your own mighty I AM Presence and request it of me, I will try to exalt all of you that the Great Law will permit into a greater unfolding of your spiritual sonship. I will bestow upon all who are worthy a greater degree of initiation than they have ever known before.

This condition will be brought about solely to assist the mankind of earth in obtaining their ascension. For, beloved ones, wherever there is a candidate for the ascension upon this planet, the radiance around that individual is a blessing to all the consciousness of life embodied here.

It was *this* power, *this* radiance, *this* glory that manifested in beloved Jesus, which magnetized the audiences upon the hillsides of Judaea, which flooded forth and quickened the consciousness of men, which produced healings of consciousness, and which gave joy to the hillsides of the world because the Christ walked upon them!

I bless you and I thank you by the power of the light from out the Great Central Sun. And I return you now to that beloved God of Freedom, your friend, beloved Saint Germain.

SAINT GERMAIN

Precious ones of the unfolding radiance, our beloved Lord Maitreya, revered in our octave, has spoken to you his words of encouragement, his words based upon the immortality of your own souls. Remember, the flame of love from his heart kindled the spark of love within yours.

It is the desire of all the hosts of heaven to fan the flame of divinity upon the heart's altar of each individual expression of God. This we do, in the holy name of freedom, to cherish the world, to encircle the world, to love the world with the peace of God.

This is the purpose of this class—to unfold the radiance of the individual, to give freedom to the individual; to unfold the planetary radiance, to give freedom to the planet; to bless mankind with their own individualized, self-realized confidence in the light of God, which never fails; that they recognize the higher way of thought; that they no longer express the limiting doubts and confining ideas of the agnostic or those who are in despair or despondency, who seek in some oppressed system or ideology, some political thought, a dream of freedom that is empty.

Rather, I say to all, let them see within the heart of their own I AM Presence the open door, the *open* door, the open door that leads to their *own* freedom in the light of God, *which never fails!*

I thank you and bless you and bid you good evening.

Spiritual Sun-Ship

There is a very exciting initiation in this dictation, the initiation of the solar radiance in the solar chambers. Where do you think the solar chambers are?

> I will bestow upon all who are worthy a greater degree of initiation than they have ever known before... to assist the mankind of earth in obtaining their ascension.

The assistance to you assists all upon the planet as you become an anchor point. It's the first time I've ever heard the word *sonship* spoken that I really felt it was spelled *"s-u-n,"* spiritual *sun*-ship.

The emphasis is on the meditation of the heart. And the

heart begins with the Great Central Sun, Alpha and Omega, being the shepherd of the sheep. He's talking about hearing the voice of the great heart of God.

I'm going to make an invocation on this initiation.

> *In the name of Almighty God, I call for the full power, wisdom, love of the Great Central Sun. I call for the absolute ray of light from the heart of beloved Lord Maitreya. I call for the drawing up of these souls now through the heart chamber, through the door of the heart unto the heart of beloved Lord Maitreya, unto the great heart of God, Alpha and Omega, in the Great Central Sun. I call for the mighty ray of light, each one's own descending light, the I AM THAT I AM, the mighty crystal cord from the Great Central Sun.*
>
> *I call for the charging and the balancing of their four lower bodies. And I call this night for the mighty transfer of the initiation of the solar radiance within the solar chambers. I call for the opening of the temple doors. I call for the opening of the solar chambers. I call for the drawing of these souls of light that they might be radiating centers of the Great Central Sun Magnet.*
>
> *The light of God never fails, and the beloved mighty I AM Presence is that light!*

Maitreya's Third Dictation, the Third Initiation

October 21, 1961, is Libra becoming Scorpio. And this dictation was given in this tiny little sanctuary in Boston where Mark came on many occasions. And this should be our third initiation.

LORD MAITREYA
October 21, 1961

Immortality and the Cosmic Sense

. . . The joy to the world that was expressed by the angelic hosts on the occasion of the nativity of the Christ flooded the entire planet with the choruses of the angelic hosts.* And the joy that expressed in the hearts of the shepherds leaped from heart to heart across the fields and plains, forests and mountains, until it entered into the heart of even a tiny shepherd boy upon the hillsides of a land far across the sea.

Precious ones of the light, you think nothing today of experiencing television and radio programs broadcast around the world. The wonders of a few years ago cease to be wonders to your minds. But, beloved ones, two thousand years ago this was a transcendent experience when the joy of the angels passed into the hearts of the shepherds and swept around the world into the pages of history and into the consciousness of mankind.

The martyrs of that era of early Christianity expressed their love through giving their all. But the comfortable experiences of present-day Christianity are a far cry from that era of sacrificial offering, when to take a stand for the light of God was almost tantamount to the loss of one's physical life.

Today, beloved ones, the world knows more about the meaning of freedom; it knows more about the meaning of peace; it knows more about the grace of God. The intellectual comprehensions of mankind have been expanded, and the theologians understand more of the ancient scriptures. The arts of printing and communication have been enhanced and expanded until the world today is not the world of two thousand years ago.

---
*The beginning of the dictation is missing from the original recording.

And the multitudes have increased. Those who heard the words of the Christ as he walked among men two thousand years ago upon the hillsides of Judaea were few in comparison to the multitudes of the earth who are hungry and who are thirsting today for the living water of Life.[3] But that water of Life is like a great river and, this very hour, is being offered to all who are athirst that they may drink.

Individuals, through habits of thought and feeling—as this beloved one told you—have become somewhat recalcitrant, and they no longer realize the inner voice of their own mighty God Presence. But they have heard the voices of discord and the voices of confusion of the world until the voice of the Christ seems far distant.

But I AM come today to charge into your midst the radiance that is familiar to your souls, the radiance that is your natural habitat, the light that will exalt you and raise you and comfort you, the light that will be a solace unto you when you seem to be separate one from another and from all forms of comfort.

For the light of God will penetrate your consciousness as you lie upon your beds and cannot sleep, when the cares and oppressions of the world seem to press in upon you and you find difficulty in finding peace. If you will turn your hearts toward the Christ and make a call unto him, he will respond and with blazing light come into your forcefield to bring you that same peace and love that he brought to mankind long ago.

You are dealing now, beloved ones, with immortality. You are dealing with the realm of the ascended masters. You are dealing with the compassion of heaven. It is no ordinary or mortal concept that comes to your mind, but it is the concept of life, the concept of *eternal* life, the concept of the grace of heaven.

The grace of heaven, beloved ones, transcends history.

It transcends the known world. It transcends your human thoughts. The grace of God is sufficient for you[4] for every occasion that you may ever face. And with the waning of all human sensibilities, mankind will find the dawning of the cosmic sense wherein they are able to cognize the nearness of the heavenly octaves and the spheres of light to their own consciousness.

The tiny babe lifts its eyes toward its own God Presence, and it smiles. And those individuals in the presence of that babe are pleased to see the smile upon the face of the child, but they do not know of the vision of the angels that appears to the tiny one.

Much later in life, when familiarity with the world scene has closed the door and the curtain that separate the consciousness of the child from the wonders of heavenly spheres, those visions come, then, no more. And the child becomes a part of the mass consciousness—guided by parents, guided by teachers, guided by companions, many of whom are fit and many of whom are unfit to guide.

The pressure, then, of mass consciousness builds up a synthetic man—not a manifestation of the eternal light, but a manifestation of carnality destined to be confused, destined to confuse, and destined eventually to perish as an individual entity and pass from the screen of life.

But this is not the plan of immortality, and God is immortal. *God is immortal!* And in his immortality there is peace and joy forever without end.

The harshness of the world, the clanging furor of the tides of mortality do not comfort mankind; and therefore, they run to and fro, seeking peace. And no peace is given to them, and yet they continue to seek. For it is the Great God Self within, which manifested in the cosmic sense in the tiny babe, that must awaken. This cosmic sense, like a rosebud, must unfold. Like a lotus it must breathe its perfume into space.

When the consciousness of man begins to unfold, it becomes as a little child. And as it becomes as a little child, the entire glory of heaven is revealed to that individual. And man realizes that outer life has been a *chimera,* and that all that the eyes have seen and that the ears have heard is nothing to be compared to the wonders of the eternal spheres!

I, Maitreya, come to you as a father would to his children. And I come to you today to breathe upon you concerning the cosmic sense, that you may awaken within yourselves to the glory of God that is present in space wherever you are. Individuals have the idea that God is far removed from them. But this God that I declare unto you today, beloved ones, is as near as your hands and feet or as close as your heart and breath.

The inflowing of the cosmic light within the body of man is a gift of the Presence of God that is perpetuated momentarily by the intelligence of heaven in action. The Christ mind—the divine power that beats your heart while you sleep, that gives to your physical consciousness, your body elemental, and your mind the understanding to govern all of the senses that control the body movements, both voluntary and involuntary—is a gift of God.

Be grateful, then, for this gift, but above all be grateful for the gift that is the eyes of your soul, the hearing of your soul, the understanding of your heart. For you are not your garments that you wear. You are not these physical bodies. You are a living soul! At inner levels you wear garments of immortality, and these are real and tangible. But because you have diverted your attention from the inner realm to the outer, you are not aware of the inner garments that you wear, and it is as though you were bereft of your attire.

Pause now and think, beloved ones, what it means to be clothed upon with immortality. Beloved Hilarion, when embodied as Saint Paul, warned mankind of the fact that they must first put off mortality if they would put on immortality.[5]

I, today, admonish you, beloved ones of the light, that you likewise recognize the need to put off the mortal senses during those moments when you desire to awaken the senses of immortality. In the name of Almighty God, precious students of the light, if you are thinking of entertainment, if you are thinking of food, if you are thinking of some accomplishment that you wish to do in order to expand your own personality, during a time when you are trying to make attunement with your God Self, how can you *possibly* make that attunement?

You must, then, put off the consciousness of the outer man, of the human self. You must come in full faith to the fount of Almighty God, believing "that he is, and that he is a rewarder of them that diligently seek him."[6]

This is a truth pursued of old by Enoch,[7] pursued of old by every ascended master who ever made the ascension. This Christ-seeking must become the goal of man if he would awaken to all of the potency and power of the sacred fire.

Beloved ones, some of you have idly dreamed of moments when you would be able to say to a man with a withered hand, "Be thou made whole!"[8] Some of you have idly dreamed of a moment when you could at a glance pass an individual on the street who was suffering from habitual drunkenness and be able to speak to that one at inner or outer levels and say, "Be thou free! Be thou whole!"[9] Some of you have been more ambitious, and you have dreamed of how you could reach out your hand as the Christ did and raise men from the dead.[10]

Well, beloved ones, this power is within you. But it is most important that you recognize that *you* as individuals must first put off the old man and his deeds.[11] *You* must put off the consciousness of the world sense and put on the new mind of the Christ if *you* are to accomplish these specific feats and enjoy these cosmic graces, these cosmic gifts.

These gifts are given to you. They are free—they are without money, they are without price.[12] They are held for you now by your own mighty I AM Presence and they will manifest in your world, and no power in heaven or earth can possibly prevent their manifestation at that moment when you are ready to receive them.

But, beloved ones, you cannot be made ready to receive them until you yourself have elected to open up the senses of heaven—to recognize the angelic hosts, to recognize the ascended masters, to recognize your own mighty I AM Presence as the only power in your world. There is no other power but God. There is no other power that can act in your world but the power of God!

I ask, therefore, that you pause as I make contact with the beloved angelic hosts and ask them to pour their radiance into the chalices of your hearts. I ask that they saturate you with the pure light rays from their hearts, charged with the essence of roses and the fragrance of pine. I ask that you be made aware, then, of the sweetness of the soul of God that is within you and of the eternal Presence of God within you.

The eternal Presence of God within you is forever and forever and forever. It is without end. Therefore accept this gift from the angelic hosts that are part of my band of light. I ask you now to be at peace. [interval of meditation with music]

Children of the light, I want to remind you that each one of you was conceived by God. I want to remind you that you came not through the gate of birth by accident, but you came by conscious, divine intent. I want to remind you that your life was as divinely intended a manifestation as was the birth of beloved Jesus and other great avatars.

I want to remind you that the hopes of heaven for you were and are great, that simply because individuals have permitted their own self-hope to become dim does not prevent the immortal concept of God from being held steadfast for every lifestream. And it is this anchor—it is this anchor, beloved ones of the light—that causes each man to feel the pull of immortality, leading him onward to seek, to understand the great cosmic laws and the great cosmic light.

I am known as the Great Initiator, and it is my responsibility to take interest concerning the unfoldment of the individual chelas in coming through the stages of initiation of the Great White Brotherhood. Today, as I gaze not only upon those lifestreams who are assembled within this room but upon the lifestreams of all humanity, I behold among mankind many who are ready for various stages of initiation. Some are ready for cosmic stages of initiation. Some are ready for less advanced stages of initiation. But many are making themselves ready by application to their own divinity.

The bonds of divinity are so far greater than mortal concepts that it is sometimes difficult to bridge the gap between human words and divine ideas so that mankind will understand the wonder of which I speak. Mankind today are plagued because of the fact that through the semantics of words, they do not always understand or conceive of the true power of the Word of God. But the Word of God is the progenitor of every individual within this place, upon this planet, and everywhere in the universe.

This Word of God, beloved ones, is ever blessed. It is tangible and real, it is intelligent, it is light! And in it there is no shadow, nor is there a shadow of turning.[13]

I would like to ask some of you who are young in years: *Where shall mankind go?* The apostles of the Christ said unto him, "Where shall we go? thou hast the words of eternal life."[14] And this is truth. The words of eternal life are given to the ascended masters by God.

Individuals have thought that God held all these secrets and all of his powers strictly for himself and the angelic band. Many among mankind have not understood that God giveth gifts to the ascended masters, gifts of hierarchical power whereby they are specifically charged with certain momentums of freedom, of obedience, of love.

This is also true of the elemental kingdom. As you gaze upon the wonders of nature, beloved ones, have you ever stopped to consider that almost every tree and bush has an angelic or elemental being standing guard over it to see that it outpictures the perfect plan of God? Have you ever stopped to realize that just as each individual has a blessed guardian angel, so every manifestation of nature has some specific God-intelligence that watches over that manifestation to see that it comes to fruition and to perfection?

Well, beloved ones, then realize that your mighty I AM Presence, the great electronic body of God from out the Great Central Sun, came forth in dazzling, blazing light as a duplicate of the magnanimous, ever-expanding light of the mighty I AM Presence in the very heart of the Great Central Sun and was duplicated for each individual's own mighty I AM Presence. And this duplicate, beloved ones, is never separated from the Central Sun itself or from the Presence of God within the Great Central Sun, so that every man, woman, and child's mighty I AM Presence is one with everyone else's own mighty I AM Presence. This makes of all life one, and there is, then, no diversity whatsoever.

And I am speaking now, beloved ones, concerning inner levels. For when you gaze outwardly, you behold individuals of various stages of development. You see them representing various age groups as far as physical aging processes are concerned. But as you look on the inner, you see no such condition. You see only the perfection of God manifesting at every point in space where there is an individual lifestream. Now that lifestream, when that individual awakens to his own cosmic identity, will find that he is able to shake off the fetters of mortality and to become *charged* with the power of divinity!

Well, when an individual awakens to the power of divinity, an initiate is born on the world scene. The star of Bethlehem appears in the cosmic sky, and the star of that nativity of divinity is manifest to the ascended masters. And immediately when they perceive this, they send forth a special protection to seal that lifestream in the protection from the heart of God coming down through the angelic hierarchy presided over by Archangel Michael.

Do you see, beloved ones, how great cooperation takes place at inner levels—how at inner levels, the levels of the spirit of life, perfection and protection ever manifest?

There are three people within this room who within the past week would have left this earth if it were not for the protection of their own mighty I AM Presence and their guardian angel. One of them is somewhat aware of it; the other two are not. But I would like to point this out to you because you do not realize just when you may need the perfection and the protection of your own God Presence.

O beloved ones, what conceit and what vanity is present in human consciousness! And yet we are not here to condemn you, for you are children of the light, and you were born to receive the glory of that birthright. We are here to assist you and we are ever here to bless you.

We will not forsake you. Your mighty I AM Presence will not forsake you. Every ascended master and cosmic being will stand by you "through thick," as you might say it, "and through thin," so long as you yourself are consciously willing to do your best to accept the plan of God, to understand the plan of God, to walk circumspectly as much as you are able.

Beloved ones, God is no tyrant. Your mighty I AM Presence is no tyrant! I would say that your Presence has been most lenient—the Presence of life has been most lenient to all mankind. But although the Presence has given men their freedom, they have not enjoyed God's universe with that freedom, simply because the freedom which they have enjoyed they have made into fetters. It is the intention of God to see to it that those fetters are *cut* and that mankind are set free from every condition that binds them to the continual round of rebirth, and that they experience those cosmic initiations that cut them free from the power of death.

Beloved ones, what is death? You understand what life is, but life, beloved ones, cannot end. For life itself is a quality. How can a quality cease to be? And inasmuch as you have life, how can you cease to be—I ask you in the holy name of God, *how can you cease to be?*

Precious ones, that which mankind know as death is only the end of a cycle. And when that cycle comes, it merely means the beginning of a new cycle. And this continual round as circles within circles and wheels within wheels[15] is a manifestation of the divine intelligence and the life plan of God. But God intends mankind to have continuity of consciousness, and therefore today I would like to point out a very specific principle to the students.

At the end of each embodiment, in mercy, the door of memory is sealed so that the lifestream coming into embodiment in most cases does not recall the events of his past life, except dimly. But, beloved ones of the light, that is not the intention of God. God intends men to have an unbroken, continuous, conscious knowledge that they *are*.

I ask you right now to ponder and consider the meaning of "I AM." *I AM,* beloved ones, means "being" and it means "existence" and it means *"bliss"!* Well, if it means existence and bliss, then that existence cannot be broken or interspersed by a series of experiences whereby you do not know anything, whereby you no longer are aware of yourself, whereby you are in shadow or darkness, for God is all light. And therefore, because he is all light, he would bestow upon every son of himself a continuous experience.

I ask you, beloved ones, if any of you are aware of the experiences of beloved Jesus from the time they removed his body from the cross until he rose again? Do you recall that the scriptures record that during the time when he was taken down from the cross until the time of his resurrection, he preached to the spirits of those who were disobedient during the days of Noah?[16]

Well I think, then, if the Christ preached to the spirits who were disobedient in the days of Noah, that he must have experienced an unbroken consciousness. And I cannot conceive that the Christ who spoke to the thief beside him and said, "Today shalt thou be with me in paradise,"[17] was himself no longer conscious of God or aware of life. The Christ was continuously aware of life. And as part of the great initiatic experiences that come to mankind, there is an unbroken series whereby an individual is aware of God—morning, noon, and night.

Through the night, at all times, an individual is never without consciousness. One is always conscious, either in the outer or the inner. And therefore, many of our initiates are assembling during the night hours while their physical bodies sleep. And they move in their white robes throughout the earth to assemble in sacred retreats and places set apart, that they might be instructed at inner levels concerning the rightness of cosmic laws by great cosmic masters and by cosmic teachers.

For it is a part of the plan of God to educate mankind continually until men are indeed as wise as gods. It is not the plan of God to keep men in ignorance or to keep men victims of untruth, but rather to illuminate mankind by the glory of the mighty I AM Presence so that the Spirit of the Great White Brotherhood will be revered by all men upon earth and will be a *living* Spirit of the *living* Christ in action among men. How can this be except it be a personal experience of each individual?

Beloved ones, when an individual comes into manifestation as a tiny babe, that individual in time comes to recognize its own father and mother and members of its household. So it is of the spirit of light. When an individual becomes as a babe in Christ—aware of the ascended masters, although dimly—there is a gradual expansion of consciousness until at last that individual is able to walk and talk with the ascended masters and the cosmic beings as freely as you have your social familiarity here among mankind. And this is as it should be.

For the patriarchs of old communed with the angels, communed with the cosmic beings. And this will happen to you, and eventually, precious ones, you will find that heaven is all around you, and the roses of heaven will blossom at your feet. The fragrance of heaven will penetrate your body and your mind. The light of heaven will lift you up in consciousness until you will feel at home beneath the stars! For you will know that they are points of light within this mighty universe of light. You will know that there are points of light—chakras within your body, and centers of light—and that in time all of these points of light will blend into one beautiful star, the star of initiation whereby you are able to pass through the star doorway and commune with nature, with the elementals, with the angelic hosts.

You will no longer be possessed with a mere sense of a physical body and the limitations of that body. You will be able to leave the body at will, and you will be able to move anywhere upon this planet or upon many planets at will. And you will find a freedom from fear, from bondage, from the need to partake of food, from the need to be subject to natural and man-made laws in an ordinary sense. For you will become subject to the great cosmic laws, and these transcend all other laws.

Precious ones of the light, the goal is mighty. The race needs the help of the ascended masters. This we are willing to give. We ask that you make the call within yourself; we do not ask that you necessarily make the statement before mankind concerning your inner intention.

Those of you who may be timid today and may not quite recognize the voice of the Good Shepherd,[18] I ask tonight, before you close your eyes in sleep, that you make a call to God, to your own mighty I AM Presence, and that you ask him to guide your footsteps that you may understand the power of light, the power of the ascended masters, the power of the Christ in action—and that you consciously elect to further your progress in the things of the Spirit, that this which passeth away, these "former things,"[19] be no longer cleaved to, but that you anchor within the veil that permanent God consciousness that no man can take from you.

And then you will be a part of our band and you will have begun in newness of life,[20] in renewing the consciousness of the atoms and electrons of your body, in charging yourself with the sacred fire. You will be eventually victors, not vanquished.

I thank you and bid you good evening.

Make the Call to Jesus Christ

I like the idea of being transmitters of joy, the joy leaping heart to heart on the nativity of the Christ. And your joy that leaps is the joy that you are born today. There is the concept that the multitudes are hungry, and many more are hungry today. And the water of Life is being offered. The multitudes are recalcitrant. They no longer hear the voice of their mighty I AM Presence, and so the voice of the Christ is distant.

It tells us of the dilemma of the density of the multitudes upon the earth who hunger, who thirst, but who are too dense to receive the answer of the Christ. And so this is the first initiation:

But I AM come today to charge into your midst the radiance that is familiar to your souls, the radiance that is your natural habitat, the light that will exalt you and raise you and comfort you, the light that will be a solace unto you when you seem to be separate one from another and from all forms of comfort.

For the light of God will penetrate your consciousness as you lie upon your beds and cannot sleep, when the cares and oppressions of the world seem to press in upon you and you find difficulty in finding peace. If you will turn your hearts toward the Christ and make a call unto him, he will respond and with blazing light come into your forcefield to bring you that same peace and love that he brought to mankind long ago.

So Lord Maitreya is giving us light. He brings light, and he asks with it that you turn your heart to Christ and make the call to Jesus Christ. It seems that he is lowering a great sphere of light, and there is a requirement for its assimilation. It is the call to Jesus Christ:

By the authority of the Father, the Son, and the Holy Ghost within us, we call to the name Jesus Christ. We call upon the Lord Jesus Christ. We call for the great light that he brought to the people of earth long ago. And we call for the light of beloved Lord Maitreya to descend now into our hearts. We call for that mighty explosion of light.

We call for that descent of that initiation given seventeen years ago. We call for it to be repeated now within this forcefield. We call for the great connecting arc of light from its original release in Boston to this forcefield, from the crown to the soul chakra of America. We ask that this light, Lord Maitreya and beloved Jesus Christ, might be released to the souls of our people, especially to the souls of light.

Let light increase this day in the souls of light of America.

Let light increase by the flame of the Goddess of Liberty, by the light of the Lords of Karma, by those of the Royal Teton Retreat. We call to the Lords of Karma. Beloved Goddess of Liberty, let the torch of Cosmic Christ illumination descend. Let it be by the hand of Lord Maitreya and Lord Jesus this day. We thank thee and accept it done this hour in full power.

The Grace of God Is Sufficient

The grace of God is sufficient. The grace of God is the Christ consciousness of Jesus. Each ascended master's grace is each one's own attainment of the Christ consciousness. Jesus said, "My grace is sufficient for you—my attainment, my light, my cosmic consciousness. *You* are my disciple. I am your master. My grace is sufficient for you."[21] This is the word of Jesus Christ to his disciples. He is stating the great geometry of being, that if there is the Guru Jesus Christ, if there are the disciples, then the Guru is the sufficiency unto them. The light that God has given unto Jesus is sufficient to save their souls, to save a world.

Those are principles of Truth. They are statements of mathematics, of algebra, of geometry. They do not fail. When you understand that they are not simply statements of faith but that they are statements of Law, and when you know the Law and you recite the Law, the Law works for you. And when you have problems and when you face terrible dragons and beasts and momentums of world energy, you need to know the Law and be able to cite the Law in your defense, in defense of your soul.

Your Christ Self is always your advocate, the attorney-at-law, the law of light who knows the Law, knows the Logos because he is the Logos, he is the Word. And you need to know that for every challenge and every initiation that you face, there is a statement of the Law that will meet that challenge. And when the Law is stated, it is a burst of cosmic consciousness; it is a burst of energy. And the correct statement of the Law will be that exact formula of sacred fire that will swallow up the discord.

Some of you have had the experience that I've had all of my life, which is to take up the Bible when you are in need, open it, read what your eyes lay upon, and always comes the answer to that moment of need. This is a very exact equation. The equation is that you have a vacuum or a want or a lack; you have a need. And that need is a desiring to be filled, and the desiring attracts that which is necessary. And so the inner being within you is an energy that gives you the corresponding alchemy.

You are the minus; you need the plus. You go to the Bible and you find the answer. Life is very exact in its measures and in what it attracts to you. You attract to yourself what you are, the vibration that you are. And when you see what is around you, it is an index of what is within you. When you see light and beautiful people around you, you know that it is the God in you and the Christ in you that has magnetized that beauty. When you see darkness around you, it is an index of the darkness within that must be transmuted. "My grace is sufficient for you."

I look upon the path that I have walked with Lord Maitreya, Morya, and Saint Germain since that hour. As I was listening to that meditation music, I remembered the little old lady who was playing that music on a little old record player, and I could very much catch the vibration of the akashic records of the room. I could visualize Mark sitting there and listening to that music in the midst of the dictation, and I thought of that first year of my path.

I had been on the Path for about six months at that point. And when I heard these dictations, I simply accepted them to be true with a great openness and that great quality of the child-like consciousness, which Maitreya says we have when we begin the Path. And being a child is something that I have always felt that I am. I was a child then, and I've never stopped being a child. And so as a child before the ascended masters, they are like father and mother and parents to me. Whatever they say, I believe—simply, truly accept it.

And the acceptance is the wide open door that Saint Germain was talking about, "Open the door to your heart." This wide open door enables the fiat and the Word to be impressed upon your heart, your feelings, your mind, your etheric body.

Unfortunately, today you can see this happening to our children in front of the TV sets. They have their childhood and they are wide open, and whatever is happening on that screen they accept. They call it *programming*. But you see, God already created the Christ Self to be a type of computer. We use the word *computer* because we know what a computer is, and we know that it can receive a vast amount of information. It can store, it can organize, it can use it, it can even be creative with it.

So the universal mind of God manifest in you is capable of expressing what God has placed within it. And if you want to use the word, he has *programmed* that mind or computerized that mind to deal with the functions of your four lower bodies—all of the complicated flow of energy through the chakras, the very breath of life itself. None of this we have to do with original thought or feeling. So for want of other words, that is how God sets a law in motion and that law continues to function.

The Little Child Who Comes

So Maitreya is talking about the little child who comes, the child who has the vision of the angels and then becomes a part of the mass consciousness and then the "carnality destined to be confused." Mark saw this in his own children. He had a family before I knew him, and he saw these children go the way of the carnal mind. It was a very, very sad experience to him. And he was greatly burdened by that experience.

He saw children who came into the world with light. He saw them as tiny babes seeing the angels. He knew their origin and their past experiences with the Brotherhood. And yet through programming, through their mother, through their environment, they took an anti-Christ attitude, anti-light, anti-the ascended masters, and became entirely programmed to the ways of this world, and to the very hour of his ascension took a stand against him and against his work.

So that family was a great burden to him and a great initiation. And he had to leave it in order to be a messenger. He would have lost his life itself, so great was the hatred and the intense opposition, which came, by the way, basically through a fundamentalist background, through a Christian background which denies the ascended masters simply because it's a new term. If you talk about angels, perhaps it would be more acceptable. But whatever it was, I saw his crucifixion. And I saw that even when people have children of light, those children of light can lose contact with the Brotherhood because of that mass consciousness influence.

So I saw the great determination in his heart to provide a better way for others who would come after him, for us and for our children. And we see what the right environment and the right training does, not only for little children but for people who've been in the world and come to Summit University.

Empty Your Cups so that God Can Fill Them

How quickly the *plasticity* (for want of another term, again) of God that is in us responds to the cleansing and to the effervescent action of the light that comes as a great elixir and purifies and purges and restores those cells. The clearing of the cells that we experience at Summit University is so that once again they can be used to receive the patterns made in the heavens, the great eternal truths, the great eternal images of ourselves. And so there is that need for the fasting of consciousness, for the giving up.

And just as we understand how much the cells absorb of what we have eaten, what we've taken into our bodies, there are cells in the astral body, the emotional body. There are cells in the mental body, in the etheric body, and they are filled with the pollutants of those planes. And they are so filled that the very fact of their being full (if there were no other factor involved) is the reason why they do not outpicture suddenly upon contact with the true message, that truth.

People have to first empty their cups so that their cups can be filled again. And that's the message of this dictation. You first have to put off the mortal in order to become immortal. You want all of these gifts. You want to be able to heal. You want this communion with the hosts of light. And here, in order to do that, you must put off your mortality if you would put on immortality.

You are not aware of the inner garments that you wear.

Be Grateful for the Great Gift

Now here's another point of initiation:

I, Maitreya, come to you as a father would to his children.

You know *guru* at one level means "father." At another level, it means "mother." We very much identify with our guru as our father and then as our mother. I can remember being exalted and in spirals of consciousness where I would call Mark "Father." And other times I would call him "Mother." I would be in such a state of bliss of his cosmic consciousness of Alpha and Omega. The guru is Father and is Mother.

> I, Maitreya, come to you as a father would to his children. And I come to you today to breathe upon you concerning the cosmic sense, that you may awaken within yourselves to the glory of God that is present in space wherever you are.

He is so concerned about us, that we also have become a part of the mass consciousness, *unresponsive* to the great light of God. He wants us to know how near God is.

> The inflowing of the cosmic light within the body of man is a gift of the Presence of God that is perpetuated momentarily by the intelligence of heaven in action. The Christ mind—the divine power that beats your heart while you sleep, that gives to your physical consciousness, your body elemental, and your mind the understanding to govern all of the senses that control the body movements, both voluntary and involuntary—is a gift of God.
>
> Be grateful, then, for this gift, but above all be grateful for the gift that is the eyes of your soul, the hearing of your soul, the understanding of your heart.

All of this, that is the great gift.

He talks about the simple point of attunement. If you're going to make attunement with your God Self, don't be worrying about what you're going to eat when you're through your meditation period. Get away from your outer self, your human self.

The Necessity that the Guru Must Ascend

I have seen these steps that God has "forced me" to take—in the sense that I have elected to be forced. God doesn't force any of us to do anything except that we have said, "I want to get back to you as fast as I can, and I'll do anything that you want me to do to get there." Then God pushes, and he pushes hard. Some people aren't quite ready for the hard push. But there is an expediency in chelaship. And I think it's good that we feel that expediency. *Expediency* is a word for "necessity," and the necessity is that the guru must ascend. *The guru must ascend.*

In the months or the year preceding Mark's ascension, I was mindful to type out and put on my mirror, "This corruptible *must* put on incorruption, and this mortal *must* put on immortality."[22] And every day I read that, many times a day. And the point of the word *must*—and it was passing through my consciousness like one of those mathematical formulas that I was speaking of—was that it was a statement of the law of the universe.

And it was healing, it was constantly healing, although it was happening at inner levels, so that the day when, like a snap of a light switch, the crystal cord was broken and the soul ascended, I read once again the writing on the mirror. And then suddenly it clicked to my physical consciousness, "this mortal" was the one that I had *seen*—God veiled in mortality—that had to put on immortality. It was the mandate of his being. It was the law of his Presence. He had to do it, and he was really telling me this every day through that verse. And telling me every day was the preparation of my soul.

Well, he had told me that ten years earlier: "I will leave. I must leave. I must take my leave of this earth. I will stay long enough to train you." So the expediency, the necessity in the training, in the chelaship, was the understanding that he was going to leave, that there would not be a messenger unless the messenger leaving personally trained another. The mantle must be handed down by someone in embodiment physically. It must be transferred physically in that case, because when it is not transferred physically by another messenger, then it becomes a much longer process. You have to be trained by an ascended master who first has to bring you to the place where you can see that ascended master and be trained by him.

And so the expediency, the necessity, the urgency of world conditions made it so that a messenger had to be there and had to be present and had to be trained. So I had the sense that I *had* to pass my initiations. I *had* to accelerate. I *had* to move at that accelerated speed because there was a necessity.

That to me is a great gift, because, you know, when we don't have to do something—either to get a paycheck or to get our degree or to pass an exam—if there's not an immediate reason why we should do something—which comes down to having enough to eat tonight, I guess; it always comes down to the economic factors of life—we don't hurry up about doing it. We'll take another day or an extra day. And another day or an extra day or an extra week or an extra lifetime could be fatal to the soul.

The World Needs You as Much as It Needs Maitreya

But worst of all, it could be fatal to the planetary evolution. The evolution of this planet needs you right now as much as it needed Jesus Christ, as much as it needs Maitreya. Maitreya wants you to know that the souls of this earth, who are waiting with their hungering and thirsting, need you, your soul, each one of you at this moment as much as they need him.

Yes, people need Lord Maitreya. Yes, they need his light and they need his attainment. But you see, if you are not there as the cup into which he pours the cold water that you serve to the one who is thirsting, then that one who is thirsting will not drink, whether Helios and Vesta be standing and pulsating in their midst. You *must* know this. This is what Maitreya wants you to get right now—this great clarity that *you* are needed today in the earth as much as he is needed.

Do not so exalt Maitreya as the cosmic being and the Cosmic Christ and so debase yourself that you're a tiny little minus sign on the blackboard, a tiny little electron, you know, that is so insignificant that it doesn't matter if you are or if you aren't.

That awareness that you are needed—I had that awareness. It was very clear to me. There were so few around Mark when I came. I was in Washington in the fall of 1961 working to support the Summit and working to support myself during chelaship. I was one of only two people earning the money to support the entire organization—myself and the other secretary. So it was very obvious that I was needed. Right?

We lose that sense when we start being the tens of thousands of souls who are coming together. But all you have to do is pick up the paper and see what is happening to the United States, what is happening to the nations of the earth, and you realize that it needs tens of thousands of souls.

But I think that it is really exciting to hear the promises that Lord Maitreya gave to the people who sat in that room, and to see that quite a few of those people have passed from the screen of life, and to see that I am here. And then I can look upon—it will be this October eighteen years—eighteen years of promises fulfilled, promises that Lanello gave to me, promises that El Morya gave to me. And, of course, we had no awareness in our outer minds of even what has transpired in the coming of Camelot and the building of Camelot.

Put Off the Old Man

Now here are all of these fiats.

> Be thou free! Be thou whole!... Reach out your hand as the Christ did and raise men from the dead.... But... you must first put off the old man and his deeds.

You've read those statements in the Bible, putting off the old man, the mortal becoming the immortal.[23] But the ascended masters are showing you how to do it. I don't think we all had a real physical understanding of how that would happen. But I see it happening in your auras and in your faces.

Each time I come back, I see a little more of you that has passed into the flame, that will nevermore be again—unless you choose to dive into the flame and take it back and say, "I can't live without you." Some people do that. But I would never have dreamed how much of the old man could be put off, how much karma could be balanced by the simple flame of obedience and the simple flame of love and the simple flame of trust.

Gossip Is the Most Hideous of Beasts

You know, I want to tell you something about the factor of gossip. I think that gossip is the most hideous of beasts and of entities that come parading across the scene to destroy the guru-chela relationship.

When I made that shout from the rooftop in Boston, crying out to Saint Germain to come and get me, a series of different contacts occurred. One of the events that occurred was that by a long, roundabout situation, I found a representative of an organization based in New York known as the Bridge to Freedom. I took a trip from Boston to New York by train to visit this representative before I ever met Mark, and I went to the sanctuary of the Bridge to Freedom.

I sat down in this sanctuary with a woman by the name of Hilda Ziegler. And I was there from morning till night, a full eight or ten hours. She sat me down and talked straight through about nothing but the teachings of the ascended masters and the embodiments of the ascended masters and all kinds of subjects that she went through. But on that same occasion, she carried on and on and on about this terrible man from Washington, D.C. She was talking about Mark Prophet, and she was talking about him in a very derogatory way.

The messenger of the Bridge to Freedom actually within about three months committed suicide and created for Morya a great burden of karma that he owed the universe because he had given his attainment to train her. During the period of her training and her messengership, she had brought forth a considerable body of teaching. She'd gotten into the psychic. She'd gotten unbalanced, and she had a lot of people around her who were not pure in their energies toward her. So she was in her thirties and she took her life, took some kind of pills and drowned herself in Long Island Sound.

Well, I went there and I heard all of these negative statements about Mark. And it seemed that this person had a very intense dislike for Mark, this other messenger, and was very critical of him. And so this was being fed to me for hours of the day, before I even was going to encounter him. It came into my consciousness, and it must have been instantaneously transmuted by my soul in my Christ Self that was sitting in such awe and wonder and gratitude after having searched for five years to find the ascended masters. And there were their pictures, and there was a sanctuary, and there was the Chart of the Presence. And there was the first person I had ever met who was a student of the ascended masters.

This level of her conversation was so negative and so astral itself that it did not even touch my consciousness. And by the time that I met Mark, I was only vaguely remembering the fact that this woman had talked and talked and talked and talked about all of these terrible things that he had supposedly done.

Well, I did meet Mark, and I had that thrilling experience

of hearing the dictation of Archangel Michael. And this other woman's testimony was very dim in my mind. But the interesting thing about it is that *then* I went to my first conference, which was 1961 (the same year that this dictation was given), and I sat in the hotel and saw this phenomenon of Mark Prophet giving these dictations. And by that time I had known him about three months. And there was a woman at that conference who took me to her hotel room and sat me down for another two or three hours telling me all these terrible stories and gossip about this man. And it was like it was fed into me and it went into the Christ flame of my heart and was consumed.

The Initiation of the Chela to Witness unto the Truth

But as I look back upon it and I look at this dictation and I realize that these things continue, I realize how clear it is that it is an initiation of the chela to maintain the trust in the guru, and that the chela must deal with this type of astral energy. And it becomes a point on the path of initiation, a very important point, a *very* important point, that if the chela is not able to perceive the testimony of the dictations and the ascended masters and the light that pours through the guru, if the gossip and the lies become more real, then he is not qualified to sit in the light. If he cannot himself witness unto the truth, and if he does not have enough momentum to perceive light and darkness, then he's not worthy to be on the Path.

Nevertheless, I feel it behooves all of us who are nurturing sweet and innocent souls to defend them against this vicious energy. This vicious energy has never ceased to attack Jesus Christ—never! And it goes on. It has gone on for two thousand years. Lies have been told about him, imputing all kinds of things to his lifestream.

Some believe and some disbelieve. Some see the glory of the

resurrection and some deny it. And it is even written in the Bible this fact of the concern of those who were burying the body, that the disciples would somehow hide the body and then say he was resurrected.[24] So they were very concerned about that body not being disturbed.

Relative Good and Evil Is Not What Is Important

So I think that it is important to come to that place where human goodness and human evil, the yin and the yang, the plus and the minus of relative good and evil, is not what is important about Jesus Christ or Gautama Buddha or ourselves or the messenger.

When I look at you as the chela, you are not accepted because you've been a humanly good person or a humanly bad person. I'm totally unimpressed by your evil deeds. And I'm totally unimpressed by your good deeds. What I'm impressed by is that you want God.

You know, we have the sheets that are filled out when you apply to attend Summit University: Have you done this? Have you done that? Have you taken drugs? Have you ever had a felony or this or that or the next thing?

It doesn't concern me in the least what you have done before. What concerns me is the purity of your heart. And what you have done before doesn't color you to me. And I think people are probably most concerned that human greatness does not impress me even as the opposite end does not impress me. It's the quality of the soul and what it is doing *now* in God.

Jesus and Mary Magdalene

But just the other day I was saying to myself, "This continual gossip that people try to conjure up about Jesus Christ having an affair with Mary Magdalene," and I felt this energy coming to me again challenging me, and I said to myself, "alright, let's sit down and analyze this."

And so I said to myself, "Would it make any difference to you if Jesus Christ had had an affair with Mary Magdalene?" And my instantaneous reply was, "Why, of course it wouldn't make any difference—it wouldn't make any difference to me at all."

He was what he was. He was the master. He was the living Christ. That was the light of his being. I saw him. I knew him then. And whatever he did with Mary Magdalene was between him and her and God. And it would never have altered his mission, because he still raised the dead, he still raised himself from the dead, he still is the ascended master.

The very next day I got a letter, and in the letter was a newspaper article. And the newspaper article was sent to me by one of the members of our retreat in Colorado Springs. It seems that in Egypt there was found a pot of scrolls the same way that the Dead Sea Scrolls were found. They were found by a boy who was in the hills. And he took them home to his mother. She was superstitious and she burned one of them and they sold the rest. And they've been around for twenty years. Finally, a museum put them all together and they translated them.[25] And there in the translation were the writings of those who they call the Gnostics.

They had all kinds of things in there about Jesus that would be quite disturbing to our standard concept of him. And when I finished reading about this book that had been recorded in those times, I felt that I had been reading about something that could have just as easily been written today by people who had been in our organization, had left our organization, and had written these things down, and had a view of what was going on that was entirely different from our view.

One of the things that was in this document, supposedly—I can only go by the newspaper; I haven't seen the book itself—was that Mary Magdalene was one of Jesus' favorite woman disciples, that he was with her a great deal, embraced her. And it said that he often kissed her on the lips.[26]

And so there was the very thing that I had dealt with the day before in my own mind. And I thought to myself, "I really cannot imagine Jesus doing this." But I had already said the day before—and I really had that sense of consciousness—that it would not matter if he had or he had not. And then as I analyzed further, I really did get the vibration that the document was not accurate.

Nevertheless, I think that there's a point in the life of every disciple when it's not, "What did he do?" but whether or not he did whatever he might have done, what is your reaction to it? That's the point of discipleship, and that's the point where you overcome your idolatry that this master has to be a perfect robot in your consciousness of what you think the perfect master is.

I think that Mark Prophet, of all people, removed from my mind the stereotypes of how we think a person has to behave or be when they are becoming an ascended master, when they have balanced their karma, and the things they ought to be doing. So I'm grateful for that experience.

Treachery, Intrigue, and Betrayal Are Always Present

I would like you to know that the person who betrayed Mark in Washington was someone very close to him who was working with him within the organization. And it was really a shocking act of betrayal.

Not long after that, Mark took a trip to Canada, and another person who was working closely with him decided to come and see me and got me cornered in a hotel and decided to ask me all kinds of questions about all kinds of things—what Mark had said to me, what Mark had told me, and all these things. She then proceeded immediately to take all of that information—which I thought I should be telling her because she was in Mark's very household, very close to him—and give it to the people that he was addressing in Canada. In the face of that information, they all resigned from the organization.

So I would like you to know that that treachery and that intrigue and that betrayal is something that is always present as the tares and the wheat, and the sheep and the goats.[27] The information that I gave her was concerning the initiations of beloved Saint Germain and beloved El Morya and beloved Jesus in which, after we'd been associated for some time, they said that in view of the difficult situation and the problems, and the fact that Mark Prophet was already in the process of divorcing his wife when I met him, and the fact that he could not be a messenger in the presence of that family, that in view of the fact that I should be trained, that we were twin flames, that we should be married.

That information came in letters addressed to me from Saint Germain and from beloved El Morya. And it was a couple of years after those letters came that we were married, because I wanted to give the fullest opportunity for Mark and his family to make it in the light and for them to have the ultimate opportunity to accept him and to accept his teachings. And they did not.

These particular people in Canada were members of the Church of England, and they did not believe in divorce. Because they did not believe in divorce, they could not accept Mark when he was divorced. And so they left him, and I think dozens of other people did also when we were married in the spring of 1963. And I think actually half of the people in the organization quit. There were probably a hundred members, and half of them quit because of that fact.

And then, of course, there was the opposition that came from all kinds of Bridge to Freedom and I AM students who thought it was an absolute disgrace that we should have children. So as we had children, people would resign from the organization. Of course, when you have a small organization, it feels like an earthquake happening when all of these people are resigning.

All of this Mark did and I did in obedience to the Gurus, to Lord Maitreya and to those who held the plan and the key for this age. And so it was a very fruitful marriage. It was a very fruitful relationship in terms of the transfer of light of the messengership and in terms of bringing in the souls who now carry the light and the aura of our beloved Lanello.

But I can tell you that right here in California and all over this country, there are people who *today* hold it against Mark Prophet for marrying me and for having those children, who left the organization then and still say that this is a false hierarchy organization because we had children. Of course, my having those children gave me the experience of New Age motherhood, of the understanding of counseling those who were in marriages, of counseling parents with children, of understanding the entire process of childbirth and the needs that must be met in our community, and also of understanding how to deal with children, how to bring up children.

Do Not Spoil the Children

The most important thing, of course, is that lightbearers have to be treated as normal children and not pampered as though they were exceptions. They have to be disciplined. It has to be expected that they have emotional bodies that are their age. When they're five, they have emotional bodies the age of a five-year-old, and they shouldn't be expected to be little Christs and little Buddhas walking around.

They need to be dealt with or else they can lose their mission. They can definitely lose their mission by being spoiled because parents think, "Well, they have so much light; they don't need to be disciplined"—or they don't need to be taught, or they don't need to be trained. And those are the things that you come to learn when you are right there in the midst of children who are behaving quite normally like other children and have the same problems that other children do.

And so I just feel that I would be incompetent to even serve with you if I hadn't been married and had those children and understood that relationship, the guru-chela relationship as Mark being father, mother, husband, brother, son, and having every relationship to me in this final embodiment. And that is what we need to have toward one another, to understand that we play many roles, and those roles need to be played, and they need to be understood.

Trust Is a Two-Way Street

So those eighteen years, then, were an opportunity for immense acceleration. And they were not without the constant initiation that attempts to destroy the trust between the guru and the chela. This trust is a two-way street. I love this concept because it has to do with the flow of electricity. There's a line of trust where the guru trusts the chela, and a line of trust where the chela trusts the guru.

Guru ⇌ Chela

The Flow of Trust
Trust between the guru and the chela flows in both directions
FIGURE 2

Now, in our path of initiation, we are expected to begin the line, to bring forth "fruits meet for repentance."[28] Bringing forth fruits meet for repentance means bring your faith, bring your good karma, bring your good works—but bring your trust. If you come to the ascended masters and you don't trust them, it's all over with. You can't even start the Path. Your trust is a line of energy, and you send it out and it becomes a little beep on the heart of the guru.

It's like a little knock on the door; it's a little jolt of energy. And you know, you awaken the sleeping Buddha. The Buddha's asleep and you awaken him with your flame of trust. The image of the sleeping Buddha is that he's asleep in this octave. In other words, he's awake and alive in the octaves of light. But because you are not aware of him, to you he is asleep.

Who you are really awakening is your own soul. You are awakening your own Christ-potential. And so you send forth the line. The guru returns it with a certain portion of trust. Just in order to have communication with the guru, the guru has to trust that you will receive it, that you will take it, that you will cherish it, that you will not trample his precious flower on the ground, and that you will be patient as he delivers to you his message.

Now there are times when perhaps the chela goes through great darkness and great doubt and great fear and is concerned and doesn't know whether or not he should trust or continue to trust the guru. That happens when you are going through the astral plane and through the initiations. But when you are a real chela who has accepted a real guru, the guru doesn't drop you the second that you have a doubt or a question.

A relationship is much bigger than that. It's a friendship. You don't drop your friend the day that your friend does something that isn't nice to you or the day that your friend may falsely accuse you of something. You say to yourself, "This is my friend. We've been friends a long time. Tomorrow he'll be feeling better." And so that's how the ascended masters are with us. They expect that we will have a sense of challenging, and now and then demanding proof and seeking that proof and being willing to wait patiently until the proof is given.

So the exciting thing about this is that you can drop the line of trust from you to the guru, and there's still a line. In other words, there are two lines that exist here. But if you have some doubt and fear, the line of the guru to you is sustained. It's sustained indefinitely, and it has a great deal to do with your past momentums, your past service to the Great White Brotherhood, your past lifetimes. When you have a great momentum of light and you may go through a period of burden, the masters keep the flame for you, just as you keep the flame for them.

The Sustaining Grace of the Guru

We do that for our children. Sometimes our children are naughty. Sometimes they do things that aren't right, or they may even not tell us the truth, or they may not tell us everything that they're supposed to be telling us about a situation because we didn't happen to ask the right question.

I've learned that a great deal about students. They'll answer every question I ask them, but they won't answer the question

I didn't ask. Well, you know when someone is not telling you the whole truth. And you know that when they do that, they've broken their line. As soon as there's a little fib or a little lie, the tie from them is broken, so they've got half a tie. Well, if you have the greater God consciousness, you know that their sustaining grace will be that you will not withdraw that tie. So you sustain it even though you know that perhaps little things are going on behind your back. You sustain the tie because you know that they will grow in grace.

When you are a parent, you understand this. When you haven't been a parent, you are much more brittle, much less forgiving, much more expecting. You'll notice that people who don't have children are always talking about how terrible children are and how terribly they are brought up and how terribly they are behaved. Well, they haven't had children, and so they think that children should be little china dolls that sit in a closet and that you dust off now and then.

Chelas are the same way. They have their ups and downs. And they are children, and they will behave like children at times. But the guru as the father and the guru as the mother has a much broader understanding. And he has a wide robe and he can contain all of that within his robe. He will not be offended. He will not feel compromised because of these little shortcomings.

So the sustaining of this great love tie when sometimes you don't do your decrees or sometimes you really are violating that guru-chela relationship, is a marvelous blessing. It is a grace. You always notice that if you, from your end, have broken your tie, when you go back to the master and when you make your calls, you find that God is waiting to answer your calls; the angelic hosts are waiting to nourish you again with love and light. And then you think of yourself as a big silly, because how could you have been so silly as to sit there and be unhappy for an hour or a day or longer. And you find out that all you had to do was make the call.

The Ascended Masters Uphold Their Chelas

So all of these gifts, which you cannot have until you put off the old man,

> They are held for you now by your own mighty I AM Presence and they will manifest in your world, and no power in heaven or earth can possibly prevent their manifestation at that moment when you are ready to receive them.

I can attest to you that from that day to this day, I have seen the power that God has expressed through me increase. And I have seen that the key to that power is getting the self out of the way. I see that the ascended masters uphold their chelas with a tremendous devotion and a tremendous defense. They defend their chelas against all enemies, against malicious gossip. They will not allow you to be judged by what you did before you came on the Path or even by the mistakes that you make while you are on the Path. They will not tolerate the gossip about you even as they will not tolerate the gossip about their messengers.

Doubt of the Teacher and the Teaching

You are, then, not a chela accepted because you are right or because you are wrong humanly, but because there's something more, because your soul is a part of the grace of God, your soul is a part of the Christ consciousness. And when we have that understanding, we are untouchable. We cannot be touched by doubt and fear.

I'd like to give you that teaching from Kuthumi, which was

recorded in the days of Theosophy, in which he says that the greatest test on the path of the chela, the greatest initiation of the chela, is when he comes to the hour when he must face doubt of the teacher and the teaching—*doubt of the teacher and the teaching.*[29] And he talks about that in his letters, and he says that if you can't get past that, then you don't make it on the Path.

You see, the teacher is your Real Self. The teacher is your Christ Self. So if you cannot sustain trust in the ascended master or in the messenger, whom you see, how can you sustain trust in your Christ Self, whom you have not seen? The person standing before you is just someone that God sets there to see if you really believe in your own Christ Self. That's the point of the test.

If you can't accept the one sent to represent your Christ Self, then you are deprived of your Christ Self as your guru. And when people are besieged by doubts and by fears, they have nothing to do with anything external. They have nothing to do with the surroundings. They don't have anything to do with Summit University, the ascended masters, the messenger, or the teachings. People like to pin their doubts on those outer circumstances like you pin the tail on the donkey.

But doubt and fear is a condition of the subconscious mind that exists prior to the student's coming to the feet of the master. And that doubt and fear will be summoned out of that subconscious just like the master calls out the collection of animals out of the zoo. He wants those animals and that zoo to come out of your subconscious so that it can be dealt with, so that you can choose between him and the zoo. And if you're going to choose your own beasts of prey, your own doubts and fears that you've created, you will live with them and you will die with them. But they have nothing to do with the teacher.

God Gives Light to Devoted Hearts That Are Pure

The trust of the children of the light in their teachers is just an amazing phenomenon. And we are taught by the ascended masters that when a child of light trusts in a teacher that is not of the light, it has no effect on his karma. If he believes and supports a teacher who is either not of the highest calling or who is actually a false teacher, his devotion to that teacher is taken by God as though it were devotion unto the living Christ—that's the absolute truth—because your trust in that teacher had nothing to do with the teacher, just as your doubt of the teacher has nothing to do with the teacher. Your trust in that teacher was based on the fact that really you had an inner tie to the Great White Brotherhood and an inner tie to your Christ Self, and so you were trusting.

So now it remains for us to see these beautiful souls of light who are trusting and who defend their teachers even when the teachers betray them, even when the teachers do obvious things that are not right. Then, because the false teachers do hypnotize them and do program them, they are there because of one of two points: either because they're hypnotized or because they are so pure that they are really devoted inherently to the Christ.

I can remember, for instance, being brought up in a religion that I chose myself when I was little, which was Christian Science. I went to Sunday school. And all of the time that I was going to church and being trained by teachers, I had absolute devotion to those teachers and absolute devotion to the teaching, but in my inner soul I was really receiving the teaching of God and the ascended masters' teachings. I was hearing what God was giving to me. And so the day that I found that there were discrepancies and certain subtle points in Christian Science that were not accurate and were not the way the ascended masters taught them, my whole world didn't come crashing down, because I was not tied to the outer form. I was tied to the inner light. I was tied to the inner light of Jesus and of the Bible and even of Mary Baker Eddy, who had a great light.

And so if the words weren't exactly right, if the teachings weren't exactly right, that wasn't what I was there about. I was there because I had a true guru-chela relationship with Jesus and Mary Baker Eddy, who is ascended.* She was ascended at that time, and I had a real, living relationship with her. And my awareness of God and of the ascended masters was such that when I came of age, it was so real that I could stand before all of the elders of the church and the board of directors and all of the people who were leaders in Boston, and I could tell them that their perception of Christian Science was inaccurate.

They had not really perceived the real divine science behind it, and their denial of angels and of ascended masters was totally false. And I had to witness in that temple, and I had to witness against people who were very powerful, very wealthy, very prominent. And all of the leaders that I had looked up to, I had to be able to tell them that their perception of truth was inaccurate.

Now had I been an idolator, had I been wed to the form of Christian Science instead of to the spirit, I could not have done that. But my world didn't come crashing down. I just had to be educated to the fact that when you are at a certain level, you receive religion at a certain level, the best that people can give it to you. God attempts to express himself in all churches. His spirit is expressing itself in all churches—even if the exact words and the exact doctrines and dogmas that the people hold are not accurate. Yet because those people are pure, there is a pure light that comes through them and blesses the congregation.

---
*Theosophia, the Goddess of Wisdom

It's a wonderful phenomenon how God, in spite of erroneous doctrine and dogma, gives his light to his sweet children. And you see that everywhere. That's true everywhere. Where people go to worship, sincerely praying to Jesus, they sincerely have his light, even if the preacher is preaching a doctrine of hellfire and damnation and denying reincarnation and saying that I'm a Satanist. You know, that doesn't mean to say that those little sweet souls are not receiving light from God if they in their hearts are pure. So God has a way of getting around mortals, and he does it every day.

A Heart Initiation

Here is the next initiation:

> I ask, therefore, that you pause as I make contact with the beloved angelic hosts and ask them to pour their radiance into the chalices of your hearts.

Again it is a heart initiation:

> I ask that they saturate you with the pure light rays from their hearts, charged with the essence of roses and the fragrance of pine.

Pine and roses are a recurrent theme with the Brotherhood and so is frankincense. So you might take a word to the wise and use those if you like.

> I ask that you be made aware, then, of the sweetness of the soul of God that is within you and of the eternal Presence of God within you.

The sweetness of your soul is the feminine polarity of your being. Your soul is the feminine polarity. And the eternal Presence is the masculine polarity. So God as Father, God as Mother within you is the awareness.

Now, even though the words are not spoken, I know that Lord Maitreya is already beginning the expression of this fantastic mathematics and science that has come to us in the awareness of the stupendous figure-eight flow of the soul and the I AM Presence and all that we have learned about that energy. Here it is, and here the angelic hosts are giving us the initiation within our heart.

Truth that is presented simply always contains the ultimate matrix of the vastness that the soul will discover, not only over a decade but over many lifetimes, over a period of cosmic consciousness after you are ascended. You will always discover more and more and more about the simple, sweet teachings of Jesus Christ, inherent in those very teachings.

And you know, the planes of consciousness between where we understand Jesus in the physical, concrete sense and where you and I understand so many of his teachings—there is such an acceleration from the point of soul comprehension to the point of comprehension through your I AM Presence, that it appears to these dear Christians in their churches that what we are saying is the antithesis of what Jesus said, that it is anti-Christ, that it is Satanic, when in fact it is but a stepped-up understanding. It's just like the violent outrage that went forth when people suggested the earth was round when they all thought it was flat.

And these perspectives that we have—you see something close up; you see it at a distance and your perspective changes—so your testimony changes, your description changes, and what looked blue might look red. You say one is right and one is wrong, but it's simply a matter of perspective. There are all kinds of things about our universe, about the planetary bodies, about gravity, about the center of the earth, about the stars, which, the more we know in science, the more we have information, the more there is a different witness, a different testimony. And people are very frightened of that change.

So that testimony of the spirit and the soul and

> The eternal Presence of God within you is forever and forever and forever. It is without end. Therefore accept this gift from the angelic hosts that are part of my band of light.

We Are Conceived by God

Here is a statement that we are conceived by God. Mother Mary showed me this stupendous revelation not long ago about the Holy Spirit being present at every conception, that there are four parties present at conception: the father and mother (the physical parents), the son, who is the incoming soul, and the Holy Ghost. And, therefore, in the conception of a child of God—remember, I said in the conception of a *child of God*—the very fact that the child is conceived means that God conceived the child, that the Holy Ghost was present.

There is no conception of a child of God without the Holy Ghost. It doesn't matter if it's rape. It doesn't matter if it was unintended. It doesn't matter if the parents didn't want the child. At inner levels they gave their consent. If there is the conception of a child of God, the Holy Ghost is present.

> I want to remind you that you came not through the gate of birth by accident, but you came by conscious, divine intent.

I hear the pro-abortionists screaming that the pro-lifers are trying to take their religious views and to make them become the law of the land. It's not a religious view; it's a statement of life. But so many people who are pro-abortion are not children of God; they are the seed of the wicked. And so they have not the life of God in them. They can freely murder that life, and they would like a philosophy that would get the children of the light to murder the one who is God in them.

Some Are Ready for Cosmic Stages of Initiation

He talks about himself as the Great Initiator and about his interest in "the unfoldment of the individual chelas in coming through the stages of initiation." He said that there are people among humanity who are ready for cosmic stages of initiation. I believe that many of you are among those people.

Do you know where you were on October 21, 1961? The fall of 1961, Maitreya was looking out from that room in Boston, the crown chakra of America, and he was looking at you. Now we are here, and he's looking at you again because when this dictation was given, he was looking at me, and he knew that Mark wouldn't be here to initiate you when you got here. So he was looking at me to be the one who would be the instrument of that initiation that he would give you.

And the masters have looked at us when we were babies in the cradle, seeing the things that we would do that we perhaps are dreaming of when we are babies in the cradle. And they look at us before we take embodiment, and they sponsor our souls. But today, the same statement is true:

> Some are ready for cosmic stages of initiation. Some are ready for less advanced stages of initiation.

Where will you be eighteen years from now? How much karma will you have balanced? Before what audience and what nation on the earth will you be delivering the message of Lord Maitreya and, therefore, giving to those people that cosmic initiation for which they are waiting? Remember, it's a cup of cold water in Christ's name.

Whenever I think of that cup of cold water in Christ's name, I don't know why, but I always see that old tin measuring cup that my mother had in her cookie drawer. And we had the same cup the whole time I grew up, and it got pretty battered. And when I used to bake, sometimes I'd drink a cup of cold water and I'd take the measuring cup. And I can remember how battered up it got. And I also remember that when I was a baby, someone gave me a silver goblet. And that goblet is very battered because it used to always drop from my high chair and drop on the floor, and all of its edges are battered.

You must remember this tremendous vision that Maitreya is the Cosmic Christ. He's pouring out the water. If you don't catch it in the cup of your being, your heart, even if it's tin and battered, there will not be a cup in which to transfer that living water of eternal Life.

And that message that he stated: You are as important to the earth, the earth needs you as much as the earth needs Lord Maitreya. You know, I would go one step further and say that the earth needs you *more* than it needs Lord Maitreya because it's always had Lord Maitreya. It's not that he hasn't been here. It's that there hasn't been anyone to give his message. Jesus was that chalice that you are, that you can be, that you can perfect.

The Word Is the Progenitor of Your Being

"The *Word* of God is the progenitor of every individual," *not* your human parents, not your human ancestry, not your race, not your religion. The *Word* is the progenitor of your being.

Now that is a statement of a law. And when you suffer in your physical body of hereditary conditions, when you suffer emotionally from emotional problems your parents or ancestors had, whatever you think you are denied because of human heredity, remember this statement of the Law: *The Word of God is the progenitor of my soul.* You say it as a fiat. You say it as your Christ Self would say it, as an attorney-at-law defending you before the world, before all of the insidious lies of this world that say that you have to live only a short time and you can only do this and only do that because you're limited by your heredity.

That is a statement of wholeness. It's a statement of healing. It's a scientific statement of your being. If you can go through a dictation and you can underline the statements that are laws, absolute laws, principles of your life, and then you learn them and you become familiar with them, they will pop into your consciousness in the hour of the greatest need.

You do *not* have to carry human limitation because of an ancestral lineage. Jesus broke that entire law by his life. The Word of God

> is tangible and real, it is intelligent, it is light! And in it there is no shadow, nor is there a shadow of turning.

God gives "gifts of hierarchical power" to the ascended masters, charged with momentums—to elementals, also. And the obvious conclusion is, well, if he can give hierarchical powers to the ascended masters, he can give them to you and me. And he has given them to us. He's given us our I AM Presence, the duplicate, "never separated from the Central Sun." You are *never* separated from the Great Central Sun, never!

The fifth dictation, which we already heard today, talks about the Great Central Sun. Your I AM Presence is a duplicate.

The Protection of Archangel Michael

> When an individual awakens to the power of divinity, an initiate is born on the world scene. The star of Bethlehem appears...

And God seals that lifestream. "From the heart of God," there is protection "through the angelic hierarchy presided over by Archangel Michael."

I can testify to that fact. I can testify to the personal presence of Archangel Michael protecting me from physical death and from any compromise of the light that might have occurred in my life before I contacted the Brotherhood and before I became a messenger. I can remember the presence of Archangel Michael so strong that I could not move my hand or my arm against the presence of that stupendous angel, who was protecting me from danger. And I did not know till after I heard his voice in the first dictation I heard, that that was the presence of the Lord that had protected me.

So he's talking about three people in the room who would have passed without the protection of their I AM Presence and their guardian angel.

There was an individual of whom I spoke to you—in fact, it was the individual that I told you about whom I saw removed from the Great White Brotherhood by removing the link from the chain—and there was a period when he was absent from our service and a period when he came back and worked for me for a time and then again left and was dismissed for good.

During the period of his absence, before he came back, I was daily seeing a projection, a vision, an image, let us say, of him having been in a very severe accident. I saw myself going to the hospital and decreeing and praying for him when he was in the hospital. And each time that I would see this vision, I would call upon Almighty God to transmute it. So the day that he decided to come back and help me and work with me, he came to the Ashram and he was almost white as a ghost.

He said to me that he had just been driving along the highway. He was on a double lane road, and he came to a stoplight. He was parked on the inside lane, and here was another car. And he looked out of the side of the car, and he saw this car barreling across the road. He was so quick in perceiving it that he reversed and went backward and pulled back out of the way. This car came barreling down and there was a terrible wreck between this car and the one that was parked in the next lane. It was a very severe accident, and he was absolutely untouched.

Morya showed me that the impending karma of that accident was due because of the individual's betrayal of the light and that because he had decided to turn and serve the light, that it had been set aside. It had been set aside through the intercession of the messenger. I had received the warning. I had made the calls. The accident was averted.

The person who had the accident was a person whose karma was not mitigated and whose energy could allow and attract that into his forcefield. So it wasn't that an injustice had been done.

And so this individual came along and he rendered the service to the organization that he rendered, was disobedient, and did ultimately leave. I pray for his soul's safety, and obviously I have not in my heart any desire to see such things happen to people. But I have witnessed that, and I must tell you that that point of protection is given when you have the tie to the ascended masters. And when you have the tie, they will absolutely sustain you through thick and thin.

The tremendous protection given is beyond even imagination. You cannot even imagine sometimes how you come out of accidents. I have seen people on this staff just miraculously spared and saved on the highways. There is a tremendous protection given. And personally, I myself would never be without the guru. Life ceases to be when you cease to have a tie to God's emissaries, because they are God. The ascended masters are God in manifestation.

Express Willingness to Give Up the Former Self

I'm very appreciative for the meaning that is given to us of the word *I AM*. It means "being," "existence," and "bliss." Those three words are given.

Maitreya is talking about continuous experience, continuous consciousness, that there is no death. The child of God, the son of God does not experience death, because he has a soul and a threefold flame. An unbroken series of consciousness, through the day, through the night, through embodiments, and that was the illustration of the tomb. Initiates assemble at night.

I urge you to accept as a little child the promise of your free communication with the ascended masters and that it will happen to you. I urge you to accept that possibility of the accurate communion—not a psychic communion, not a psychic experience that you do not want, not going through your electronic belt, not confusing your human consciousness with the ascended masters, but the direct face-to-face contact with the Brotherhood.

> The race needs the help of the ascended masters. This we are willing to give. We ask that you make the call within yourself; we do not ask that you necessarily make the statement before mankind concerning your inner intention.

That is a very important point of wisdom, before you go to sleep,

> that you make a call to God, to your own mighty I AM Presence, and that you ask him to guide your footsteps that you may understand the power of light, the power of the ascended masters, the power of the Christ in action—and that you consciously elect to further your progress in the things of the Spirit, that this which passeth away, these "former things," be no longer cleaved to, but that you anchor within the veil that permanent God consciousness that no man can take from you.

And then you will be a part of our band and you will have begun in newness of life.

Again showing that you have an initiation—you have an opportunity to be a part of the band of Maitreya and his angels.

But he's asking you to do something. Naaman the Syrian was asked to dip into Jordan seven times. He almost didn't do it, if it weren't for his servant.[30] Sometimes the little things the master asks us are so simple that we forget to do them.

Will you remember from 6:30 p.m. to whenever you go to bed tonight to

> make a call to God, to your own mighty I AM Presence, and that you ask him to guide your footsteps that you may understand the power of light, the power of the ascended masters, the power of the Christ in action—and that you consciously elect to further your progress in the things of the Spirit, that this which passeth away, these "former things," be no longer cleaved to.

In other words, you're asking that you can put off the old man and put on the new, that you're expressing your willingness to God to give up the former self, "that you anchor within the veil"—in other words, that you anchor here in this octave the "permanent God consciousness that no man can take from you." If you will make that call, "you will be a part of our band and you will have begun in newness of life."

And he already told you what happens when an initiate is born. Then you have the absolute protection of the Brotherhood. You will eventually be victors.

> And then you will be a part of our band and you will have begun in newness of life, in renewing the consciousness of the atoms and electrons of your body, in charging yourself with the sacred fire. You will be eventually victors, not vanquished.

The Full Initiation of Your Ascension Is Offered

So we had a number of initiations in this: the radiance of light and the request that you make the call to Jesus Christ, bringing the blazing light to your forcefield, breathing upon us the cosmic sense that may awaken within your cells to the glory of God, which is present wherever you are. That's the initiation where he comes as a father to breath upon you concerning the cosmic sense of the glory of God right where you are. He doesn't want you to be the victim of that mass consciousness density. He gives us the pause for the initiation to make contact with the angelic hosts, pouring their radiance through the heart. And the purpose of that is so you can make contact with God as your soul, God as your spirit.

There are quite a number of initiations offered here. The full initiation of your ascension is actually offered. If you'll just put off the old man and put on the new, you can raise men from the dead, you can heal the sick, cleanse the lepers, and so forth. You need to know that that is true.

And now, the promise: If you make the call to God to guide you—to give you understanding of "the power of the light, the power of the ascended masters, the power of the Christ in action"—and if you do determine to progress in the things of the spirit, and if you will put off the old man and put on the new, "you will be a part of our band."

I'm going to ask you to rise now so that I can make an invocation.

> *Beloved Lord Maitreya, I call for the full power of the Great Central Sun Magnet to accelerate within these souls the great cosmic sense of Almighty God present here and now, and the sweet sense of the soul's rapport with the I AM Presence*

through the Mediator, blessed Jesus Christ, and their own Christ Selves.

I call for the intensification of the understanding of the sweetness of the guru-chela relationship that we share. I call for the initiation of trust, absolute trust in only one, Almighty God. In God we place our trust. I place my trust in the God of the chela as the chela places his trust in the God in the ascended masters and their messengers. And therefore, as we trust in God within one another, we are never let down by human idolatry within the self or within another self.

Almighty God, we ask for the sending forth of the light of Mighty Astrea. Roll back all harmfulness coming to souls of light on the Path. Roll it back! O beloved Archangel Michael, in answer to the call of the great avatars of the ages, I ask you to bind the demons of condemnation that would stand in the way of the approaching chelas of the light.

Blaze forth the light of our hearts! Blaze forth the mighty Summit beacon! Blaze forth that intense light ray! Blaze forth that intense light ray! Blaze it forth, O light of God, and let the beacon of our Camelot be the beacon of the entire Spirit of the Great White Brotherhood amplified by our souls for souls of light in America to come swiftly to the awareness of their own mighty I AM Presence and the ascended masters.

In the name of the Father, the Son, the Holy Spirit, in the name of the Cosmic Virgin, Amen.

January 26, 1979

CHAPTER FIVE

The Initiation of the Holy Spirit

Some of the greatest chelas that I know are let's-do-it people. It's exciting to bring forth from the Brotherhood a plan of action and to be meeting with a group of chelas and then to have one say, "Let's do it!" It breaks through the level of the etheric body, the memory body, the mental body, the emotional body, and puts you right there on the nine o'clock line. It's the line of action—a tremendous line of action. It's an exciting place to be.

Have you heard the lecture on the karmic clock from July 1976? We'll see that you get that one morning this week. It's got a lot of great slides with it, and we're putting it together in the book of that conference that's a paperback book that's nearly ready.[1] That was a great lecture. The karmic clock basically shows you where you are in balancing 100 percent of your karma.

One hundred percent is the whole pie, right? So if you were going to divide it up, each quadrant would be 25 percent. Usually you have to have about 25 percent of your karma balanced to even have any desire to be on the path of chelaship. And when you get that 25 percent balanced, you awaken to the Cosmic Christ mind and you want to know "Who am I?"—who I AM.

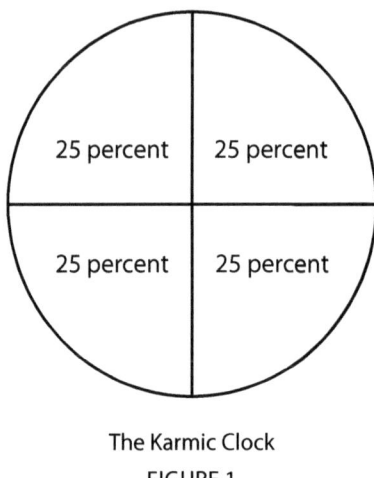

The Karmic Clock
FIGURE 1

Under 25 percent, you're so dense, you're almost like animals. The animal people of the earth are so full of animal food and animal vibrations that they haven't even discovered the fact that they don't know who they are. They're just part of the herd, part of the mass consciousness. And they're just about as content as the cattle that they eat, grazing on the hillsides. They have become what they eat.

When you can get rid of that much density, you can come to the awareness, "Hey, I don't know who I am. It's disturbing me. I want to know who I am. I've got to find the guru who can tell me." When you get to the six o'clock line of the Mother, you've balanced 50 percent. You go one degree past the six o'clock line, and you've got 51 percent of your karma balanced and you qualify for the ascension.

Strive to Balance 100 Percent of Your Karma

Well, Lanello gave that famous dictation on one of my recent birthdays. He said, "I want chelas and staff members to strive to balance 100 percent of their karma. I don't want you coming home with 51 percent. You can make that. I want you to go beyond."[2] But when you go beyond, this is where you really hit all of the sufferings and everything that we've seen Jesus go through.

This is the whole astral plane, the dark night of the soul, the carrying of the cross of world karma, the descent into hell, the dealing with the momentums of insanity, the exorcism of demons. This is where you need the Holy Spirit. This is where you need action. This is one of the most difficult periods in the existence, in the initiation of any chela.

When Mark ascended, El Morya announced that I had balanced 51 percent of my karma, and that meant that Lanello was willing to leave. He was willing to leave because he knew that I'd get Home. He wasn't willing to leave this plane before he knew that I could get there. But that's not the absolute guarantee, because you can go back and make more karma and lose that. So when you volunteer to stay beyond your 51 percent, you're taking a big chance.

When we arrived with Sanat Kumara, we had that much momentum of light. We had that light. We lost it. We lost it at the place where we were no longer eligible for the ascension.

Of course, the 51 percent eligibility is a dispensation of this century. Prior to that, it was always a requirement of 100 percent balanced in order to get back to God. With the coming of the Cosmic Christ and the gurus and Jesus Christ, finally in this century, we've had the requirement reduced to 51 percent. That's a bargain price for your ascension. It's the greatest bargain in the world today.

Initiations of the Third and Fourth Quadrants

Well, obviously I stayed around and I'm not standing still. So I know what I'm talking about. That third quadrant is a great initiation. But the great boon of being willing to stay with it and go through it is that after you've swum in this astral sewer for however many years that it takes you to get through it, you come out on the nine o'clock line of the Holy Spirit.

It's a very important line because you don't have to have balanced 75 percent of your karma to stand there. You can stand there wherever you are on the clock provided that you have a tie to the gurus, provided that you have a tie to those who *have* gotten there, who *have* made it. You need someone standing with you who *has* put this astral sea under his feet. And the intent is that you shall one day become that person, that you shall stand there.

When you reach that place, you have some *very severe* initiations in the physical quadrant, on the nine o'clock, ten o'clock, and eleven o'clock lines. But you've got a 75 percent momentum behind you. And the thing you have over every other saint who's ever been there is that you have a supreme enlightenment. You've got an enlightenment such as the saints of the churches of East and West have never had. We have so much teaching that tells us what is happening. It is so incisive. It's the teaching of Omega. It's the great gift of knowledge of the understanding of forces working in the world and what our position is in them.

The additional gift you have is community. We're together. We reinforce and understand one another. We understand each other when we're going through this dark night of the soul, the astral plane. We understand its symptoms, and we stand shoulder to shoulder and we help each other. And that's something that a lot of the adepts in ages past have not had. They stood alone.

We also have the presence and the intercession of the Great White Brotherhood and the knowledge of its existence. The science of the spoken Word is the gift of Saint Germain in this century. It's a tremendous boon.

Those factors are why you can go further than your 51 percent. Until you get there, I cannot stress enough that the tie to hierarchy is all-important. You can't make it without being on the chain of those who have made it. These are *very* disturbed waters in the third quadrant. They are treacherous waters, and you need the lifeline to carry on. But to have the authority to precipitate in the physical, you need to be with the ones who've done it.

Chelaship Begins on the 9 o'Clock Line

So, say you're over here on your four o'clock line or anywhere in this 25 to 50 percent quadrant, which is where the majority of students are. This is where you are positioned. Wherever you are in that place, you can relate to that Libra sign, that Holy Spirit experience, as long as you've got the Brotherhood, as long as you've got the chain of hierarchy.

So the Libra line is the action of the Holy Ghost. And that is the action of the sacred labor, and it is the action of the chela. Chelaship does not really begin unless you can stand on that line. And since we can't stand on that line until we've balanced that karma, we must have the guru. *We must have the guru.* The Eastern teachings are so emphatic on this. No matter what stream of teaching you'll pick up, if it's the real teaching, that is the stress. You need the lifeline, and the ascended masters provide that lifeline.

So when Maitreya comes and says that we must have the sacred labor, he is understanding that unless you can occupy the position of the Holy Ghost and be God in action, you're not really fulfilling your chelaship, because it's love. Love is the fulfilling of the law of the guru-chela relationship.

Now look at the children of Israel. They had an interaction with Father. The Father principle in Abraham and the prophets was guru. Father laid down the Law. You obeyed that Law; you were protected. You disobeyed that Law, and swift and sudden destruction came upon you. That was a teaching of karma, but it was not the fullness of the guru-chela relationship. There were not too many chelas in Israel. They were children learning a law and being spanked when they disobeyed the law. It was the learning of the relationship to Father.

The coming of Jesus Christ—he is the Mediator, and he is the great Guru that through his Christ consciousness bears the karma of the world, bears the karma of his disciples so that the disciples can go out two-by-two, door-to-door, town-to-town, city-to-city wheresoever he will come. So they become evangels of Jesus Christ, and they become carriers of the Holy Ghost because he, in the position of the Christ, is holding the balance for their untransmuted karma. And he tells them when he washes their feet that he has to wash them; "If I wash thee not, thou hast no part with me."[3] And he tells them that they are not yet wholly clean; they're not yet wholly cleared of their karma.

So Maitreya's introduction is the opportunity to stand at the nine o'clock position before you've earned it. It's the opportunity to wear the mantle of the guru, to try it on for size, to have the Electronic Presence of the gurus. And because you choose to be a chela and to be one with the guru who is standing there, you can carry on his work in his name. And doing his work in his name accelerates this spiral of transmutation of the misuses of this quadrant, this mental body, as well as the etheric.

Karma in the Four Lower Bodies

Now I don't want you to think from the karmic clock that the first 25 percent of your karma is only balancing your etheric body, the second is only balancing the mental, and so forth. That's not how you think of this clock. You think of it in terms of the fact that all karma that you make through the misuse of the fire element affects the entire clock. The first 25 percent of the karma that you balance will be distributed evenly over your whole subconscious. And so is the second, so is the third, so is the fourth. But we clock it this way so that you can understand the levels of mastery and the hierarchies under which you are receiving your initiations of the Cosmic Christ.

In other words, when you have balanced 25 percent of your karma—fire, air, water, earth; etheric, mental, emotional, physical—you are coming under the initiations of the hierarchy of Aries to establish I AM WHO I AM by the flame of God-control, and you will be meeting your momentums of the ego, the not-self. But you will be meeting those momentums as they have affected every other line of your clock, every other phase of your human consciousness. So that will be the point where you stand at the point of your initiation.

But obviously, every act of karma affects all of the four lower bodies—especially mental karma, because when we perform actions, we are using our minds. So there isn't any karma in the whole 100 percent of energy that you've ever used that you are not responsible for its use through your mental body.

The period in this mental quadrant is the period of Summit University, is the period of training. It's the period of the wisdom flame. And the more wisdom you have, if you have a pure motive, the more that wisdom itself is transmutative.

Wisdom is transmutative. The yellow flame transmutes ignorance. All of the seven rays are transmutative in and of themselves *if* the will be pure, if the desire be pure. If your desire isn't pure, you can be bathed in a flame and after the flame passes by, you can still have the stench of arrogance or of ignorance in your forcefield.

So the reason for the guru-chela relationship—if there are not thousands of reasons, this is one very key reason—is that in order to make it on the Path, you must be *actively* integrated with the Holy Ghost. Your karma does not allow you to be integrated. Hence you must be with someone who is integrated in order for you to pass the very initiations that you must pass to make your ascension.

The Figure of the Guru Is Found in All the World's Religions

The guru has not disappeared from any of the world's religions. Whether it is Mohammed or Mother Mary or Jesus Christ or the prophets, people are aware that they need a leader. They are aware that they need someone to follow. And those who have gotten so discouraged with life and with the world and who say, "I'm not going to follow anyone, because I'm so discouraged with all of the false teachers," they really have lost the thread of hierarchy.

However, it can be a very healthy period and a healthy experience to withdraw from those who you know are not adequate, and then to wait in the peace of the Inner Self for the right teacher to come or for the coming of the dawn of the day of your own Christ Self or your I AM Presence. I think we've all been through that.

But there are those who do not do that in humility or sincerity, with sincere supplication to God for answers. There are people who do that in an absolute defiance of the entire hierarchical order. And they say that they are doing it because of the terrible behavior of leaders they have known: "Because so-and-so and so-and-so and so-and-so have been so terrible, I'm not going to be a part of any organization. I'm not going to follow anyone." That's just taking other fallen ones and their antics as an excuse for one's own defiance of Almighty God.

I've seen that done by any number of people. "I don't go to church because the priest did so-and-so." "I don't go to church because the minister was a hypocrite." And thirty years later they're still telling their story and they still don't go to church. That's just nothing but downright rebellion, because it doesn't take too much development to realize that God is there and that you don't have to fall down and worship the idol of your minister or your priest and because he fails you, you evermore will fail God.

That's just a very weak argument, but it is one of the arguments of the fallen ones, one of their excuses for not being faithful to God and his servants. And you'll find that when you examine their excuses in the light of truth, all of their excuses are pretty weak. But they deliver them with such a ferocity and such an intensity that their emotionalism that's behind their weak excuses seems to carry the day.

Don't Be Intimidated by Those Who Have No Christ Mind

It's like the abortion arguments. There's no real argument that can be given that will hold water. But you deliver the entire pro-abortion argument with the intensity and the energy of these fallen angels and it grips and it paralyzes the nations. It paralyzes people. People are not really convinced of the arguments, but they are being hypnotized and gripped, literally *gripped* by the energy, the wallop behind it.

I think that you need to understand not to be intimidated by individuals who really have no logic, no Logos, no Christ mind and they're delivering their diatribe and their denunciation and their emotionalism, but their logic, their mind of God consciousness is so weak. And so when they come across with all that energy, you have to learn to recognize that sudden impact on your solar plexus, on your bodies. It comes through the TV set. It comes through the mass consciousness. And after a number of years of going through that, all of a sudden you say, "Hey, wait a minute. I'm going to stand up and roll it right back."

That is when you need the *firm* voice and the *firm* energy of God, which thrusts from you and makes the statement of truth with authority. Jesus spoke with authority and not as the scribes.[4] And the authority of his voice carried the two-edged sword that rolled back this very carefully calculated psychology of the wicked. They *know* that they're delivering a solar-plexus punch behind their lies. And they know that their lies do not stand up when held up in the light of the sun.

Now, you do not become emotional or emotionally charged, but you are very *firm* and you are very resolute in your statement of the Word. And you make that statement, and you make it with *utmost* simplicity, because the truth that defeats these lies and this energy is very simple. So you can speak with the Word that comes forth from me now—from my soul, from my Christ Self, from my I AM Presence. And it comes forth from my guru because my guru and I are one, because I'm obedient to my guru to the best of my ability. And because I'm one with my guru, I'm one with the entire Spirit of the Great White Brotherhood.

And therefore when I speak, I speak with the full authority of the ascended masters and the entire momentum of the victors of the age. When you walk in that light and speak with that light and do not compromise your honor or your personal dignity, you will grow and grow and grow in your own self-respect, hence in the respect that you draw from others.

Speak with the Authority of the Holy Ghost

The word you speak when you are in that authority is the Word of the Holy Ghost. It is the combination of the momentum of the Holy Ghost of everyone who has ascended. And that multiplication factor is why the Great White Brotherhood has the ability to deliver the power to its chelas. That is the power that Jesus wielded. He was totally in touch with every angel, every cosmic being. That's why he said in the hour of his crucifixion, "Don't you know that at this moment I could call to my Father and he would send to me twelve legions of angels? But nevertheless, so it must be. The scriptures must be fulfilled."[5] And he said, "You have no power to destroy me except it be God who give you the power."[6]

The instantaneous contact with the Great White Brotherhood gives you the authority on the instant to have standing with you, as you face the world, twelve legions of angels or whatever ascended master's Electronic Presence that you invoke. That is the authority that it takes to defeat the word of the antichrists as they go in and manipulate society, education, and all of these human fields of endeavor. And these various fields of human endeavor require people educated as well as endued with the Holy Ghost to penetrate them, to bring the truth to light, and to bring the error to light.

I do the best that I can in investigating information on the various fields and bringing it to you at conferences, giving one- or two- or three- or even four-hour lectures on a concentrated area, bringing to light some of the more obvious problems.

But there are areas to be studied and research to be done that require specialization.

For instance, I had a plea today in writing from a woman who said, "Will you please give an exposure at a coming conference on the medical profession and the entire momentum of the use of chemicals to deal with disease and the pharmaceutical companies sponsoring the medical schools, hence the treatment of disease instead of health prevention—all that is going on in the tyranny of preventing people from treating their bodies, whether it be with laetrile or whatever else they would do?"

The exposure of *evil* as an "energy veil" in the medical profession is something that must be done. The masters have made general comments in dictations. I have never done a complete exposé on the medical profession, because I know that should I begin to do so, it's an enormous body of research, and I don't consider myself qualified at the human level to go in and explore all types of methods of healing, to look at the field of chiropractic, of orthopedics, of all of the different forms of naturopathy and different types of sciences that are being used today. And so for me to attempt to give such an exposure, I have not done so because I would want to bring to bear a greater quality of professionalism than I have the desire or the opportunity to put into such a message.

I know what it takes. And I *know* what I'm tackling. I know the beast that I'm tackling when I'm tackling the medical profession. These are the princes of this world. These are the power elite, this profession. What I do is that I give the invocations for the binding of these forces at inner planes that are the source of their power. It's the crumbling of the system from within that happens by the use of the science of the spoken Word.

The Use of the Holy Spirit Is the Role of the Chela

What I'm saying is that the use of the Holy Spirit, the action of the Holy Spirit, in all of these fields of human endeavor is the role of the chela. It's the role of the one anointed by the guru with his mantle. And according to your causal body and your divine plan and your development, you can take the great skill of the two-edged sword and go farther than I have gone—whether it's in the exposure of Marx or of the KGB. Even a two- or three-hour lecture is just the beginning of what is really needed to ultimately precipitate the defeat of that darkness. So chelaship becomes the translation of the intense white-fire light of the guru to humanity.

I just want to keep this figure-eight before your remembrance. The guru sits at the point of the I AM Presence. The chela is attempting to sustain the point of the Mediator and Christ Self. And the souls of humanity are on the other side of the figure eight.

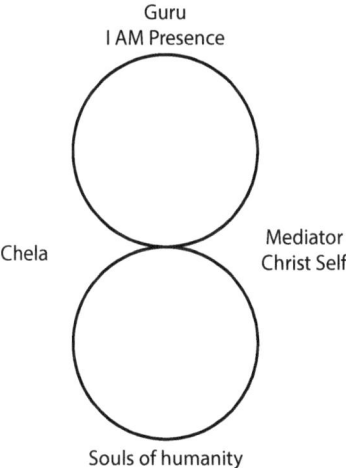

The Figure-Eight Flow between the Guru and the Souls of Humanity
FIGURE 2

We know that the I AM Presence never deals directly with the soul. The I AM Presence always deals with the soul through the Mediator, the Son. So the guru that is manifesting the pure energy of God gives that energy as the understanding and the statement of the Law and the application of that Law in human affairs.

But there's a certain point at which the torch is passed. The mediator who is the chela takes that energy and again translates it down for the souls of humanity. And so you have a figure-eight flow: the person who stands at the level of the Christ is drawing the first sheaths and veils of darkness off from the world.

Did you ever see cotton candy made? You know how it's made up of wisps. You keep drawing that substance off from the world, and it's getting transmuted in your decree sessions. And so you are raising the level of humanity so that you can then feed them the light that they need to have without being hurt. What you are feeding to them in the teaching comes to you in very, very concentrated capsules in dictations and high-powered and intense lectures. They must go through the hopper of your mind. They must go through your heart flame in order to reach people.

The Exposure of Embodied Evil

We were talking this morning about the "Confidential Files" from *The Touch of Shiva*. Those tapes cannot be produced in any other way. That's the statement of the Darjeeling Council. They must contain the invocations. They must contain the Shiva calls. They must contain all that would deter normal people from hearing them—because the message is so heavy. It's the exposure of embodied evil.

People who have tried to expose that in the past without dipping into the flame of Alpha have been destroyed. They've been murdered; they've gotten sick and died. They've disappeared from off the face of the earth. They have not been able to handle that which they were exposing. They'll do a good job for a number of years, but they can't sustain it.

So the great key is that you do it as an extension of hierarchy. I do it, myself, as an extension of the gurus. Their mantle is a swaddling garment around me. And those invocations draw down this intense power in the midst of our meetings so that even you can take the intensity of contacting the original records of the Satanism of Karl Marx. That Satanism carries you in vibration right back to Satan and all of his legions. They're in the world. And there's no way that you can challenge their evil and expose it and win and heal the earth of their menace without the balance of that figure-eight flow.

So these tapes would not be understood by prominent people in our society, because of the yelling of "Shiva!" and the dynamic decrees and the invocations. Their ears are not attuned to that kind of energy. They're not attuned to the Holy Spirit. When the Holy Spirit spoke through Saint Stephen, they covered their ears and they gnashed their teeth, and they just couldn't stand to hear it. They couldn't stand the energy. It was such a pain to their bodies.[7]

And so the translation down is what we are about. The guru releases the Trinity and the action of the Mother, and the chela carries it. But the delivery of the punch that goes from the Lawgiver of the Father to the wisdom of the Son is the Holy Ghost. It's love—love in the most *intense* fire that can be delivered.

So the program of Lord Maitreya is to put you right at the point of where chelaship has ever been. The great gurus of the East, the great teachers in the tradition of the Buddhas as well as in Hinduism, are the outstanding examples of the chela becoming the guru.

Matter Is a Mirror Reflection of Spirit

Gabriel was mentioning that Matter is a mirror reflection of Spirit. And you'll notice that in one of the diagrams that's coming out in the *Pearls of Wisdom*.[8] When you have a mirror reflection, everything becomes opposite. And so everything is not simply repeated, but it's like it's turned over. It's the negative polarity of the positive Spirit.

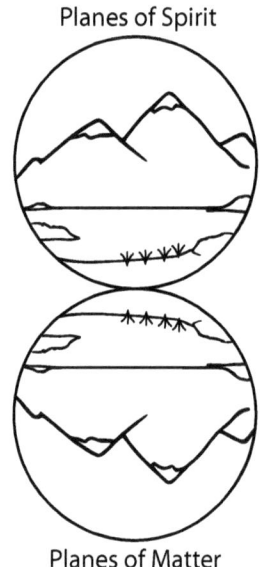

The Mirror Image of Spirit in Matter
FIGURE 3

So if I have in my upper sphere a mountain and lakes and grasses, when I draw it in the lower sphere, it's the other way. So we are that mirror opposite. We don't think we're upside down, but we're told that we see everything upside down and retranslate it.* Maybe we see everything right-side up and retranslate it to

---
*As light passes through the lens of the eye, the image projected on the retina is upside down. The brain processes the image so that it matches our perception of "up" and

our upside down state. Whatever it is, these two spheres are guru and chela.

You know, people tell me that when they look at certain pictures of me, I look like Morya. Well, I'll tell you, they're surprised. But I'll say this, if I didn't look like Morya, I'd be worried.

The term you find in *The Chela and the Path*[9] for the origin of the word *chela* is the Sanskrit *ceta,* which means "slave," and that gets really scary to people. But that is its origin, and it has nothing to do with the denial of free will or you becoming a zombie. It means you are becoming the hands and feet of your master. It means you understand that he is holding the focus of Spirit, or of Alpha, and that for his energy to be translated, you have to put it into action. And how best can you put it into action? You learn his movements, you learn his energy flow, and you imitate it.

That's what the imitation of Christ is all about. This understanding has always been with the true tradition of the churches of East and West. But as soon as we state it in our terms of today, people become hysterical.

The World Rejects the Representatives of God

I was reading a letter today that was sent by a father to a son who had sent him *Prayer and Meditation.*[10] He said, "I asked Grandma what she would say if somebody said that they had gotten a message from Jesus, written it down and signed 'Jesus' as the signature. And Grandma's answer was, 'I'd say he was nuts.'"

What it made me think of was, How come somebody isn't saying that John the Revelator was nuts? He did exactly that.

"down" in our physical interactions with the world. In 1896, American psychologist George M. Stratton devised some glasses that caused the image entering the eye to be inverted. After a few days, he found that his brain automatically corrected for the anomalous input and caused everything to appear right way up again. When he stopped wearing these glasses, everything appeared to be upside down for a few days before his brain adapted again.

He did it two thousand years ago, and everybody accepts it as holy writ. And what's more, what he said is nuts: dragons and serpents and beasts and all kinds of crazy things going on. Ezekiel must have been nuts, too. He had beasts and eyes and all kinds of fires going on. It was beyond the imagination of science fiction —absolutely beyond! I haven't read a better science fiction book today than the Book of Ezekiel and the Book of Revelation. And it has become holy writ, and it's exactly that process.

You have to shake people awake to that. You have to shake them alive. They're like some kind of doormats. You pick up your doormat and you shake it, and you get this big cloud of dust. People have been doormats for the fallen ones for so long that they don't even have an original thought in their heads. And anybody who's really thinking, they think that he is a far-out revolutionary, or they've got to label him the Devil or a Satanist.

When Saint Germain walked through the streets of Paris healing the little children, the parents would pull them away and shout at him that he was the Devil, *Diable*. They called him a devil when he was healing them. So don't be surprised when you have your healings and your miracles that it is said, "Aha! Now that proves that he's the Devil."

You'll never convince people with a sign. They told Jesus that he cast out devils by Beelzebub, remember.[11] They could not accept that he did the work by Almighty God. So how much less are they going to accept what you're doing? That point of the communion with God has been denied, and people have become a doormat for the lie that you can't commune with God.

Chelaship Training for Staff

So here we are, the guru and the chela. Originally Summit University consisted of following Mark Prophet around all day and watching what he did. And when people came to La Tourelle or to Virginia and said, "I want to serve. I want to be a chela," that's just what they did. They followed him around—in the car, in the house, wherever he was from morning till night. It didn't matter what he was doing.

After we got more and more staff and we began to build up a greater and greater body of understanding and teaching and the chelas accelerated to a certain level, it became quite noticeable that the new person at the door, especially the person who had been through drugs and through a lot of other teachings, could not suddenly hop up to the level of where the guru now was with his original circle of chelas.

So Mark said that we had to have a program so that people could understand the steps from where they were to where he and his chelas were. That began staff orientation. Staff orientation consisted of a number of tapes to hear and things to read. You could get through them in a few days, and you were in. Well, it's no longer possible. Now it's twelve weeks of Summit University before you can deal with the energy that the chelas in this community are dealing with. And it's all a question of energy. The bigger the rolling momentum of this cosmic snowball, the more of the mud ball that's thrown at it, and the bigger the momentum has to be to counteract it.

Persecution by the Anti-Cult Movement

When we were in La Tourelle in Colorado Springs,* we were not handling the menace of an entire nation of fanatical, frightened people who are persecuting everyone from the Moonies[12] to I don't know who. I think it's just absolutely terrible. I think the persecution that the Unification Church is going through

---

*La Tourelle was the headquarters of The Summit Lighthouse from 1966 to 1976.

is absolutely outrageous. I personally don't like Moon. He gives me the chills. I wouldn't want to be in the same room with him. But his people are beautiful, and they are being persecuted. And I think it's *absolutely outrageous.*

So today we are dealing with, for instance, the energy of that Senate hearing yesterday, which was closed. Even our representative didn't get in. You had to be there at five a.m. to get in the door, there were so many people there. It basically dealt with Unification Church and Guyana[13] and the general discussion of "cults" and whether or not it's going to go into a full-scale investigation. The National Council of Churches and the American Civil Liberties Union made very strong statements that they were not in favor of these congressional investigations happening, because they felt it was an encroachment on the First Amendment right to religious freedom, it was unconstitutional, and it was bordering on being a witch hunt.

So you find yourself with strange bedfellows. The National Council of Churches and the American Civil Liberties Union are notably left wing. And, of course, I've always thought that I get along a lot better with left-wing people than I do right-wing people. That's always been true, because they're more easygoing. They're more tolerant. They always have a better understanding of New Age religions and Eastern teachings. Whereas right-wing people have the right ideas on many subjects, they tend to be ultraconservative in religion as well as in politics, and they have a quality of rigidity that is sometimes bolstered by fear and hatred.

And so it's a funny thing. El Morya sees to it that there's no point in us perching anywhere from Right to Left. But it's good to have friends in all camps because you never know who's going to be on the right side of the ascended masters' teachings.

Calls to Archangel Michael Have Cleared the Nation

The most astounding event to me about this whole weekend was the fact that the rallying of Keepers of the Flame across this nation in the invocation of Archangel Michael calls has so cleared this nation of substance and of doubt and of fear that there has been a literal translation of America by the intensity of the decrees of the students. I am just gratified. The winds that blew on Saturday and Sunday, they swept away substance. The crackling of the legions of Archangel Michael is tremendous!

It was a one-day hearing. It's over. And there are so many people against having hearings that I doubt very much that it will be brought up again. Their conclusion was that they've gotten so much flak on this persecution of religion and violation of the First Amendment that the way they're going to go after cults now is to investigate to see if they are in violation of their tax-exempt status through the IRS. So that is the angle I would suspect that they are proceeding on.[14]

When people are harassed to the level that the Hare Krishna people have been harassed or the members of Unification Church, I think it's a desecration. I know what it is to live in fear and torment that your telephone is being tapped, that you're being followed, that you're being watched, that any minute somebody's going to write an article about you, that any minute somebody's going to tell another lie about you.

I don't feel that people should live in America today in that kind of fear and torment. I think it's a terrible climate. It's a diseased climate. And when people stop having the freedom to experiment with any kind of a culture or any kind of a religion, you stop them from making the mistakes that are necessary for their growth, for one thing. I cannot defend the false gurus and the false teachers, but I absolutely cannot see the persecution of our people in this manner.

The Persecution of a Man in Utah

Yesterday the story in the newspaper that so burdened me was an example of the ultimate persecution of one man in the state of Utah. He was a Mormon, and he had a wife and four children. And in the past year he took another wife and her four children because he believed in practicing to the letter the original teachings of Mormonism. And they were living on a farm. He built the house. He built the schoolhouse. He was educating his own children. He pulled them out of public school because he didn't like the drugs. He didn't like what is happening in the public schools.

He was educating his children at home, and he decided that they needed to get some very important experience in practical life such as farming and weaving and cooking and baking and all of these things that take the child back to the earth. The children were given IQ tests that were given to the public, and the children didn't score so well. The parents scored as having high IQs, but the children were generally lower than their peer groups. So it was considered that he wasn't giving them a proper education, because the psychologist who examined them said that they didn't know how to interact socially in today's world.

Well, who can put a value that's more important? The state is saying that it's more important for these children to learn to be social animals and to learn to be with the in crowd than it is for them to learn the flame of the family and the plowing of the field and all of these things.

Whether or not that man's a bigamist, I couldn't care less. I mean, his children couldn't care less, either. He's their father and he loves those children and he's the authority figure of Alpha in their lives. He's doing the best he knows how to do. They were so self-sufficient, he delivered all of their own babies. They produced all of their own cloth, and yet he had the modern things of electricity and so forth.

They ordered him to put his children back in school. He wouldn't do it, so he was in contempt of court. The second thing he did was that the second wife he took had a husband who wanted the kids back and was challenging him for alienation of affections. They wouldn't send the kids back, because the kids wanted to be with the mother. So he was in violation on two counts.

So, two men came to his farm and said, "We're from the L.A. Time" (without the s). He was going to give them an interview, then they told him they were from the law enforcement agency, whichever it was, and they were there to arrest him and take him away because he was in contempt of court. He pulled out a gun and he said, "If you lay a hand on me, I'll shoot you." So they left.

At that point he and his two wives decided that they were being persecuted, and they did not leave their farm. They all carried guns. They decided they were under siege, and they were not going to give in. They were not going to put those children in school. The state was not going to force them to do so. The brother of this man knew full well his temperament and his psychology, and the brother said, "If you people go up and try to get him, the blood is going to flow on that farm."

Now, he was wrong in disobeying the law, but the law itself has to be challenged. The right of the state to force an individual to educate his children according to the lines of the federal government and society today, that has got to be challenged or we are all going to find that our children can be taken from us because they don't happen to pass the tests that the world is giving them.

The things that make the IQ of the children in the world are their bombardment by TV and their interaction with each other and their movies. They pick up a certain general awareness of information that even I don't have. You can name people, you can name songs, you can name all kinds of things about life in America today, and I wouldn't know what you were talking about. I don't listen to it. So if I took an IQ test, I might not be where the rest of the world is, and my children might not be.

Well, here it is. This man was willing to fight that battle all by himself. And because he was a Mormon and the original Mormon teachings tell you to be a bigamist, he felt that what's wrong with the world today is it's not going back to the first principles. And there are quite a number of Mormons like this. And so they're going back and they're being bigamists.

And that, you have to understand, is a problem of a false teaching and a false hierarchy teaching within the Mormon Church. It doesn't make the person evil. It just means he's trying his best to find truth and that's the way he's pursuing truth.

People Ought to Be Free to Pursue Truth

People ought to be free to pursue truth even if we disagree with them, as long as they're not hurting anyone. And these people aren't hurting anyone, because children aren't hurt by that when they don't know any different. What they're hurt by is people having affairs and swapping partners and being immoral and leaving their kids home and going out and being drunk and all of these things that society condones.

As soon as you announce that you're a bigamist, everybody's down on you. But the children weren't suffering, because those children were loved intensely. They had a real family love. It showed their picture in the paper. The women were properly attired in a very conservative dress. The children's hair was cut short. Their faces shone. They were with their father, and there's a real love scene going on between this father and his children. The two women who were standing there were obviously totally in harmony with each other.

So what happened? The authorities decided to go out and get him. About ten or twelve men went out to his farm. They all had shotguns. And he came out to get his mail in his mailbox, and they announced that they were coming to get him. He took his gun out and started shooting, and they shot back and they shot him dead. Those children are now fatherless. And those women are there, and they have said, "We're not moving from this farm. We will educate our children on this farm."

I think that is one of the greatest tragedies I have heard of in years. I think that it is so terrible. I think that it's just pure communism. It's pure fascism in this nation when we have lost our sensitivity to appreciate that another person's culture can be valid.

And then the paper brings out the fact that this man was born in Brooklyn of German parents, highly industrious, as you can well see. He totally created his whole little family life there. And his father had taken him as a child back to Germany. During Hitler's rise to power, this man was a part of Nazi Youth. Well, what people today who are in their fifties in Germany were not a part of Nazi Youth? They all were. But right away everybody thinks, "Oh, well, he was a fanatic anyway."

German people have a certain intensity, and they have given that blood and that intensity to a lot of nations in the earth. They have traveled around the world. They've intermarried. And that

German strain is always hardworking, hard-hitting—and yes, it's stubborn and it's proud and it's pigheaded and it's all that, too. But you'll find that that German strain contributes to the total strain of humanity. It's an energy of work that has been a foundation in the building of America. It's a very intense energy.

People who are totally German always have that initiation. They've got to get over that pigheaded, stubborn, proud vibration. But their qualities of work and intelligence and industriousness and freedom and individuality are stupendous. And that's why they get pigheaded—they're always defending their individuality.

He came back from Germany, he moved out West, he settled down and became an American citizen just like the rest of us. And now he's gunned down and he is no more, because nobody could think of how to handle that guy except with guns. Nobody could think of how to deal with an individual. We've come to be an animal farm. We've all got to think and look alike. It's such an outrage, I tell you.

We Must Demand Cosmic Justice

Rather than scream in the marketplace, I go to my closet and I give my outrage to Alpha and Omega and I demand cosmic justice. And I've been around long enough on this planet to know that that is the recourse we have and it's the recourse that works and it is changing the world. And you need to know that that's where you need to be, also.

But when I tell you about these things, you've got to get out and stump and translate that message to your people—*your* people who understand *you* because you're at the same social understanding or economic level or whatever it is. The people who relate to you and you relate to, they've got to hear that cry.

Fortunately, the people in the nearby community have demanded an investigation of the killing of this man, and they are also outraged. I am simply delighted to think that there's that spunk and spine left in the American people, that even though they disagree with him, they can champion his right to choose a way of life.

This way of life we're pursuing in America today is producing nothing but disease and psychologically impotent people. It's producing homosexuality. It's producing immorality. Who is to judge him to say he hasn't found the right way of life? Who is going to say that? Who is going to be the ultimate God on earth that's going to tell everybody how they can live and how they can't live? I'll tell you, I'm not going to. People have to be free to evolve toward God.

Persecution of a Woman in Los Angeles

But do you know something? This very week an identical thing happened in Los Angeles. Did you read about the woman who couldn't pay her gas bill? She couldn't pay her gas bill, and it was under ten dollars. She was a woman alone. How many thousands of women are suffering today because we have never created a proper male image for our men in America?

We have never explained to a man what it means to be a man, what it means to be a Joseph, what it means to have the supreme honor of bearing the seed of Alpha. Man doesn't have his right image, so he leaves his woman because he never feels he can be quite good enough, because he can never father the Manchild.

That's man's original and primal office—to sire the Christ Child. But he's told it was a virgin birth. Joseph wasn't necessary; so he's not necessary, either. He might just as well go off and play with whores as to be Joseph. So we have all these deserted women in America because women themselves have failed to endow man with his proper and true image.

This woman is alone, for whatever reason. She's got two little kids. She's working hard to make ends meet, to send them to school, but she can't pay her gas bill. So the gas company sends down the police. Two policemen come to this woman's house. She didn't live in a slum. She lived in a decent neighborhood. It wasn't wealthy but it was a decent neighborhood. They said, "We're coming in to turn off your gas."

She felt threatened. Doesn't anybody understand the psychology? When you put somebody in a corner, they've got nothing to do but fight. She was threatened. It was cold. She didn't want her gas turned off. So she got upset. She got emotional. She grabbed the first thing she could find, which was a butcher knife, and she went out to attack the policemen.

That's just a natural thing that a mother bear does to protect her cubs; it's a natural human instinct. She threw the knife. Can you imagine two policemen not being able to handle a woman out of control throwing a knife? Wouldn't you think that they could seize her, give her a karate chop, and handcuff her? No. In front of her two little kids, they pulled out their guns and they shot her dead.

That happened in Los Angeles in the last week. Look at this world. And people are after cults. Why aren't they after this insanity? That woman is dead, and those children are orphans. And they stood there and watched their mother be murdered. That happened in the United States of America. There's no way you can tell me that those policemen could not have handled that woman. They should have ducked the knife that was flying through the air and seized the woman. There's nothing to that. Any one of you could have done that.

Now you understand why the left wing calls those policemen pigs. That is such an outrage against God. I just have to cry out to Almighty God to come into this earth. And the only way he can come into this earth is through his chelas, people who can carry enough light to counteract this injustice. Everybody is powerless to stop it because they don't have the tie to the ascended masters.

You Can't Get Anywhere Without a Tie to a Guru

Maybe I'm playing Fa-Mi-Re-Do, Fa-Mi-Re-Do every day when I come in here, but it's the same theme. It's my same tune. I never got anywhere in thousands of years and nobody else ever did unless they had a tie to a guru. There's no other solution. You need the power of God. You absolutely have to have the power of God. And the only way you can do it is to become the shadow, the negative of the positive.

The chela has to become the essence of his guru. When I see your faces looking like El Morya, I tell you, that's when I light up. So that's why Maitreya came with his program—there is such an intensity of energy out in that world that has to be counteracted and challenged.

What has to be done to challenge the police system that will go in and murder people in their own homes in cold blood like this? You can't fall back and say, "We can't do it." You *can* do it. We have a most wonderful program at our Montessori school. It's going on in Los Angeles. Seven of our students are going all day Saturday from six thirty in the morning on this police training program. They go through all of the training of becoming policemen. They ride around in their cars; they do their office work; they're with them. They get absolutely total training to become policemen, but they're doing it while they're teenagers. And so they understand how the law works. It's exciting.

We've got people in Montessori who want to become policemen. They understand it's Archangel Michael's legions. And they understand that Archangel Michael's legions have been infiltrated by the fallen ones, and that they're the ones who behave like pigs. Then the children of God imitate them.

The reason that people are so insensitive is this heavy, heavy meat intake, the pork, the beef, the beer. They get so like cattle that they react like cattle. They have no fine feelings. They have no respect for life. And the vibration over the country of butchering babies in an abortion mill puts an aura of insensitivity over all of the people. So they can kill each other. Life is so cheap; it's too cheap. They've forgotten that life is God.

So you have to become specialists. You've got to look at what are the evils in the world and what are the things that really affect you the most. The more talent you have, the more gifts in your hand, the more things you can affect. Of course, the obvious place to be is in the state legislature and in a lawmaking body. But that's not the only answer. Police departments need flames. Police Chief Davis, who's been famous in Los Angeles for all these years, has a real flame of Archangel Michael. He's not the police chief anymore.

But these little nuclei, these little molecules of energy that affect communities, all they need is one lightbearer in the middle of them, one person qualified. It doesn't matter what you want to do. Position yourself strategically where you can be that keystone in the arch that holds up the whole arch. That's what the guru is, you know.

The Keystone in the Arch

I think that this is an amazing concept. You know the principle of the arch and all the bricks in it. All of the bricks are in position, but the arch doesn't hold up unless it's got its keystone. It's the wedge at the center. The guru is the key in the "higher-arch" of being. He's the *hierarch* because he's the keystone in the *higher arch*. This is the arch of being, and all of the stones in the arch are chelas. They are all together because that one individual is the keystone. Everything leans on it and everything holds together. And without the keystone, the whole thing comes tumbling down.

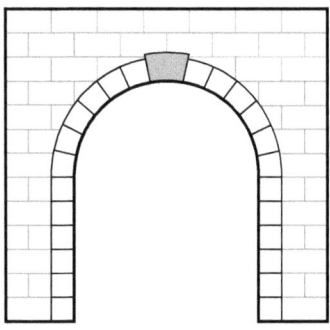

The Keystone in the Arch
FIGURE 4

There are all kinds of people in very important positions. But the keystone is the one who governs the energy and governs the matrix and holds the geometry together.

You have to find out where you are going to become a keystone. You can't become just any one of those stones. It's not for you anymore. You're going to be a keystone. You might be a keystone on the farm out here or a keystone in the printing department. You could be a keystone, and nobody might ever hear of you. But you might also have to be a keystone in your local PTA or your local pro-life group.

Wherever you are a keystone, everybody who is a part of

that mandala depends on you. Even if you don't happen to be the most important person in the group, you may be the power behind the throne or the heart behind everyone else. Even if they don't know that you're the keystone, all energy of that endeavor flows through your heart chakra. Your heart becomes the heart of that activity. And you need to do your work at night, your violet flame.

You need to be aware of everybody who's involved. Sometimes it's thousands of people, but you need to know whose energy you're handling, because that energy passing through your heart must be transmuted. Your heart is the furnace of your alchemy on earth. And that furnace has to have enough fire to burn the fuel. And if it doesn't, you can pass out of embodiment of too much energy in your heart—it's a great danger—but you will not if you're tied to the gurus.

It's a very important point. You can stand out and face the multitudes and challenge evil as long as you do it in the name of your I AM Presence, your Christ Self, and your guru and his mantle. Then he's standing with you with his Electronic Presence over you.

But if you decide, "I've got the teaching. I've got the information. I don't need hierarchy. I don't need the Brotherhood. I'll just go out and do this myself," that's where you fall. That's where you can't make it, because you're trying to stand at the nine o'clock line at that Holy Spirit action level of challenging the whole world, but you don't have your own attainment yet. And that's why you need the humility to know that you need the Great White Brotherhood. You need those saints. You need the ascended masters behind you.

And you always have to know that you're acting as the instrument of your Christ Self and your I AM Presence and the hierarchy. You can't indulge in momentary bursts of pride in your own attainment, because that's when you become vulnerable.

You Must Become a Keystone

You must become a keystone. And the only way that you're going to become a keystone is to become a chela. And the only way that you're going to become a chela is to become the Holy Spirit. And the only way that you're going to get the Holy Spirit is to get into service and action. That's where you're going this afternoon. And I'm not going to talk too much longer so you can get there.

I wanted to tell you that there's no other way I would have understood the teachings. Words are meaningless. Do you know what you find out when you start teaching little children? They haven't had the experiences of life to know what words mean. They don't know what sensuality is. They've never had the vibration in their bodies. They have no idea what you're talking about. They don't know what jealousy is. They don't know what these vibrations are unless they mix with people and say, "Oh, that's what it is." And then the word on the paper that they read in a book has meaning.

We've got that problem in Montessori International today. They're hearing all kinds of teachings, but they haven't been in the world long enough to understand that the world is challenging, to understand the "energy veil" of *evil*. They're so pure in their innocence that you look at these children in their purity and they don't understand the difference between good and evil. They don't understand the difference between light and darkness. They can move back and forth in their views and their understandings because they haven't had the experience of living.

Teenagers Must Learn to Become Economically Independent

Yesterday I introduced to Montessori International the fact that in the teenage years, they must become economically independent. They must learn how to earn their daily bread. They must learn the free-enterprise system. Saint Germain says that we're bringing up a generation of teenagers on handouts from their parents without teaching them how to run their own businesses. By the time they're twenty, they're ready for the welfare state. He says that if this goes on much longer, we won't have a free-enterprise system, because we're educating our youth right out of it by giving them everything they need.

What Saint Germain says is that the reason children rebel and take drugs is that they're not fulfilling their inner calling that they must become economically independent. They must know that they can earn by their hands, their heart, and their head. They must know that they can provide for themselves. Otherwise they feel insecure in the universe. You have to know that given the raw material of your earth, you can make a go of it without your parents. And the teenage years is the time to learn that.

If you're not learning it, there's an unfulfilled element of your nature and you rebel. You rebel against the parents who are giving you what you know you should be earning. And later you're going to rebel against the welfare state that's giving you what you know you should be earning. That rebellion is being inbred into our children—carefully calculated by the fallen ones and their psychology. They're inbreeding rebellion because we're not giving our children the real education that they need. And when they rebel and take drugs and speak out against their parents, they don't know that it's because that particular hunger is not being fulfilled, because we've already destroyed their soul sensitivity of being aware of their soul needs.

People don't know why they're sick. People don't know why they get cranky when they eat the wrong foods. We feed them the wrong foods and we condition them to sugars and all of these things so that when they're hungry, they get sugar. So they're conditioned. So they cry out and they want the real food. By the time they're conditioned, if you give them the real food, they don't want the real food. People don't know what's good for them anymore.

Children know that they have that sensitive period. They want to be up and doing, and they want to be independent, and they want to be conscious contributors to the community. But they need the free-enterprise system, which gives a reward for good service. That's the whole lesson of capitalism: it's a guru-chela relationship. Children are not ready to surrender an identity, because they haven't earned an identity yet. They don't know who they are yet. They have to find out who they are, and so they're on the path of Christhood.

The Community of the Holy Spirit

I've given lectures where I've shown that the path of Christhood on the three o'clock line is a system of capitalism, and the nine o'clock line is the community of the Holy Spirit.[15] The nine o'clock line is where you have made it. You have become an individual. You have been successful. You know that if you put your time and energy into something, you can conquer. You have a firm sense of individuality. That is your Christhood.

When you've earned that Christhood, you don't need it anymore. You can give it away because you can get it anytime. If I'm broke today, I'll be rich tomorrow. It's no problem. I'm not worried. You're not worried, either. If you've proven it, you know it.

So what do I do? I lay it all at the feet of my guru. I lay it at the feet of the community, and I say, "I don't need this stuff. I want my brothers and sisters to have it." America's supposed to be a community of the Holy Spirit. You can't get there unless you let people fulfill themselves in the guru-chela relationship in terms of the fact that Jesus said, "The labourer is worthy of his hire."[16]

The job that he does should be compensated. He should have money that he sees as energy, the fruit of his labor, that he can then have by free will to decide what he will do with, how he will spend it. Whether he will give it all away, whether he will support his family, whether he's going to buy a new car, or whatever he's going to do with it, he's earned it and he's got a freewill choice to make. And hopefully that free will, will be educated to a higher and higher degree.

Maitreya's Program for Teenagers

Yesterday I introduced at Montessori International Maitreya's program for the teenagers, where they are going to run and totally manage a business and have complete training in business education. They're going to have a snack bar on campus here. It will be all Montessori students, nobody else will be involved. They're studying business. They're studying accounting. And if they earn money, they'll make money, and if they don't, they won't. That's the risk of the free-enterprise system and starting your own business.

Well, they're all hopping up and down with excitement. We put an application into Fullerton, which is a place where we get all kinds of things for almost nothing that the government is selling. Just yesterday we found out that we can buy a pizza oven that is enough to have a whole, big pizza parlor. They are thousands and thousands of dollars, and we can pick it up for three hundred dollars.

So this is going to be the excitement of today, I can tell you, these kids finding out they can have a pizza oven for their snack bar. You never saw a group of kids so turned on and so excited as that group of students is today, and it's because they have a need. This is a need in their education. They need to know that when they get out of school, they can go out in that world and they will not be bulldozed down by all kinds of people taking advantage of them. They will understand what it means to have a corporation, an association, a partnership, how you keep your books, how you run a business, how you have to figure overhead when you're charging for things, and the whole thing. So they're going to be doing that, grades seven to twelve.

The Charity of the American People

You are at a different level. Unfortunately you didn't start here when you were ten years old. Hopefully you've been through a little bit of understanding of the enterprise system. You're at the community of the Holy Spirit level. You're at the nine o'clock level, and you have the opportunity now to realize that when you have been God-victorious and proved that you could do what they are now doing, then you say, "What's the point of it? What's the point of making this money? What's the point of my mastery and my attainment? So I've made ten thousand or a hundred thousand or a million dollars. It's sitting in the bank. That's not life. That's not what I really wanted. What was really important to me was the fact that I could do it. But the money isn't making me happy, so I'll make other people happy with it. I'll go ahead and I'll help a community where I believe in what it's doing, et cetera."

Many wealthy people in America sponsor hospitals, they sponsor all kinds of things for children. And that's their real reward.

That's why we have such freedom in America. We have the greatest system of charities of any nation on earth. Our charity system today shows that people in America are a giving people. They give more money away than any other nation in the whole world. We are the great givers of the entire earth. We give and give and give.

That's why we don't need socialism. That's why we don't need a welfare state. The people are so stingy in other countries that they have to tax the people so that the churches can survive, because they don't contribute to the churches. Out of your taxes come your church contributions in many Western European nations today. And people are rebelling against that because they say that they don't believe in God and they don't want their taxes to go to the churches. And that's the kind of problems they're having.

We don't have that problem because our churches are wealthy. Our charitable institutions are wealthy. That's because when people pass the initiation of their Christhood in America, they're generous. They want other people to benefit, and they can see that the poor in spirit need those who have attained to the abundance of the spirit.

The Word Must Be Translated into Action

So in chelaship, both positions are lawful. You may be fresh out of high school. You may need that three o'clock line. You may need to go out and do what you have to do. That's your inner soul development. You may be at a place where you are fresh out of high school but you've had that experience in so many embodiments, you want to get into the community right now. You have such a strong identity that you don't need to prove that identity by the conquest of that free-enterprise system. So the community of the Holy Spirit, of which World Communism is a perversion, is the place where you invest your labors. And the rejoicing of the fruit of that labor, is the expansion of cosmic consciousness.

The reward I have for every work that I do is to see an individual in front of me who has become more of God. That's the increase. That's my joy. That's why I don't need anything—because I contain all of God. Who needs anything when they contain all of God? Until you know you contain all of God, you do need things. You do need an opportunity to master a trade and to master a sacred labor. Jesus did it and you have to do it, too.

So mastering a trade and a sacred labor or giving yourself to the community—both of these are fulfilled in Maitreya's program, which will be now carried on three afternoons a week in addition to Saturday.

We want to get you out of the classroom and into action because one word of the Brotherhood is worth millions of other words. The Word is so powerful that Maitreya says you don't have to sit here all day. You reach a saturation point. You're going to hear lectures and get teachings from eight to twelve, and the teachings are just going to have to be condensed. And if you want more, you know where to get it. You have our library of recordings, you have books, and you can study on your own.

But the Word that you receive is a tremendous transfusion of energy of the Father and of the Son. And in order to receive more, it has to become the Holy Ghost. It has to be translated into action. It's the simple burning up of daily energy. You eat food; you need to exercise. You eat food, and so forth. That's the way it is.

You all have assignments in various departments and out on the land. And within a week we'll have about two hundred eucalyptus trees that have to be planted around the whole border of the property.

Some of you will get right into publishing and other various departments. I want you to leave Camelot with a sense of the flame of the community, that people here are just like you with their abilities and disabilities, with their virtues and their faults, but pulling together we've created a community. You might be the keystone of a community in New Zealand or Australia or communist China or Taiwan. That could happen in a few months. And you're going to have to get the flame of community in the sense that you have been a part of building that community.

Now, if anybody thinks he's getting shortchanged because he's being put to work and would rather sit and hear lectures, that's alright with me if you think that you've been promised to be in class all day long at Summit University. But I'm telling you that the real classroom of the guru is to be his flame in action.

Questions and Answers

Student: Is there a name for a food entity?

ECP: You mean gluttony? Well, I tell you, I'll be so glad when we won't have to eat anymore. That's the worst thing about leaving Eden. We had to start eating all that food. Eat the food and you have to fast it out. Then you have to eat again so you can function. Just encircle the whole mess. Encircle the whole business.

Be sure you get the right nutrients so your craving is not something that you're missing in your body. Take plenty of vitamins, jog around, take in the air, and try to give yourself alternatives to eating. It's basically wrong programming. You're un-programming your desire body and your physical body. Stimulus, response—the cells demand; you give. They've been demanding all kinds of things they shouldn't have for a long time. So you have to pull the reins tight.

Do We Have to Give Similar Invocations when We Expose the Darkness?

Student: Mother, when we go stumping, if we want to do the exposure on Satanism, will invocations be necessary when we are there in the same way that you gave them with your exposés?

ECP: Well, I imagine you in small groups giving the information that's in the lectures. And I imagine you keeping up your decree momentum, your communion with God, your communion with the Brotherhood, and your communion with my Christ Self and Lanello sponsoring you, and then going to a group of people and speaking exactly at their level, telling them what they can hear and not telling them what they shouldn't hear. And you can offer a simple prayer to God that they would understand when you start.

I've done the invocations, and the energy on that recording takes care of that information. When you present it, you do not have to give those same invocations and you don't have to shout Shivas. That's what you do at home, that's your preparation. As long as you know you're standing on that platform with the masters, you will be able to deal with it. But you'll find that you will have to give some sort of prayer, some sort of meditation. You'll find the whole audience will get so bogged down, or they won't be able to take it, because there are so many demons around that they react against you.

I stopped giving so much exposure of the conspiracy on my second and third stumps because people walked out. They were angry. They shouted and screamed at me. They yelled, "Heil, Hitler!" while they were leaving. As soon as I was exposing the conspiracy, they went into a complete outrage.

These are New Age people that you'd call left-wing New Age people—free thinking, peace loving, you know, peace, peace,

peace people. And they just are so shocked by the Holy Ghost delivering that message that it upsets them terribly, disturbs their entities. And, of course, some of them are fallen ones. Some of them are leaving because they're the ones that are being exposed.

I think there's nothing like experience to teach you what you can and cannot do in teaching people. I learned it all by experience myself. So let's be up and doing.

The Significance of Joseph As the Father of Jesus

Student: In speaking about the psychology of fathers and their being robbed of their Alpha image, you mentioned the virgin birth and that they have been trained to think that Joseph wasn't necessary in bringing about the Christ. Could you expand that and say what it means?

ECP: Jesus has stated that Joseph was his father. Jesus stated that in a recent dictation.[17] That is dynamite information. Mother Mary gave a dictation many years ago through Mark in which she said Joseph was *worthy* to be his father.[18]

If you look at the revelation of the Archangel Gabriel to Mary, it says, "The Holy Ghost shall come upon thee, . . . and . . . that holy thing which shall be born of thee shall be called the Son of God."[19] I understand the Holy Ghost as a person and so does every Christian. If I say that the Holy Spirit is energy, Christians will challenge me and say, "Don't you know that the Holy Spirit is a person?" I say, "Of course, the Holy Ghost is a person. He's also an energy." Person and principle are energy and person in one.

So I understand that my interaction with the Father has to manifest in the Father person. When you have enough of Father consciousness in you, you attract first Father as energy, Father as Law, and then finally you see Father face-to-face. He is a person.

Brahma is a person—inside of you, in the Great Central Sun as Almighty God, and also in father figures that come into your life.

The next point is the Son. The Son is a consciousness. He is also a person. When you become enough of the Son, you behold the Son face-to-face. Mary was the bride of the Holy Spirit, not just of twin flames descending upon her but of the person of the Holy Ghost. Saint Joseph as Saint Germain was the incarnation of the *person* of the Holy Ghost.

Whether God transfers to Mary by "intravenous" tubes a direct line of energy from his throne to give the energy for the conception of a child or whether he does it through Joseph, it doesn't matter to me. It doesn't make it any less holy. But the world has labored under this idolatry that Jesus could not be the Son of God unless God was his father and bypassed Joseph—because Joseph was a mere mortal.

Well, Mary was a mere mortal until she was translated, until she was assumed into heaven. So the diabolical plot of the fallen ones is to say that man is not good enough to sire the Christ, and when woman is going to bring forth the Christ Child, she's got to get it directly from God because man is not good enough. That is a psychology that we have lived with for thousands of years.

So what does man do? He's not good enough to be with his virgin bride. He's not good enough to be the father of her child. Joseph didn't do that, of course, because Joseph was there. He was the supreme keeper of the flame of Alpha. He was the supreme bearer of the seed of Alpha. Mary did not descend from the house of David, Joseph did. Joseph's lineage was from the house of David. It's traced right in the Bible, if you're going to look at human genealogies—but Jesus doesn't.

There is another passage in the Bible that talks about Jesus being Joseph's son. Here it is. I found it the other day. It's amazing what people don't read in their own Bibles. This is Luke 4:22.

> And all bare him witness, and wondered at the gracious words which proceeded out of his mouth. And they said, Is not this Joseph's son?

Here's the other one. This is Luke 3:23.

> And Jesus himself began to be about thirty years of age, being (as was supposed) the son of Joseph, who was the son of Heli, . . .

It goes all the way back to David. There's a parenthesis in here that says "as was supposed." Now you can take those words "as was supposed" as a later edit of biblical scholars, but you can even take it in two ways.[20] It says he was the son of Joseph "as it was supposed" because a lot of people thought he was the son of Joseph. Or you can take it the way Christians take it, that they *thought* he was the son of Joseph, and the writer is making a commentary.

In other words, for the purposes of being taxed, for the purposes of knowing who they were, he was listed as the son of Joseph. But I think that's very interesting. I have come across a Greek New Testament, and I was going to go back and see what that was in the Greek.

Man and Woman Bear the Light of Alpha and Omega

But you see, there's no greater plot of the fallen ones. To deny that you are the Christ, they have to make Christhood unavailable to you. If it's only available through the virgin birth and we're all stuck with a normal birth, then who's ever going to give birth to a Christ Child?

It's a whole damnable philosophy of the fallen ones, who

refuse to admit that anybody but Jesus Christ can be the Son of God. But Mother Mary showed me very clearly, one day in the last few years as I was meditating, that the reason that man is not fulfilling his role is that he does not esteem himself as the bearer of the seed of Alpha.

Even if he's not having children, even if he's not married, or even if his wife is not bearing children, the fact that he carries in his body the seed of Alpha means that he is carrying the energy of Alpha in the white-fire core of the Great Central Sun. He bears that in his body. As he walks the earth, the physical focus of that seed is the very energy that makes him *man*. And the fact that the woman bears the egg of Omega is the very fiery-core energy that makes her *woman*.

That bearing of that seed and that egg is why God has so pronounced his judgment upon homosexuality and masturbation. The spilling of the seed upon the ground is the desecration of this high, intense light, which is intended to be borne in the body and not expended from the body and not desecrated. It's like man is the carrier of the wine of communion as the essence of Spirit, and woman is the carrier of the bread. And both are needed to produce the Christ Child. We need the Body and the Blood of our Lord.

God has appointed us male and female to carry the two halves of the whole so we will remain humble and not become self-sufficient and say, "We don't need each other"—because we do need each other. We need the polarity of those two energies.

So when man does not know he carries the seed of Alpha, what is his worth? His total worth is denied. We have no greater worth than the fact that we are the temple of the living God. In us lives the Christ, but the Christ in each of us serves the office of that incarnation.

I bear the Mother egg of a cosmos. I'm very conscious of that fact, of this tremendous pulsating light. I bear it in my causal body. I bear it in all of my physical chakras. But I also bear it uniquely physically because I am woman.

You bear the energy of Alpha, you who are man. And you bear it in your causal body, you bear it in your chakras, you bear it in your energy, and you also bear it physically because everything that is goes from Spirit to Matter, etheric, mental, emotional, and finally physical.

When we do not see the two parts of the whole as being sacred, we don't see the child as sacred either. So we abort the child. The holiness goes back to the very seed of life itself and the egg. So, what we're saying is that the seed of man isn't good enough to bear the Christ Child. Well, subconsciously within the soul of his being, he knows that his supreme worth is that while he lives on earth, the seed that is in him is his physical, tangible focus of Alpha. And it is totally desecrated in homosexuality, and it is lost and dissipated in masturbation.

If you tell a man that he's not good enough to bear the Son of God, he leaves the home and goes off with other women. And it is subconscious. It's reinforced by domineering women. Because of the longevity of men thinking that they're worthless, they tend to become weak, spineless, without the masculine ray. Because they don't appreciate what the masculine ray is within themselves, they don't respect their own masculinity. That comes across to women. So women become "henpecky." They become tyrants. They become domineering.

We have problems with battered husbands. I never knew that before. I've heard of battered wives. But the police department will tell you that there are battered husbands. Women beat up their husbands. Would you believe it? But this is what's happened to our society. That is why women are abandoned.

And you have this problem among the blacks because of the experience of slavery. Slavery didn't start in America. Blacks enslaved blacks in Africa long before slavery got to America. It's the cheap price of the male. The male who is bred like an animal to produce better and better slaves loses his self-worth. And so this is a tremendous problem in the nations of Africa today. All the African women I met told me that it is the worst problem they have.

But the women have overcompensated. They have become so domineering, so full of criticism, condemnation, and judgment, that the husbands can't make it in the home anyway. They'd rather go out and receive the comfort and the praise of a prostitute than stay at home and be criticized all day long for what they're not doing. So it becomes a vicious circle. This keeps going round and round.

It's got to stop here. And it never stops till you have enlightenment. Mother Mary gave me that precious jewel of enlightenment. And it is tremendous when you think of it, when you feel in your purified body that not only your spiritual centers but every part of your body, every cell of your body, the center of every cell is the light of Alpha and Omega.

When I meditate in my body, my body is just scintillating pulsations of light. It's full of millions of stars. Every cell is a star, and every star is the light of Alpha and Omega. And through any one of those stars I can contact God in the Great Central Sun. I prefer to go through the great star of my heart chakra. But every cell has that basic component of life.

The sensitivity to the seed and the egg gives you the sensitivity of being the co-creator with God. And as I say, it doesn't necessarily mean having a physical child. It means carrying that polarity of energy to create, wherever you are, whatever you're doing, whatever your age.

It is exciting to be alive when you understand your fundamental mission. And my sense of appreciation of man—whether it's Mark or my husband or chelas in the community—is that I bow before your flame for having the courage to be on earth the bearer of the seed of Alpha. And I'm so grateful for that one role and that one office holding the polarity of the Blood of Christ, that I can go into *samadhi* over that single contemplation.

The man who has the courage to be the bearer of the seed of Alpha with all of its attendant responsibilities is the man or the group of men or the group of chelas who make my mission possible, because I could not have been on this mission from day one without the physical embodiment of man. And it continues to be so to the present hour. The men in this community are the ultimate supports of my mission—first and foremost, because they'll carry the masculine ray. Secondly, because of all of the fabulous work that they do, a tremendous amount of work.

So we won't take any more questions. God bless you. They'll be answered as you strive.

So it's: eat, come back, get your assignments, and go. And you can whistle while you work. You can **decree** while you work. You are a decree.

God bless you.

February 6, 1979

CHAPTER SIX

The Mantle of the Christ

In the name of the light of the Holy of Holies, in the name of the light of God that never fails, I call forth the light of beloved Helios and Vesta. Beloved Lord Maitreya, quicken now within these hearts infinite *self-awareness,* infinite *self-awareness unto the Guru. I call for the great God-awareness of the guru to descend now within each heart. Let each one's own self-awareness be realized through the Self-awareness that thou art.*

In the name of Brahma, Vishnu, Shiva, in the name of the Cosmic Virgin, Amen.

I'd like to read to you a poem of Henry Wadsworth Longfellow, which he translated from the Spanish of Lope de Vega.* I'd like you to meditate on it.

---

*Lope Félix de Vega Carpio (1562–1635)

To-Morrow

> Lord, what am I, that, with unceasing care
>   Thou didst seek after me, that thou didst wait,
>   Wet with unhealthy dews, before my gate,
>   And pass the gloomy nights of winter there?
> O strange delusion! that I did not greet
>   Thy blest approach, and O, to Heaven how lost,
>   If my ingratitude's unkindly frost
>   Has chilled the bleeding wounds upon thy feet!
> How oft my guardian angel gently cried,
>   "Soul, from thy casement look, and thou shalt see
>   How he persists to knock and wait for thee!"
> And O! how often to that voice of sorrow,
>   "To-morrow we will open," I replied,
>   And when the morrow came I answered still, "To-morrow."

The name of the poem is "To-Morrow." It speaks of the procrastination of the welcoming of the guru that has been the guilt of humanity for thousands of years.

Maitreya has come because he is welcomed. Let us not feel that because we have placed our physical bodies at Summit University that automatically we are bringing the Christ in from outside of our gate. Let us realize that every day we need to re-welcome Lord Guru Maitreya into the inner temple of our heart, and in so doing, to allow him to remove from our temple those conditions and circumstances of consciousness that are not comfortable to his meditation and to his action.

The first *Pearl of Wisdom* from Lord Maitreya is dated January 29, 1960. I would like to read it to you:

> What is it you mirror, O children of earth longing to be free? Is it the ephemeral fashions of the day or the eternal garments we wear? In this great duality of active life that

derives its motion and energy from an inner flame, where goes your *attention,* beloved ones?

Your petitions and requests pass often in review before me, and I am so reminded at times, in some instances, of these words of two thousand years ago: Ye know not what ye should pray for as ye ought (to know)!¹

To pray, to petition or to decree is all an attempt to call forth that which *you* desire. If your manifold desires mainly exclude the inner but include much of the outer, you are eating the husks of life even if you receive all that for which you ask.

Seeking the Right Gift

This is a most important point of the Path—that when you correctly exercise cosmic law, you may ask for material things and get material things. You may even ask for physical health and be healed of sickness, but unless you ask for cosmic consciousness, you will not have it simply because you prayed and received physical things or physical health.

People in Science of Mind, even Unity or Christian Science, many people in the Los Angeles area who are following such movements consider that they have attainment because they have learned a form of scientific prayer whereby they can surround themselves with all of the things that they need. If you look in the Sunday papers, you can see ministers of Science of Mind or Divine Science. They place their pictures in the newspaper seeking to become someone important and popular, and it's all about how you can get what you want out of life.

So there are people who use God and use him very selfishly. He has already told us, "Seek ye first the kingdom [consciousness] of God and his righteousness [right use of the law], and all these things shall be added unto you."² And "Take no thought for your life, what ye shall eat, or what ye shall drink."³

When you seek God consciousness for the purpose of giving it to others, you are seeking the right gift. You are seeking to become God. To seek to become the guru is the purest desire. When you seek to become the guru, the guru provides you with all things.

I would not like to consider that in fifty or a hundred years our decrees should become used generally by the masses of mankind as this Japanese mantra is used to get wealth and whatever people desire. So let us be careful that we do not allow our impure desires to come to the surface and that we do not use prayer to God to fulfill these impure desires. Rather let us pray that our impurity be consumed and that God place within our consciousness his pure desire.

When we desire to have his pure desire, just one drop of that energy within us will be the healing of our physical infirmities, will be all the supply that we need. It's very important that we do not ask amiss but ask rightfully in prayer.

E Pluribus Unum: *One Out of Many*

> But if you turn your attention, beloved ones, more and more often upon the ascended host, ought it not to mean that you *shall mirror us* even if at times somewhat imperfectly? For it will still be our image, God's image, the Christ image, your own individualized flame of *immortality* that is being magnified within you for the pristine purpose of taking at last its rightful dominion, which will set you free in accordance with the original divine plan!
>
> You see, Where your treasure is, there will your heart (your full attention) be also.⁴ And inasmuch as the words, "by their fruits ye shall know them,"⁵ unto the present day

do have patent meaning, so shall that meaning be exemplified and called forth into *living reality* by your own Christ-like daily conduct, my earnest ones.

"Earnest ones"—earnest disciples.

Now the Great White Brotherhood is not a fable, nor is it a mysterious organization to be dangled before the uninitiated as something that sets you apart from others or distinguishes you with temporal honor. Neither is it intended to extinguish you in the ignominy of sincere but abject humility, but rather in the dignity of divine providence to provide an avenue or protected outlet where the Christ light of the many can go forth in ordered service, divine dignity and ever-living purity. This will glorify that precious spirit of divine unity that good fortune has so wisely inscribed in these words from the Great Seal of the United States of America as *E Pluribus Unum,* "One Out of Many," which in its greater meaning comes full circle to read: *Many* Out of *One* in *Unity of Action*—political, educational and religious—who shall draw nigh unto their Creator in a feeling of such oneness as will glorify the ageless Christ of all whose active unity is ever dwelling in the *one light* of every man!

E pluribus unum, "one out of many." You should know the word and know how to spell it. It is on the dollar bill. It's on the Great Seal. But what it teaches us is that the United States of America was founded to be a community of the Holy Spirit of the twelve tribes of Israel and all who would be converted through them to the Messiah. *Gentiles* means those who are of the light who are in other nations. It does not mean an inferior group of people. All souls of light—no matter what their race or nationality or religion or background—are a part of this community.

But the laggard evolutions are no part of the real, living

community of America. And today America is being destroyed by the hatred, the jealousy, the resentment of laggard evolutions, both within her borders and outside her borders, who are jealous of the light of the seed of the Woman, the seed of the Woman clothed with the Sun.[6] This is the dilemma that we face, the dilemma of the Lords of Karma.

So inscribe upon your heart, "We are one Christ consciousness made out of many souls, and in that oneness we share the great plenty of our land, the great abundance." We must cast out the moneychangers and those who seek to control us by the distribution of food, the distribution of money, the control of industry, the control of the government. If we do not successfully challenge and bring to judgment these individuals, America will be destroyed by them, for that is their intent.

It is the intent of the Carter* administration to make out of the United States part of a collective order of nations where we are one nation among equals. This is why Carter will go to Nigeria or to Mexico and receive insults and not even defend the office of the Great White Brotherhood that he holds. He holds the mantle as the head of the tribes of Israel, and he is allowing his mantle to be trampled upon and is thereby dragging all of us through the mud of his inferior consciousness. He worships the power elite, who are the fallen angels. He worships them and they control him.

America is not a nation among equal nations. America and her people are the lightbearers, the torchbearers to the earth. A superior endowment gives them a superior responsibility. And this has nothing to do with white racist supremacy in the various doctrines you will hear coming from people and religious organizations that speak about the white race as the superior race.

There is one superior race on the planet. It is the I AM Race.

---
*Jimmy Carter was president of the United States from 1977 to 1981.

It is composed of people of every religion, every color, every origin, every planetary system, no matter where they are from, who worship the I AM Presence, the living God, the individualized God flame, in other words, "God with us." *Immanuel* is the word that means "God with us."

Those Who Espouse the Right Cause for the Wrong Reason Are the Most Dangerous

Those who do not worship God with us or God in us are the idolators who would destroy the true religion of the I AM Presence. So a member of the I AM Race knows that God is indwelling and bows before the Messiah, who is the messenger of Lord Maitreya—Jesus Christ.

Now, when people for generations and thousands of years have had the opportunity to bend the knee and confess the guru of the Garden of Eden or the guru in Jesus Christ or the guru in Gautama and have not, we must say that we know them by their fruits of consciousness, and they have identified themselves by their vibration. These individuals, then, need to be challenged by light, turned over to the archangels without even the slightest vibration of condemnation coming forth from us. They need to be isolated by their doctrines, and the electorate must be educated so that through their own individual Christ Self they will vote for the right people who espouse the right issues.

We have said before, there are people who espouse the right issues for the wrong reasons. And they are the most dangerous of all. The wrong reasons are self-gain. They will be for the causes that should liberate America, but they use those very causes as political climbers. You have Jerry Brown* in this state, who is

---
*Jerry Brown, a member of the Democratic Party, served as governor of the state of California from 1975 to 1983 and 2011 to 2019.

hollow as a black hole in space, who espouses now every conservative wind that blows, because he feels that that is the politically expedient thing to do. And he is being challenged by Democrats and all people alike.

These people are most dangerous. They have one goal. That is power. They have no personal loyalties. Better that he be loyal to a fallen one and express that loyalty and come out and declare it than have no loyalties whatsoever. He is probably one of the most dangerous individuals walking the United States of America, ranking only second to Ted Kennedy in terms of the power madness of the fallen ones.

If you'll notice Ted Kennedy[*] in the newspaper, he's always raising his arm when he's making a speech, exactly as the fallen angels have exhorted the children of God in imitation of the seven archangels. And he will come out with his pronouncements, and he will use this hand to drive them home. He is using the perverted power of the Sacred Spear.[†] Both of these individuals would like to unseat Carter, who himself is programmed to bring America to her utter destruction.

Now, when you have a political game of combatants all composed of individuals who come from the fallen ones, you have the greatest challenge to *E pluribus unum,* because only the children of the light can blend their Christ consciousness into one blazing Manchild, one blazing community of over two hundred million people who move together for the glory of God.

---

[*] Ted Kennedy, younger brother of John F. Kennedy, served as a senator for Massachusetts from 1962 until his death in 2009.

[†] The Sacred Spear is also known as the spear of Longinus, which according to legend pierced the side of Christ during the crucifixion. The spear has been housed in the Imperial Treasury of the Hofburg Palace in Vienna since the eleventh century. Its mystical power derives from its contact with the blood of Christ. The spear is also a symbol of the light of the raised Kundalini. The messenger gave a lecture on the Sacred Spear on February 18, 1979, during a seminar titled "The Path of Initiation under Maitreya Buddha." The lecture has not yet been published.

We, therefore, see our answer not in pitting ourselves in the midst of this struggle, not in sending you or other Keepers of the Flame forth to run for political office in contests where the people are programmed to select one of several fallen ones, where the political understanding is immature, where their knowledge of the issues is inadequate.

You Are Powerful Merely as Extensions of Lord Maitreya

We have to understand that there is a tremendous timing that comes to us from Lord Maitreya and Gautama Buddha. And at this moment, many of you here and in the field are far more effective working in government employ where you do not have to battle the fallen ones in a political race for office and where you can be abused and exposed as having a tie to the ascended masters' religion or having a particular guru, especially Guru Ma.

It's a very important moment to realize how powerful you are merely as extensions of Lord Maitreya very quietly making the most powerful exhortations unto the LORD God for the resolution of our problems. And when you have to spend vast quantities of energy in the pursuit of votes from a people, an electorate who is uninformed, you need to understand that that battle at this moment is being waged in the right- and left-wing circles.

There are plenty of right-wing people who are out seeking those offices at this moment, and they have enough human substance in them that they provide the yin and the yang of human relative good and evil. And, I don't see that this moment in this very year is the time for our people out of our teaching centers or out of this group to suddenly run for a major congressional senatorial seat or even in their state legislatures, unless they already have an established career along those lines and are certain that they can win—because the amount of light that you can draw forth for the saving of America is weighed. And the exposure and the condemnation and the confusion that arises when a lightbearer jumps into the middle of the fray with the fallen ones is not only devastating to the chela and the teaching, but it also deprives the individual of the certain victory that he can have by his invocations and by the strength of our community.

How to Save America and the Earth

Maitreya says that the world cannot have forced down its throat what it will not have. You couldn't force the shah of Iran down the throats of the Iranian people. And when people do not want what is good for them, then they must experience for a time what is bad for them until they get fed up, cry out to the living God, and ask for a deliverer. When the people's voice demands a leader like the Ayatollah Khomeini, then the best lesson of karma and the guru is to withdraw and let the people have him.[7]

This is the dilemma we are seeing. The challenge of Lord Maitreya to us is how to save America and the earth in the face of an overwhelming popular indoctrination of sympathy for the fallen ones, support for the fallen ones, and an outcry against the real sons and daughters of God. It has not changed. In fact, it has increased since the hour of Jesus' crucifixion. The world cries out, "Give us Barabbas!"[8] We've seen it again and again.

And so if America is intended to be a community, and we cannot solve that problem because of the invasion of America by laggard, anti-Christ generations who are in every race and in every sector, then we must form our own community as an archetype, as a nucleus. And by creating a perfect matrix in the most perfect guru-chela relationship that we can establish, we are providing a leaven for the leavening of consciousness. We're providing a magnet to magnetize individuals who will understand the priority of that community as *the way* to save America.

And it is not the long way around. It is not the impractical way around. If it were not for the presence of this community in America today, you would, first of all, have had cataclysm in Southern California, but you would've also had economic cataclysm.

You Have What God Needs: A Physical Temple

This is the anniversary today of the transition of our beloved Mark Prophet. On this very day six years ago, he surrendered his life to God and bought time and space for you and me to become the Buddha. And so our weekend celebrations are upon the glorious gift that he gave. He laid down his life for his friends, and he considered all of the American people his friends and all of you who were coming but not quite here, worthy of that sacrifice. Without the buying of that time, we would not be here. We would have had the cataclysm and the economic collapse.

Now we see the buildup of darkness again. And again, God is asking us to make a *living* sacrifice—not to go through the transition of death, not to take our ascension, but now to realize that the living sacrifice is to be the instrument of Lanello. Since he was required to lay down his life, even as Jesus was, he and Jesus both need your body temple. And if you have ever asked yourself, "What do I have that the ascended masters don't have that I can give to them that is useful in service?" it is your physical temple—the fact that you can operate in the Matter planes, the fact that you can provide the vehicle for their teaching distilled to the level of those whom you meet.

So we anticipate a tremendous release of light this weekend as we appropriate the great mantle of our beloved Lanello.

Maitreya says through Mark:

The coming days should be exalted as priceless days of opportunity when the cosmic seed of our endeavors should sprout and expand the results of the recent far-reaching deliberations of the Darjeeling Council, which are presently being revealed in many ways to the eyes of every sincere and alert student of the light whose own zeal and faith thus widen the panorama of Life's love and the consequent loveliness of Life itself, which will then expand to include the greater meaning of the lilies of the field and their glory;[9] the sanctified life and its glory; the golden ripening grain and its glory; the heavenly manna and its glory; the Christ-victory that overcomes the world and its glory; and the *nearness* of the Presence of God to you hourly as you are held *every moment* in the keeping of his real and tangible holy angels and their glory!

Glory is the "glow-ray" of the I AM Presence.

I, Maitreya, wish for each one that all these glories of God, and many more, may become daily more real to you than even the changing skies themselves or the climate of earth!

Behold, in the many planetary mansions of our Father and of his Christ, the light of every world twinkles its individual welcome across the starry realms of space right into each heart where that blessed anchored ray connects all with the same Christ-reality of immortal life.

I AM ever your attention to God each day in the victory of freedom's unfoldment.

Lord Maitreya

Whenever one reads dictations that were given before one found the light or came into the service, one always has that comforting, nestling feeling that right in the very moment that the dictation was being given, God had his eye upon one, upon each of you as his eye is upon the sparrow. And that dictation and the release of light was sent forth in order to be a sphere hurled into the Matter plane, bursting as light, the light going forth contacting your heart and drawing you a little nearer.

When I heard about all of the tremendous decrees given by the I AM movement as I was being born and growing up, I felt such a tremendous gratitude for all of those people and for the dictations that were given then, which I knew were the sustaining light in those formative years. And so, all of you have been drawn in by these nets of light that are strengthened each time a dictation is given.

Your Desires Must Be Transmuted or Outpictured

Another *Pearl of Wisdom* was given on September 23, 1960:

> Thought must ever be governed in order to produce the harvest of perfection intended by the Father of all life—and yearned for by so many unascended today! The etheric record, the span of memory from each individual's first and earliest embodiment until the present day, contains within it an indelible record, which must either outpicture on the screen of life in order to produce cosmic balance and justice in the affairs of mankind, or else be transmuted by spiritual alchemy or by a mystical process such as the blessed and proper use of the violet fire of freedom's love and forgiveness.
>
> While many men idle away hours in "developing their negatives" (that is, their human tendencies—much in the same manner in which a photographer develops a photographic plate), mankind would do well to use instead every method that God affords whereby they may transmute, heal and bless the "Book of their Life" (their own etheric memory body). To begin again—to begin anew countless times—is better by far than to be blown off course or to follow the whims

of those blind leaders of the blind who refuse to hearken to the voice of conscience or to listen to the voice of God!

Truly, the laborers are few, and the harvest is plenteous. The time of threshing, the time of purging and of purification in this golden age is at the very door! Love, however, not fear, should be the welcome to draw men to the harvest festival with rejoicing. The cultivation of joy in contemplation of divine possibilities that are the blessed hopes of heaven is a wise way of expanding the light activities of our dear chelas who understand the hourly need to bring the practicality of a mystical Christianity into daily action before men that they may see the good works of the children of light and desire to be like them.

"The cultivation of joy" is the point of that sentence, "in contemplation of divine possibilities."

I AM the smile of God bestowed on all the Children of Faith.

Maitreya

The most important point about your psychology made here is that *everything* that is in your consciousness within the span of memory, which is the recording of your desire body, must outpicture on the screen of life, for good or for ill. So we watch the screen play, don't we? And we say, "Who is the author of the drama of my life? Why, I am the author, and what I see upon the screen is what I have within the nucleus of my being." It is either outpictured or we transmute it by the violet flame.

Thirty Minutes of Violet Flame Each Day

So it is not a question that somehow it will go away or somehow you will suppress within your subconscious those things that are not pleasing. They *will* outpicture. They may outpicture as want, as lack, as an inability to hold the light of cosmic consciousness. They may manifest as all sorts of conditions from which you suffer. Or they can go into the flame. Remember, Saint Germain told Godfre that thirty minutes a day of violet flame is the requirement for the individual who would be chela and who would ascend in this life.

I know I AM students who have been obedient to that requirement, some of them for twenty and thirty years. And I would like to tell you that there is a radiance and a mastery as a result of that, regardless of any other condition of their being. There is a radiance and a mastery that you ought to seek and emulate.

Already your own decrees and your own energy in your auras makes you head and shoulders above chelas of other teachings who do not give the violet flame. That doesn't make you better than them. It makes the violet flame better than their methods. It means that they ought to espouse the same method.

You Were Chosen to Express the Fullness of God upon Earth

Now I'd like you to hear a few words from Maitreya given on February 10, 1962:

> O benign ones, thou who art chosen from the Beginning to be as the only begotten of the Father, I AM come tonight into your forcefield to bring to you a sense of your soul's unfolding as does a flower.
>
> The bud of your own God Self is waiting to unfold. And you are expected to respond to the vibratory action of this Christ mantle, which from within out seeks to array you in immortal garments of strength, power, purity, adoration and complete realization that God is All and in all.

With a sense of the completeness of divinity, I wish to tell you tonight that there is a golden thread woven through every circumstance of your lives, which is not always apparent because it is underwoven between other threads and it seems to disappear for a moment from your view. But nevertheless, that golden thread of perfection is ever present with each of you, and it assists you in finding—if you will pursue it—the way back Home, the way back to the victory, the glory, the purity, and the power of the Cosmic Christ and of the Buddha.

You, blessed ones, seated upon the lotus throne of your own heart, may unfold your latent divinity with all of the safety of a Buddha and of a Christ. The opportunity is yours. No man can take from you this crown.[10] No one can defraud you of this opportunity except yourselves—by feeling that you are unworthy, by feeling that you are unwilling, by feeling that you are *not* chosen. And yet, I, Lord Maitreya, have assured you in full faith that each of you and all of mankind *were* chosen to express the fullness of God upon earth!

Take, then, this opportunity. Consider it most precious. And so the Spirit of God shall so exalt you as to bring you into our presence at night, while your physical form sleeps, and confer upon you those cosmic initiations that will raise you and set you apart from mankind as a peer in heaven's eternal courts.

Oh, how mankind love and adore, even to this hour, titles and nobility. And yet I tell you, of a truth, the greatest titles and nobility of all are waiting to be conferred by heaven itself upon mankind. And when they are given and bestowed by God, no man can part you or sunder you from them, for they are your eternal portion and inheritance.

Now, O cosmic fire, blaze thou within these children! Intensify within them the mantle of life's perfection, the unfolding radiance of their purity and of their budding divinity.

Let this light so expand within the forcefield of their being that they shall from this night on be able to give to all they meet a greater than ordinary love—the love of God without limit, the love of the ascended masters, the example of the sacred fire in physical manifestation!

I thank you and bid you good evening.

Your Soul Unfolds as Does a Flower

Thou who art chosen from the Beginning to be as the only begotten of the Father.

The ascended masters who come out of the East repeat this message over and over and over again because the mass consciousness of the earth has accepted the denial of that message. And the belief that they are *not* chosen to be as the only begotten of the Father is the greatest enemy of the children of light upon the earth.

This is what Jesus Christ brought home to us from India, from his oneness with the Cosmic Christ, from his great cosmic initiations even before his incarnation—his initiation, to bring to you a sense of your soul's unfolding as does a flower.

Now, we have not seen a flower budding. We only see from time to time as we watch the flower that it has expanded. We take a camera, and we can put a rose under a heat light and accelerate it and watch it and take photographs so that we can have a series. We have an inner knowing about what is happening in the unfolding of a rose. Spiraling from the center is a white light of Alpha and Omega in balance. And it is ever so gently released, the same gentleness with which the earth and worlds turn without disturbance to life. It is a warmth that exudes because an energy is released. And so there is a warmth and a glow and a light as this spiral of energy comes out from the heart and produces the physical counterpart, the flower's unfolding.

Now our spiral of energy coming forth from our individual heart must have its counterpart in manifestation as beautiful temples and great creativity. But the intensity of that spiral can also affect every other part of life upon the planet, as it does through the Christs and the Buddhas. And so that same gentle energy is for the balancing of Alpha/Omega, the healing of all those upon the planetary body.

So to have the sense of our soul's unfolding as does a flower is to have the sense that God is perpetually releasing this gentle yet omnipotent spiral of energy. It is as powerful as a raindrop upon a rock. It is an invincible, intense energy, and yet so gentle—gentle as velvet.

And *sense* means "cosmic awareness." It means the Cosmic Christ awareness of Lord Maitreya himself. This is the perpetual awareness of our gentle Buddha, that the spiral never ceases to be unfolding and releasing its perfume, its fragrance, and the gentle power that draws all of life into that same cosmic awareness.

> The bud of your own God Self is waiting to unfold. And you are expected to respond to the vibratory action of this Christ mantle.

You are expected to respond. It "seeks to array you in immortal garments of strength, power, purity." The sense "of the completeness of divinity" is a part of this unfolding sense.

Find and Pursue the Golden Thread

And then he tells us of the golden thread. Finding the thread, we may pursue it. It is a thread of perfection, the perfect Christ image, and we can follow it back Home. And so, God has not left us without a treasure map so that we could find our way back to his Home. It's the golden thread.

You, ... seated upon the lotus throne of your ... heart, may unfold your latent divinity.

Take the opportunity.

He guarantees you the safety of a Buddha and of a Christ.

He promises that you will come to him if you take this opportunity while you sleep at night.

He speaks again of nobility, titles and nobility, showing that when there is conferred initiation, then there are not equals among equals. There are those with greater light and those with lesser light. And those of greater light must be honored as the gurus.

Self-Awareness of the Sacred Fire

You must become an "example of the sacred fire in physical manifestation." How else will anyone understand the words *sacred fire?* How can anyone else know it? And so, if you're going to become the sacred fire, you see, it is a part of this initiation. A sense of your soul's unfolding as a flower includes self-awareness of the sacred fire.

How many of you experienced a physical burning in your heart at some time during the Maitreya seminar?*

I have experienced that burning in my heart reaching such an intensity that I would have to discontinue my meditation in order to stay in this octave. That is quite a frequent experience. So I'm glad that God gives me many things to do so that I have an excuse to stop my meditation.

There is *no* denying that God is present. And you remember, "Did not our heart burn within us?"[11] When the disciples saw him on the road to Emmaus, they did not know who it was and chided themselves for not recognizing him, saying, "We should

---
*A seminar titled "The Path of Initiation under Maitreya Buddha" was held from February 16 to 19, 1979, at Camelot.

have known because our hearts were burning within us." That is a clear, clear sign of the presence of the Lord.

While we have the Lord's Body and the Lord's Blood, we also have—yesterday, for instance—the seminars on cults that went on in Los Angeles with various deprogrammers passing out their literature against this organization and this messenger. So you see what a world of benighted ignorance that requires the thrust of the sword of your sacred fire to unveil the living truth.

Where Do You Place Your Trust for Survival?

I'm going to read to you another *Pearl of Wisdom,* March 10, 1961:

> With the coming of the New Age, old things shall indeed have passed away!

That is the new age of your own personal Christhood. The old things of the old self literally simply pass gently away. It is not always so violent and so painful. You simply no longer enjoy the things that you used to enjoy, and it is a relief to have a new table to sit at with the Lord's hosts.

> Men have thought destruction for so long that the main part of the whole prophecy mentioned above, upon which most have thought, has been in connection with destruction —and especially planetary destruction or the downfall of civilization. Let me hasten to assure all mankind that while cataclysms do occasionally manifest by natural law, the passing away of the old order is purposefully to clear the way for the building of the new. This always brings the birth in consciousness of the Christ tendencies, or divine propensities.
>
> You have perhaps heard it said even by your earthly mothers, "As the twig is bent, so the tree is inclined to grow."

You see, the inner intent of the heart in man is in part inherited. Of course, whenever the war entities or hate entities and other mass-created malign influences that cause the world so much personal and planetary unhappiness are removed or transmuted, the world or individual breathes free for a moment—but only long enough for someone to again start the chain reaction of misqualified free will in the same old discordant pattern that for centuries and millenniums has made suffering on the earth and in mankind's experiences. Therefore, only by universal acceptance by the world at large can final victory come to the earth and its multitudes. And only by rising in consciousness to your own ascension can you find personal escape. There is no other way!

That is a very profound answer to today's dilemma about which we were just speaking. "Would you, in fact," Maitreya is asking in this moment,

> plight your troth or put your trust in the world for your survival? Do you see anyone in the world in whose hands you could place your soul or physical survival or even your health or even your education or the path of your soul?

We look to the ascended masters and to our Great God Presence. So we see the signs of the times, many of which preceded other revolutions, other upheavals in which we lost our lives. For example, people have lost their lives suddenly in Iran today because they waited too long to exit the country. They waited too long to see the signs of danger.[12] We see these signs all around us today. And the signs were very present before the crash of 1929 or the Russian revolution or the coming of Hitler into power. The massive buildup of armaments by Hitler before World War II was a clear index that war would come.

Prepare Your Body to Transcend the Dimensions

So today we see signs that tell us that we must have an alternate way, an escape. And there is only one alternative—to prepare your body to transcend the dimensions.

The ascended masters told you that I live in the etheric plane, and they told you that that is an option for you.[13] When you came to Maitreya's seminar on initiation, you came to my house. And so you came to my level. The master released the radiation necessary for you to live in the etheric plane for the hours that you spent in his radiation.

The great key to survival in transition is to so purify your four lower bodies so that you can move in and out—even in your physical form—of the ascended masters' retreats. Would Saint Germain save you in time of cataclysm? Of course he would. But he cannot bring you to a place that is just as lethal to your being as an atomic bomb. That lethal place is a place of highly concentrated sacred fire. The retreats of the Great White Brotherhood are anchored in the physical plane, in the heart of the earth, in the heart of the mountains. If you are not going there, it is because your vehicles are not ready.

Your Need to Survive in Transition

Your stay at Summit University is not an attempt to put you in a hothouse and to force-feed you with so much light for anyone's benefit. It is an attempt to give you the maximum opportunity to appropriate light because of coming changes. Changes are inevitable.

Immediately following Lanello's ascension six years ago, I held a conference after the Easter class in Los Angeles about how to survive in transition. There was great darkness in Los Angeles.

I left as quickly as I could leave following that conference. It was almost as though cataclysm was upon my heels, so great was the weight. And not until Jesus gave the dispensation for us to come here would I even dare come to Southern California.

Changes will come. We are not concerned what form *they* take. We are concerned what form *we* will take. God wants you to survive. He wants to provide you with an out. There are psychics who have gleaned from their probing of the mysteries that somehow God would come in this end of the century with spaceships, or by allowing them to enter subterranean caverns in South America in the Andes, and that would be the escape hatch. Well, it is not the psychics who will survive. It was not the psychics for whom those prophecies were given. Those prophecies were given for the lightbearers who could accelerate their temples.

And so, if you feel that it has been a strenuous period of fasting and diet and decrees, it is because of the tremendous love of Maitreya and his realization of your need to survive in transition. Whether in the physical body or out of the physical body—even if it's out of the physical body—the purification that you go through is recorded upon the physical body and even assists you to get out of the mayhem and the mass chaos and terror that occurs on the astral plane during any kind of planetary upheaval, because of the enormous shedding of blood and the hordes of night attempting to gain control of the people through fear.

Fear is the great instrument of revolutions, and superstition aids and abets fear and anxiety. And so, we clear the physical body even in the presence of danger to that physical body. We still pursue our purification because it gives liberation to the soul.

Balance Your Karma and Be Ready to Make Your Ascension

So Maitreya says that mankind with their war entities and their hate entities, they are cleared and cleansed by the gurus and the chelas only to find that they recreate them again. He says,

> Only by universal acceptance by the world at large can final victory come to the earth and its multitudes. And only by rising in consciousness to your own ascension.

You do not need to *make* your ascension. You simply need to be *ready* to make your ascension. You need to be *ready* with the balancing of your karma.

There is no faster way to balance karma than the preaching of the Word. The preaching of the Word is to your personal benefit. It is not for the gain of an outer organization or an outer group of people. When the Word passes through you, you are accelerating your bodies. When you speak the Word, you are partaking of the Body and Blood of Christ, not selfishly but giving it to others. And as it passes through you, you become it. You become the Word. You are transformed by the Word. When he says, "There is no other way!" and he is the guru of all ages, we must take so deeply to heart and so seriously his message.

Your True Family Is Grateful for Your Light

Is there a desire not to ascend? Clear it! Transmute it! Is there a death wish? Plunge the spear into death and realize life. But don't play around and dally with a lengthening of your chelaship because you are concerned about being too different from families and loved ones too quickly. One day you will be the Rock of Christ and you'll be walking on the water of the astral plane, when they would sink beneath the waves. And the hand that you extend to your loved ones will be the hand that enables them to cross over those waters.

And if perhaps they misunderstood or maligned or criticized you while you went through the discipline of gaining that attainment, when their souls and their lives are saved because of the sacrifices you have made, then they will rejoice. And you will be glad that you were not tempted to step yourself down for the benefit of their human comfortability.

You know, people are very uncomfortable around me. Shall I say, "God, take back your light. People are uncomfortable." No, I'm very content to withdraw so that they will not be uncomfortable. I withdraw to places where they will not be disturbed by my presence. But I will not relinquish the light, because I know it is the balance.

You can always find people who are comfortable and are grateful for your light. And those are your true ascended master friends, and that is your true family.

The Most Shadowed Hour Is Just Before the Dawn

The inner intentions of the heart are developed only in two ways: either by hallowed attunement with your own God Presence I AM or by listening to the mass voices of discord from the megatons of misqualified energy that mankind have created. Seed produces in kind. Therefore, the only safe counsel comes from Above, where all cosmic virtue and purity are born. That which raises you into your ascension comes from Above; that which pulls you down into discord is from below. It is that simple. Forget, then, personality, even injustices. Forget even your own needs for a moment, if need be, and concentrate on service to others in the holy name and power of the Christ. Do this and you shall find life even among the illusions of so-called death. The Great Law cannot be broken!

Every day is a portion of the holy season of eternity.

Through externalization of God's kingdom in your own hearts and upon this dear earth, you shall in dignity and wonder unravel the sweet mystery of life that is my own keynote.*

In the name of Almighty God, I call for the quickening of the inner ear of these chelas to the sweet mystery of life of Lord Maitreya.

Rending the cosmic veil, you shall come face-to-face with your own divinity without end. And in the magic circle of the Presence of God, you shall know that charmed existence that, while making all life one, also gives to each one an endowment of such peace, power, and protection as only God can give.

Remember, I had a like existence upon earth to your own present state and by the transcendent power of my own God Presence was raised to where I now wear such garments of eternal life as you shall one day wear. It is absolutely essential, then, that you do not faint or become immersed in states of hopelessness where you begin to feel out of touch with God. For all such feelings are only the result of too much thought about the illusions of self and mundane life, with not enough contact with the reality of your own Holy Christ Self and Great God Presence I AM.

The remedy must be applied constantly. You did not wander away from the light in a moment. Sometimes it takes more than a moment to find your way Home. But it is dangerous to delay the journey when life offers such grand opportunities.

So blessed ones who have delayed or postponed, begin again. And you who have long plodded, continue! Keep on, and on and on! The most shadowed hour is just before the dawn of initiation. Many of you are nearing great cosmic

---

*Victor Herbert's "Ah! Sweet Mystery of Life" is beloved Lord Maitreya's musical keynote.

initiations. Hold fast the light, the doorway into the eternal day of God.

I AM Your Friend, Companion, and Brother,

Lord Maitreya

Now as we prepare for the Easter conference, we will listen to beloved Lord Maitreya's offering of March 28, 1964, fifteen years ago, his Easter release of the resurrection fire.

The White Cube
The Coming of the Avatar

One by one, they have come. One by one, I have gazed upon their faces. I have read the record. I have perceived the intent. I have given my love. One by one, they are raised. And yet, the Law calleth forth torrents and multitudes.

The sweetness, the gentle simplicity of the pure God-design is so captivated by the strands of the human personality that it is as though they were bound hand and foot, caught in a mesh of their own weaving from which they cannot extricate themselves.

And yet, as an acetylene torch will cut through steel, so the power of love, the blue-flame power of the holy will of God, poureth forth its radiance and severeth, strand by strand, the fetters of human making until, at last, the soul goeth free as a bird from a cage and soareth into the heavens to reunion, to initiation, to understanding, to bliss. In the stillness of the holy radiance that poureth forth God's love—in the stillness of that love, all form vanishes in a burst of light!

I AM come. I AM come to represent the mighty hierarchy, conferring upon those who would serve our cause a more than ordinary honor—the honor of the ages—anchoring them in the cleft of the Rock of Ages, extending over them our white mantle, consecrating them to the pure edict of light.

Understanding floweth forth as a sharp sword, a cutting sword, a piercing sword. It severeth, as it were, the unclean from the clean and divideth clearly the light from the darkness. Initiation conferreth upon all the mantle of the Christ and the holy portion that is every man's allotment of the Holy Spirit.

Be thou still. Be thou at peace. Be thou aware of thy God. It is not in mere words, the release of holy sound, but it is in the release of holy substance that men are made clean by the clean flame of devotion, the clean flame that purifieth and sweepeth away all that is not clear and radiant and pure and lovely, until that which remaineth is God, is Good, the basic Christ Child simplicity.

The holiness of Saint Francis and of the anointed Christ consciousness manifested by Jesus, the World Teachers who stand by my side to serve—these are tested men of God, men of cosmic honor, men of cosmic virtue. These came long ago and were presented to me. And as I gazed at their young faces, I knew then that I beheld an avatar.

And I will tell you something about those who have the office that I hold. Those who have the office that I hold are as thrilled with a manifestation of the supernal radiance of the elect as God would have us be. Our delight is in these tiny things: to gaze upon a face and to know that here is a victor, to initiate such a one into the mysteries of heaven, to place upon such shoulders the clean, white linen, the arrayment of our office. This is an honor conferred upon us, and we are indeed grateful for the manifest opportunity of doing this for all who will come as a sweet child to receive the olive branch of peace and the holy dove descending upon their consciousness.

There was a cry that went forth in the past, but it was negative. It pertained to human degradation; therefore, I shall not use it this day, even though it is recorded and written.

But instead, I shall utter the message of its antithesis, of its opposite, of its manifestation as God intended.

Do you remember the shepherd king David? Do you remember the psalms that flowed forth from his heart?

"The Lord is my shepherd; I shall not want. He maketh me to lie down in green pastures.... He restoreth my soul.... Yea, though I walk through the valley of the shadow..., I will fear no evil: for thou art with me; thy rod and thy staff...."[14]

And so, the psalms of David have brought a sweet music to the souls of men, and it has come to pass that the release of his energy has mounted to do honor to the King of kings and the Lord of lords.[15] The tensions of the world are lessened, far lessened, by holding the focus upon such holy words, by cherishing the outpouring of his wondrous heart.

And so, I pay tribute today to those lonely souls, as Tabor did this night past,[16] and call to your attention that these are not lonely souls in reality but are souls of divine union who have passed through the tests, the trying crucible tests of life, and have attained a manifest victory that cannot be denied by man, nor by their contemporaries, nor by their own families or their friends. I would call to your attention the statement that was made by beloved Jesus pertaining to friendship, stating that whosoever doeth the will of God was his friend and, in a sense, his brother and mother and endeared one.[17]

Blessed ones, as you go forth to keep the flame of your divinity, you must recognize that some of you are as untried knights by comparison, and some of you are squires in the learning process, desiring to stand as the Knights of the Table Round but remaining yet completely untested and untried.

Were you to come to me today where I am—for I am in the Cave of Light in Chananda's retreat[18]—I tell you that a very special dispensation could be given. For we have summoned a tremendous radiance. And this radiance is to be released tomorrow, in accordance with the divine intent, with the breaking of the dawn and is intended to accelerate its tempo until at the hour of twelve it shall reach its zenith in the time zone where you are. This has been coordinated by the Darjeeling and Indian Councils in order to confer upon the students assembled here the rising crest of that holy momentum, releasing it to the heart of America and dispensing it for all nations to drink of the cup of its radiance.

Of course, if you were here today and could bathe in the accumulated radiance, I am certain you realize that it would indeed strip from your being layers upon layers of densified substance until, by its power and pressure, you would find yourselves so much closer to your precious goals.

I regret that I could not open my arms and form a pathway of light over which you all might walk to come here today to partake of this momentum. But I think by telling you of it that some compensation shall be given. For in your thoughts, your mental body and your emotional body can, in a sense, be projected to us here and receive the mighty flame passing through your mental body, through your emotional body, to still the feelings of frustration and distress there, to wipe away from your being the cause and the effect and the record of memory that is sordid and destructive, and by divine discrimination to enable you to feel the anointing that was placed upon David's head[19] and upon the head of Jesus[20] and upon the head of all avatars who have ever come to our retreat and who have ever knelt before me as the hierarch that I AM.

O precious ones, my love for you is so great this day that it is as though I would give another million years of service to this blessed planet if I felt that by so doing I could free this generation. And yet, the Karmic Board will not permit it; the Great Law will not allow it. And so we are all tempered, you see, in our moments of high inspiration, by the greater wisdom flame of God, which demands the best course for all.

Therefore as I speak to you now, I advocate that in the

stilling of your consciousness, you cognize the meaning of quietness and contemplation and purity. Visualize now with me in a special manner, so that you may have conferred upon you a mighty blessing. Before each one of you, visualize a cube one foot square. This cube is white and resembleth alabaster. At this moment it is like unto a bulb through which a current is not passing. We will in this experience cause it to glow, but not yet. We must first tell you of what significance this cube is.

The cube is foursquare. The cube is indicative of the New Jerusalem. The cube is indicative of the Holy City celestial that descendeth from God out of heaven. The cube is significant of the white stone and the new name that is given to all who are able to receive it.[21]

The cube represents your potential entrée into that Holy City of God, builded upon the prophets and teachers and avatars of all ages, builded upon the lives of the saints, builded upon the cosmic unity of the Foursquare City, builded upon the initiatic system of the Great White Brotherhood. This great cube of light represents also, then, your own precious contact with the Great White Brotherhood.

This cube is symbolic and factual—factual in the sense that in God's eyes and by his power he may make the largest offering of any relative size according to his desire. And therefore, this cube appearing before you in space, which you hold with your hands, is in essence as big as God would choose to make the New Jerusalem—a place of limitless light and consciousness and purity, a place where all of the saints of the universe and of all universes can abide. Could it then be small? Could it then be too large? It is exactly the correct size.

And as you recognize that this is your portion—your stone in the eternal temple, representative of the crystal-clear perfection of your identity—you will realize that were it surrounded now with mud and slime and human refuse, it would be unfit to place in the temple all bright, all light, all pure, all holy. And therefore, this temple must of necessity be held in spiritual dimensions, for it cannot yet be trusted to the flesh.

Ere the cock crow, thou shalt deny me thrice.[22] Know ye not, then, that the aspirations of men and their intents are so frequently cast aside in desperate moments? Individuals have actually forsaken this fraternity without realizing the potential that is within it. This is most unfortunate for themselves and for us, too. For had they remained, they would have had conferred upon them the eternal promises in a greater measure and a greater outpouring.

And yet, this shall not deter the faithful. For in all ages the lonely ones have walked the pathway of initiation. They have understood the meaning of dedication and selfless service. They have understood that they alone must pass through the gate of initiation, that no one upon earth could do this for them, that no other person could substitute.

Mothers have knelt at my feet and pled that they might pass through the most horrible of tests in order that their sons might be given a higher place in the kingdom. But the Great Law would not permit it, and I have turned them away one and all.

All must come alone to this place where they recognize that in their hands they hold their own cosmic destiny, that this white stone that now is before you is a symbol of that potential which lies within you.

El Morya, with all of his mighty love and light that blazes forth through me now because I have mentioned his name, is aware of the fact that he could not with all his love push you through and fit you into that temple perfect and beautiful. Only your own God-given free will, continually driven against all the forces of opposition, can hold a perfect balance—the key to your own soul's salvation.

"In your patience possess ye your souls"[23] is the power

that will enable you to hold the God-design and God-direction that will make it possible for you to enter into the temple that is indeed more within your own hands than in the hands of God, for he has given it to you!

Do you see, beloved ones? It has always been yours. It was the enriched cosmic design that God entrusted to you in the Beginning, which has always been there and has never been taken from you, except that it was raised into a higher pattern not only in your Higher Mental Body, but in the very center of the great God flame within your own individualized I AM Presence. And it has descended this day from your own Presence as the gift of life.

It is possible for you to contact that Presence. It is possible for you to contact that perfection. It is possible for you to be fit into the eternal temple and to keep the flame of your divinity blazing—not only now, but ever hereafter!

And for this reason I say to you—as you hold this seemingly inert temple of life, which is your own being foursquare, within the power of your own hands—know that at one given moment in this service we shall light it with the great cosmic flame. And then as that cosmic flame blazes in tremendous whiteness and radiance, it shall come to pass that all of you shall offer to your own God Presence this white stone that is your own true reality containing your name, symbolizing your service to life forever. And you shall offer it to your Presence, knowing that only your Presence has the perfect key that will enable you to work out your perfection.

And therefore, as you return it to your Presence, all splendid and shining with the holy radiance, you will always remember that you have held this divine treasure right within the forcefield of your own physical hands, and also that it has passed through the hands of your Holy Christ Self and is retained for you within the heart of your great God Presence within the very central flame of God's own heart.

Now, precious ones, the moment draweth close when the angels of initiation shall draw very near. Therefore, I shall ask that music be played, first in a soft manner and then coming to a crescendo where the radiance can blaze forth and awareness can dawn upon your blessed consciousness this day.

You have journeyed here in contemplation of greater light, and you shall receive that light. But the degree that shall manifest shall be determined by determinative factors in your own being and world. All are not the same, and yet we have given to all the same cosmic cube. All are not the same, for all have not cognized the use of that which is within their hands.

And yet, the possibility of equality lies as a gift in the hand of all. As men bear this responsibility and knowledge well, they shall no longer blame another for their own shortcomings or failures. Neither shall they blame themselves, but they shall say to their own God Presence:

I AM ready! In all of the ages that have passed when failures have plagued me, generated by my own lack of understanding, I know that thou wert there and that thou have guided me unto the present hour. Therefore, I stand, waiting my own cosmic initiation. I desire a place in thy great sheepfold. I would be a stone in the temple pure and holy and immortal. I offer myself and all that I AM to thee! Take me and use me, assimilate me and direct me.

And observe, dear hearts, how the cosmic response will generate in your minds a new law acting—a law that will fulfill your design with the speed of light, the speed of lightning, and the power of the angels. This will happen if you expect it. This will happen if you direct it, knowing that it is your Presence that will act through you to bring about the manifestation you crave and desire and want so very badly.

O precious ones, go forward in the light! Hold thy cube now more closely and draw thy hands together until it is as though thou canst feel this cube and the pressure thereof restraining thy hands, until it is as though thou couldst not place them together, for this cube is the tangible light substance that is within them. And around this cube thy hands may feel the pressure of that immortal life which is the glory of the saints of all ages and the power of the eternal Principle made manifest. [music played]

URIM THUMMIM[24]

Glow, radiant cube of light
With immortal substance white—
Let thy brilliance flash in fire
And let thy love all hearts inspire!
For Victory's Presence here is manifest
And God himself is blest.

O holy cubes blazing white,
Be offered now to God's pure light;
Lift thy hands, O blessed ones,
Toward the Sun of thy Presence.
O angelic hosts, take up these cubes of light
Glowing with all the light of the firmament.

O mighty God Presence, thou I AM of all,
By thy light and love we call
For the virtue of the light
And the power of God's might
To manifest in human night
And see that all things are made right.

'Tis God's delight, O blessed ones,
That firms the resolution strong
And arms the heart to distinguish right from wrong
And offer in the name of God so fair
The love and light of a maiden's prayer.

A beauteous soul of joy comes down,
Descending, then, to wear his crown;
And all men everywhere rejoice,
For light and power in God's voice
Shall blaze forth from the mighty Son,
The cosmic being, God's holy one.

And all men are the fullness then
Of that great flame ablazing there,
The answer to the maiden's prayer,
The Cosmic Mother whose love shines round
And fills the circuit with the sound
Of heavenly rejoicing and the chord
That is the fullness of the LORD!

May the Great Sun Prince Michael, Lord of the Archangels, sever from thee, blessed ones, forever, all that is not of the light of God. May the Great Sun Prince Michael be thy special guardian forever. May the Great Sun Prince Michael protect every Keeper of the Flame.

O Archangel Michael, take command of these blessed ones. Give them thy love, and may they give thee their love.

Your Own City Foursquare

How many of you recognized Jesus' music that was being played? Just a few of you. Music composed by Godfre, "'I AM' Come in Full Glory," which was played by the pianist.

Now, the first initiation is to confer

> a more than ordinary honor . . . anchoring them in the cleft of the Rock of Ages, extending over them our white mantle [of light], consecrating them to the pure edict of light.
>
> Understanding floweth forth as a sharp sword, a cutting sword, a piercing sword. It severeth, as it were, the unclean from the clean and divideth clearly the light from

the darkness. Initiation conferreth upon all the mantle of the Christ and the holy portion that is every man's allotment of the Holy Spirit.

So, the conferrence is the honor of the ages, and that honor is the mantle of the Christ and the holy portion that is your allotment of the Holy Spirit.

That initiation took the tangible form of the white stone, the one-foot cube. It's your own being foursquare. It is your City Foursquare.[25] It symbolizes the New Jerusalem.[26] It

> represents your potential entrée into that Holy City of God, builded upon [the Truth voiced by] the prophets and teachers and avatars..., builded upon the initiatic system of the Great White Brotherhood.

It might be interesting for you to just take with you now your meditation upon the cube and see how many different points about the cube you can remember—what it is, what it can do—and then listen once again to the portion where he gives the cube.

The Descent of the Christ Self into Your Temple

> A beauteous soul of joy comes down,
> Descending, then, to wear his crown;
> And all men everywhere rejoice,
> For light and power in God's voice
> Shall blaze forth from the mighty Son,
> The cosmic being, God's holy one.

Now, for me that was a very personal message. It should also be a very personal message for you, for your own Christ Self descending into your temple.

> And all men are the fullness then
> Of that great flame ablazing there,

> The answer to the maiden's prayer,
> The Cosmic Mother whose love shines round
> And fills the circuit with the sound
> Of heavenly rejoicing in the chord
> That is the fullness of the LORD!

Your own "maiden's prayer" for the Christ to descend in you is fulfilled as you become the Cosmic Mother who gives birth to the Manchild. So your soul is the maiden, the feminine portion of your being, calling for the Manchild to be born within you. And each time that great ritual is reenacted, it evokes the great blessing of the Cosmic Christ.

> *In the name of Brahma, Vishnu, Shiva, in the name of the Mother, it is done.*

February 23, 1979

NOTES

CHAPTER ONE: The Restoration of the Thread of Contact
1. John 8:58.
2. John 1:5.
3. John 13:34.
4. Gen. 2:7.
5. Matt. 16:22.
6. See Archangel Gabriel, *Mysteries of the Holy Grail,* chapters 10 and 11.
7. John 6:53.
8. Matt. 7:21.
9. See Acts 10:42; II Tim. 4:1; I Pet. 4:5.
10. The date of the dictation was later determined to be September 18, 1960.
11. At the Sunday Service on January 7, 1979, Maitreya's dictation of December 31, 1978, was replayed, "The Initiation of the Law of the One."
12. Matt. 22:15–22; Mark 12:13–17; Luke 20:21–26.
13. Luke 22:41–44.
14. Isa. 40:3; Matt. 3:3.
15. John 20:17.
16. Isa. 45:22, 23; Rom. 14:11; Phil. 2:10, 11.
17. Matt. 6:10; Luke 11:2.
18. John 8:25, 58.
19. Luke 2:49; 18:1; II Cor. 4:1, 16; Gal. 6:9; Eph. 3:13; Heb. 12:3–5.
20. John 4:24.
21. See Mark L. Prophet and Elizabeth Clare Prophet, *The Science of the Spoken Word,* chapter 11, "The Power of the Ten Thousand-Times-Ten Thousand."

N.B. Books listed here are published by Summit University Press unless otherwise noted; available at http://Store.SummitLighthouse.org.

22. John 14:15.
23. Matt. 6:10; Luke 11:2.
24. As defined in *Merriam Webster's Collegiate Dictionary*, (tenth edition), the verb *stump* means "to travel over (a region) making political speeches or supporting a cause." According to *The Oxford English Dictionary*, the noun *stump* in early American usage referred to "the stump of a large felled tree used as a stand or platform for a speaker"; hence, the word came to be used to refer to "a place or an occasion of political oratory." In a landmark dictation given June 30, 1976, in Washington, D.C., Pallas Athena inaugurated the Coming Revolution in Higher Consciousness. Soon after, El Morya called the messenger "to stump." He said: "Stump as though you were running for election. Stump for Jesus and Saint Germain and the message of the eternal Christ." The messenger's Stump lecture from her tours in 1978 was published in an audio album, *I'm Stumping for the Coming Revolution in Higher Consciousness.*
25. John 19:30.
26. "The Man Who Would Not Die" was an episode in the television series *In Search of...*, hosted by Leonard Nimoy. This episode, which was about the Count of Saint Germain, the Wonderman of Europe, included commentary by the messenger about Saint Germain and a portion of Saint Germain's dictation of June 11, 1977. It first aired on December 31, 1977.
27. The messenger is referring to Lord Maitreya's dictation of December 31, 1978, in which he said: "Did you think that it was a process of evolution and that Maitreya had not yet passed his initiations?" This dictation is now published as "The Initiation of the Law of the One," *Pearls of Wisdom,* vol. 33, nos. 35 and 36.
28. John 9:39.
29. Josh. 24:15.
30. Matt. 7:14.
31. I Sam. 15:22.
32. See *Catherine of Siena: The Dialogue* (New York: Paulist Press, 1980).
33. Idi Amin was a commander in the Ugandan army who ousted President Milton Obote in 1971, abolishing parliament and declaring himself president for life. As many as 300,000 Ugandans are said to have died during his eight-year reign, another 250,000 fled to Kenya, and many others lived in exile in Britain.

    "Big Daddy," as he liked to call himself, a 270-pound former military boxing champion, drew worldwide attention by his flamboyant eccentricity in foreign policy, outspoken belligerence toward other nations and their leaders (particularly Israel and neighboring Tanzania), and his ruthless purges. These included the periodic liquidation of prominent Ugandans and several thousand Lango and Acholi tribesmen who had supported Obote. "On any given day it was not unusual for 100 to 150 Ugandans to be killed," *Reader's Digest* reported in January 1980. "Entire villages were wiped out. Bodies floated down the Nile by the hundreds."

Described as a man who could turn in a moment from gentle and charming to demonic, Amin's bizarre conduct led to persistent rumors about his mental stability. In a blatant show of racism, Amin expelled the 50,000 Asians living in Uganda in 1972, only to strip the country of the trained personnel vital to its economy. When Britain cut off all aid following renewed reports of torture and brutality, Amin confiscated British businesses in Uganda without compensation—later claiming that relations with Britain went awry because he would not marry an Englishwoman. In 1977, Anglican archbishop of Uganda Janani Luwum and two of Amin's cabinet ministers were killed, beginning the persecution and slaughter of many Christians and non-Muslims (Amin was a convert to Islam).

Amin's downfall came when he invaded Tanzania in October 1978 in an attempt to draw attention away from internal problems. In April 1979 Tanzanian troops with Ugandan exiles and rebels took the capital of Kampala, welcomed by its residents. Amin fled to Libya, leaving the nation once dubbed the "pearl of Africa" with bitter tribal divisions, a bankrupt economy, and a population demoralized by his reign of terror. He eventually went to Saudi Arabia, where he died in 2003.

34. "Whom the gods would destroy they first make mad." This phrase has been used widely in English literature, including in the poem "The Masque of Pandora," by Longfellow. Its origins can be traced back to antiquity. Sophocles' play *Antigone* includes the line "Evil appears as good in the minds of those whom god leads to destruction."

CHAPTER TWO: **A Transfer of Power**
1. Rom. 8:38, 39.
2. Matt. 26:26; Mark 14:22; Luke 22:19; I Cor. 11:23, 24.
3. John 6:31–35, 41, 47–58.
4. Isa. 40:3; Matt. 3:3.

5. Isa. 30:20, 21.
6. Matt. 6:25–34; Luke 12:22–32.
7. Isa. 11:9; 65:25.
8. Dictation by Daniel Rayborn, October 14, 1963, available from AscendedMasterLibrary.org.
9. Jer. 13:23.
10. Matt. 27:46; Ps. 22; Mark 15:34.
11. John 14:12.
12. est was an organization founded by Werner Erhard in 1971. It offered very intense weekend seminars supposedly with the goal of enabling participants to free themselves from the past and their own self-limiting patterns. In his *Exposé of False Teachings,* Kuthumi described est as "brainwashing, soul-smashing sessions" and warned of the "initiations which take place when a would-be student formally enters into a relationship with an unauthorized teacher, a self-elevated initiator." (*Pearls of Wisdom,* vol. 19, no. 8, February 22, 1976)
13. Rev. 6:16; Luke 23:30.
14. Luke 21:26.
15. Part of the curriculum of the twelve-week Summit University sessions held at that time was a series of lectures by the messenger on different types of entities. The lectures included invocations for the clearance of these entities from the students.
16. *Lord of the Rings* was an animated film version of Tolkein's trilogy released November 15, 1978. The film was financially successful but received mixed reviews from critics. The gray creature that crawls on the ground is Gollum, and the astral hordes depicted in the film are orcs. Peter Jackson's *Lord of the Rings* trilogy, released in the early 2000s, similarly depicted these aspects of the astral plane using live action and computer graphics.
17. Acts 26:14; 9:5–6.
18. Luke 24:49.
19. John 14:9–10.
20. John 20:17.
21. David's relationship with his Christ Self is a theme in the Psalms. For example, Psalm 110 includes the following verses: "The LORD [the mighty I AM Presence] said unto my Lord [my Holy Christ Self], Sit thou at my right hand, until I make thine enemies thy footstool.... The LORD hath sworn, and will not repent, Thou art a priest for ever after the order of Melchizedek."

CHAPTER THREE: **The Goal of Chelaship**
1. These *Pearls of Wisdom* by Archangel Gabriel are published in the book *Mysteries of the Holy Grail.*
2. Matt. 11:12.
3. Isa. 6:8.
4. I Cor. 15:41.
5. Kuthumi was developing mastery in the field of psychology in his final embodiment. Born in the early nineteenth century, he attended Oxford University in 1850 and spent considerable time in Dresden, Würzburg, Nürnberg, and finally Leipzig, where he studied at the University of Germany in the 1870s. At Leipzig he visited with Dr. Gustav Theodor Fechner, the founder of modern psychological research.
6. See chapter 2, this volume, note 11.
7. Mark L. Prophet and Elizabeth Clare Prophet, *Understanding Yourself: A Spiritual Approach to Self-Discovery and Soul-Awareness.* The messenger's commentary on this book delivered in a series of lectures at Summit University has been published in *Advanced Studies in Understanding Yourself.*
8. Archangel Gabriel, "On the Mystery of the Sacred Eucharist," *Pearls of Wisdom,* vol. 22, no. 5, February 4, 1979; also published in *Mysteries of the Holy Grail,* chapter 11.
9. Matt. 9:12.
10. See sermon by Elizabeth Clare Prophet, January 21, 1979. Available from AscendedMasterLibrary.org.
11. Matt. 5:3.
12. I John 3:17.
13. Matt. 3:8; 7:19.
14. Mark 10:18; Luke 18:19.
15. From January 11 to 20, 1978, the messenger traveled to Ghana and Liberia, presenting lectures on the teachings of the ascended masters. She met with the leaders of the governments of both nations and appeared on national radio and television. In her lectures and meetings with government officials, she warned of the dangers of corruption in government and society and of dangers of communism. (At that time the Soviet Union was aggressively seeking to expand its influence in third-world nations through establishing political and economic ties and also through active support of Communist guerilla movements.)
16. Exod. 17:12.

17. The International Cooperation Council was established by Leland Stewart in 1965. It was reorganized in 1980 under the name Unity-and-Diversity World Council.
18. The messenger's lectures on Karl Marx and Jesus Christ have been published in the book *The Economic Philosophy of Jesus Christ vs. the Religious Philosophy of Karl Marx*. The lecture "Psychotronics: The Only Way to Go Is Up!" (October 5, 1978) is available from Ascended MasterLibrary.org. The lecture on the Club of Rome, "Limits to Growth, Exposed" (January 1, 1979) has not yet been published.
19. Swami Satchidananda (1914–2002) was an Indian religious teacher, author, and yoga adept. He taught a system he called Integral Yoga and founded an ashram called Yogaville in Virginia. He first came to prominence in the West in 1969 when he opened the Woodstock rock music festival.
20. In this dictation, Shiva gave extensive teaching on rock music, including the following: "Beloved ones, these fallen ones have invaded the very temples of the lightbearers through the misuse of energy and rhythm. You have been told again and again and yet I say it again: that which has perverted life has come through the misuse of rhythm of the white-fire core. It steals into the subconscious mind by the abuse of the body.

    "The presence of sugar, alcohol, nicotine, drugs of every description and kind within the temple are a weakening of the very fibers of the spiritual body whereby that body can contain light—all of this aggravated by the rhythm of that rock music and the acid rock that is projected upon the youth. And, beloved ones, the very serious consideration of the representatives of the Holy Spirit this day is whether or not this generation shall be lost because of the rebellion against love in the misuse of the rhythm in that perverted sound which is invading almost every household where there are young people, and it occurs in youth because of the very energies of the sacred fire.

    "The invasion of the temple, the invasion of the holy of holies by these unclean spirits through the perversion of sound was the cause of the sinking of Lemuria and Atlantis.... Let the teaching, then, concerning the misuse of music be spread abroad.... Beloved ones, there is nothing, and I say *nothing whatsoever* that is constructive in *any* form of jazz. And I say this unequivocally." (Shiva, "The Rhythm of Shiva: The Trial by Fire," Part 1, *Pearls of Wisdom*, vol. 21, no. 37, September 10, 1978) The dictation is also available from AscendedMasterLibrary.org.

21. Elizabeth Clare Prophet, *The Science of Rhythm for the Mastery of the Sacred Energies of Life,* available from AscendedMasterLibrary.org; also published on DVD as *The Power of Music to Create or Destroy,* including illustrations of the effects of different pieces of music on the aura.
22. Matt. 10:41; 11:27; John 12:45.
23. In a dictation on May 7, 1967, the Great Divine Director said: "We petition, then, in the holy name of God to the Karmic Board that every lifestream who shall find our work and service of contact and communion distasteful to them be given their freedom to hear our voice no more for the space of one hundred years.... I trust that this petition, unless it be contrary to some specific action of an individual lifestream, will be granted and that those who turn away from the hearing of our words will find that we will make no effort then to seek them for at least one hundred years, which in the main would place it beyond the pale of that lifestream for the balance of their entire embodiment." Available from AscendedMasterLibrary.org.
24. Jesus' two commandments are found in Matthew 22:37–40: "Jesus said unto him, Thou shalt love the Lord thy God with all thy heart, and with all thy soul, and with all thy mind. This is the first and great commandment. And the second is like unto it, Thou shalt love thy neighbour as thyself. On these two commandments hang all the law and the prophets."
25. Exod. 20:13.
26. Elizabeth Clare Prophet, March 18, 1973, "Obey Immediately!" Available from AscendedMasterLibrary.org.
27. Rev. 3:16.
28. Gal. 6:5.
29. "Every man shall bear his own economic burden" was the rule for community members when our headquarters was at Camelot, outside Los Angeles. Most members of the community were not paid a salary. They met their financial needs through part-time employment in the local area while they worked full-time on the messenger's staff. When the headquarters moved to the Royal Teton Ranch, this was no longer feasible, since part-time employment opportunities outside the community were limited in the remote rural location.
30. For information about twin flames, see Elizabeth Clare Prophet, *Soul Mates and Twin Flames: The Spiritual Dimension of Love and Relationships.*
31. John 16:7.

32. Acts 2:1–4.
33. Luke 24:49–53.
34. John 14:26.
35. For information about plotting cycles of the cosmic clock in your life, see Elizabeth Clare Prophet, *Predict Your Future: Understand the Cycles of the Cosmic Clock*.
36. On May 8, 1977, Gautama Buddha inaugurated a ten-year plan for the turning of the tide of darkness in the earth. "It must be heard by the people of God on earth that the hour is at hand and that the Lord Buddha has extended to you as people of God one decade for the turning of the tide—one decade from this hour for the spreading abroad of the teachings, for the contacting of hundreds of thousands of souls who will take the teaching and the science of the spoken Word and use it for the salvation of earth. After the decade has passed from this hour there is no guarantee forthcoming from the Lords of Karma or from the Keeper of the Scrolls that the tide can any longer be turned from the fate that has been plotted by the dark ones." Gautama Buddha, "One Decade for the Turning of the Tide: The Great Central Sun Messengers, the Cosmic Christs, and the Buddhas Come Forth," in *Pearls of Wisdom*, vol. 21, nos. 28 and 29, July 9 and 16, 1978.
37. On January 14, 1979, Archangel Gabriel announced Mission Amethyst Jewel for the gathering of disciples at community teaching centers of Church Universal and Triumphant. Mission Amethyst Jewel is based upon the principle of the violet flame burning within the heart of the chela. The chela is the jewel. And as the chelas come together they form clusters of amethyst jewels that become the new study groups and teaching centers around the world.
38. II Cor. 12:4.
39. Rev. 2:17.
40. See Virginia Fellows, *The Shakespeare Code*.
41. Matt. 10:6; 15:24.
42. See Acts 10, 11.
43. Gen. 1:26.
44. The first book in the eight-volume series of the dictations of Jesus was published in 2021. See Elizabeth Clare Prophet, *The Word: Mystical Revelations of Jesus Christ through His Two Witnesses, Volume 8*, covering the years 1993–1998.
45. See Elizabeth Clare Prophet, *Teachings from the Mystery School — The Maitreya Discourses*. Also available in MP3 and DVD formats.

46. "Victory in the Holy City" was the name of the campaign for raising of the funds for the development of Camelot.

CHAPTER FOUR: **The Initiation of the Solar Radiance**

1. The seminar titled *Become the Buddha* was held in San Francisco December 2–4, 1977. The Buddhas who spoke there were Milarepa, Maitreya, Gautama, Lanello and Padma Sambhava.
2. John 6:32–35.
3. John 4:10, 14; Rev. 7:16, 17; 21:6; 22:1, 17.
4. II Cor. 12:9.
5. I Cor. 15:53, 54.
6. Heb. 11:6.
7. See Elizabeth Clare Prophet, *Fallen Angels and the Origins of Evil*, containing a translation of *The Book of Enoch*.
8. Matt. 12:9–14; Mark 3:1–6; Luke 6:6–11.
9. Mark 5:34; Luke 17:19; John 5:6, 8, 9, 14, 15.
10. Matt. 9:18–26; Mark 5:22–43; Luke 7:11–15; 8:41–56; John 11:1–44.
11. Eph. 4:22–24; Col. 3:9, 10.
12. Isa. 55:1.
13. James 1:17.
14. John 6:68.
15. Ezek. 1:16; 10:10.
16. I Pet. 3:18–20; 4:6.
17. Luke 23:43.
18. John 10:1–18.
19. Rev. 21:4.
20. Rom. 6:4; 7:6.
21. II Cor. 12:9.
22. I Cor. 15:53.
23. Eph. 4:22–44.
24. Matt. 27:62–66.
25. The Nag Hammadi library was a collection of early Christian and Gnostic texts that was found in 1945 near Nag Hammadi, Egypt, about sixty miles north of Luxor. The first English translation of the texts was published in 1977. See James M. Robinson, ed., *The Nag Hammadi Library in English,* 3d ed., rev. (New York: HarperCollins Publishers, 1990).
26. The Gospel of Philip includes the following: "The companion of the [savior] is Mary of Magdala. The [savior loved] her more than

[all] the disciples, [and used to] kiss her [often] on her [mouth]." (Gospel of Philip, 63, tr. Marvin Meyer, http://gnosis.org/naghamm/GPhilip-Meyer.html) Words in brackets are the best guess of the translator to fill in portions of the text that are missing in the original manuscript. The passage has also been translated as "Mary Magdalene was the companion of the Savior. He loved her more than all the other disciples, and kissed her on her [. . .] more often than he kissed the rest of the disciples." (https://gnosticismexplained.org/the-gospel-of-philip) It has also been suggested that the missing word may have been cheek, forehead or feet, with the kiss representing a sign of respect.
27. Matt. 13:24–30; 25:31–46.
28. Matt. 3:8–10.
29. See *The Mahatma Letters to A. P. Sinnett,* Letter No. 65.
30. II Kings 5.

CHAPTER FIVE: **The Initiation of the Holy Spirit**

1. This lecture is published in Elizabeth Clare Prophet, *Predict Your Future,* chapter 10, "The Psychology of Wholeness."
2. Lanello, April 8, 1979, available from AscendedMasterLibrary.org.
3. John 13:8.
4. Matt. 7:29; Mark 1:22.
5. Matt. 26:53–54.
6. John 19:11.
7. Acts 7:54–60.
8. The diagrams follow chapter 17 in Elizabeth Clare Prophet, *Mysteries of the Holy Grail.*
9. El Morya, *The Chela and the Path: Keys to Soul Mastery in the Aquarian Age.*
10. Jesus and Kuthumi, *Prayer and Meditation.*
11. Matt. 12:24.
12. The Unification Church, sometimes colloquially called the Moonies, was founded in South Korea in 1954 by Sun Myung Moon, who claimed to be fulfilling the uncompleted mission of Jesus Christ. In his *Exposé of False Teachings,* Kuthumi described Moon as a "son of Belial," In the 1970s, the church became a target of the anti-cult movement. Members of the church were kidnapped by deprogrammers, held captive and subjected to psychological pressure until they renounced their beliefs in the church's teachings. Similar coercive

deprogrammings were also carried out against members of many other new religious movements in the 1970s and 1980s.
13. On November 18, 1978, 913 members of the Peoples Temple at Jonestown, a quasi-religious/socialist commune in Guyana, South America, committed a mass suicide-murder at the direction of leader Jim Jones. In the aftermath of the tragedy, many religious organizations were forced to defend not only their beliefs but their right to exist. Self-proclaimed "experts" on one or a number of new religions took up the so-called "cult menace" as their cause. As a result, a growing suspicion—based on the underlying fear that all "cults" used brainwashing and therefore any one of them could become "another Jonestown"—spread across the country. With increased pressure for government regulation of "cults," a number of investigations and hearings were held by committees in Congress and state legislatures.
14. In 1982, Sun Myung Moon was prosecuted by the IRS and convicted of tax fraud, serving 13 months in a federal prison. The practices Moon was convicted of were commonly used by other churches, and many Christian religious leaders protested the case as politically motivated selective prosecution. Prosecutors offered to drop the case if Moon surrendered his green card, which he refused to do.
15. For example, see Elizabeth Clare Prophet, "Where Do We Go from Here?" April 5, 1977; available from AscendedMaster Library.org. An excerpt is published in *The Path of Brotherhood*, pp. 95–101.
16. Luke 10:7.
17. Jesus, "The Communication of the Word," November 23, 1978; available from AscendedMasterLibrary.org.
18. Mother Mary, "Renew Your Sacred Covenant," October 12, 1963; available from AscendedMasterLibrary.org and published in Mark L. Prophet and Elizabeth Clare Prophet, *Mary's Message of Divine Love*, part 3, chapter 2.
19. Luke 1:35.
20. For an in-depth historical and theological analysis of the Biblical passages referring to Jesus' birth, see Elizabeth Clare Prophet, *The Lost Years of Jesus*, chapter 1, note 2.

CHAPTER SIX: **The Mantle of the Christ**
1. Rom. 8:26.
2. Matt. 6:33.

3. Matt. 6:31, 34.
4. Matt. 6:21.
5. Matt. 7:20.
6. Rev. 12.
7. A campaign of protests against the rule of the shah of Iran began in October 1977, culminating in the shah fleeing into exile on January 16, 1979. The regency government that replaced him invited the Ayatollah Khomeini, a hardline Islamist and leader of the opposition movement, to return to Iran from his exile in Paris. The government collapsed on February 11, 1979, as guerrillas and rebel troops loyal to Khomeini overwhelmed government forces in street fighting, bringing the Ayatollah into power. A referendum in March voted overwhelmingly for the creation of the Islamic Republic of Iran, and a new constitution adopted in December 1979 established a theocratic state with Khomeini as "Supreme Ruler." Khomeini was rabidly anti-American, branding the U.S. as "the Great Satan." He transformed what had been one of the most modern and Westernized societies in the Middle East into a repressive, fundamentalist state, sponsoring terrorist groups throughout the region and suppressing political dissent and individual freedoms (especially for women).
8. Luke 23:18.
9. Matt. 6:28.
10. Rev. 3:11.
11. Luke 24:32.
12. See note 7, this chapter.
13. Sanat Kumara, February 18, 1979, "Our Sphere of Oneness," *Pearls of Wisdom,* vol. 42, no. 19, May 8, 1999.
14. Ps. 23:1–4.
15. I Tim. 6:15; Rev. 17:14; 19:16.
16. In his dictation of March 27, 1964, God Tabor honored the "Silent Ones" or "Lonely Ones," whose "hearts in silent communion behold in the quietness of their being the infinite reality of God"—those who have drawn apart "to commune with the power derived from their eternal Source."
17. Matt. 12:46–50; Mark 3:31–35; Luke 8:19–21.
18. Chananda is Chief of the Indian Council of the Great White Brotherhood. His retreat, the Palace of Light, is located in the Himalayan mountains. He is also hierarch of the Cave of Light (focus of the Great Divine Director in India), situated in the mountain behind the Palace of Light.

19. I Sam. 16:12, 13.
20. Matt. 3:13–17; Mark 1:9–11; Luke 3:21, 22.
21. Rev. 2:17; 3:12; 14:1; 21:2, 10, 16; 22:4.
22. Matt. 26:34; Mark 14:30; Luke 22:34; John 13:38.
23. Luke 21:19.
24. *Urim and Thummim:* Hebrew, lit. "lights and perfections," the oracular brilliancy of the figures in the breastplate worn by the high priest; also significant of Truth. See Exod. 28:30; Lev. 8:8; Deut. 33:8; Ezra 2:63; Neh. 7:65.
25. Rev. 21:16.
26. Rev. 21:2–4.

408 pp   ISBN 978-1-60988-355-3

Teachings from the Mystery School
The Maitreya Discourses
Elizabeth Clare Prophet

Come and Find Me...
Welcome to the Mystery School of Lord Maitreya—
the Buddha of mercy, love and compassion.

Two thousand years ago, Maitreya sent forth the call to his disciple, Jesus, to come and find him. And so Jesus set out for the Himalayas to find the Father, Maitreya, and to receive the teachings that would be the key to an age. Now, once again, Maitreya sends forth the call. Are you one of these fiery spirits that Maitreya Buddha is calling?

In this book you will find keys to anchoring the consciousness of the Cosmic Christ in your life. Maitreya beckons: "Come and Find Me."

Welcome to the adventure of the ages.

212 pp   978-1-60988-381-2

Initiations of the Heart

Elizabeth Clare Prophet

Did our hearts not burn within us...

The mystics have always known that the heart is the most important center of consciousness. We can gain visions through the third eye, enlightenment through the crown. But the true fount of cosmic consciousness is always the heart. How do we develop our heart—the chakra of Divine Love? How can we increase the fire of the heart? How can we expand the threefold flame, the very source of Life within us?

Within *Initiations of the Heart,* the ascended masters reveal the mysteries of the heart. Most importantly, as we enter into their Word, each one offers a transfer of light—a unique initiation of the heart.

The apostles felt the fire of the heart in their encounter with the risen Christ on the road to Emmaus. May you also experience that fire through your encounter with the masters in this age.

246 pp   ISBN 978-1-932890-04-4

Maitreya on Initiation
The Coming Buddha Who Has Come
by Elizabeth Clare Prophet

Maitreya, the Coming Buddha, the Future Buddha, plays many roles in the various Buddhist traditions throughout the Far East.

Maitreya on Initiation is a compilation of Elizabeth Clare Prophet's lectures and writings on Maitreya throughout the years. Also included are five messages on initiation from the Great Initiator himself.

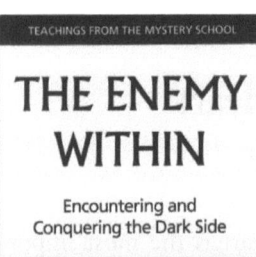

232 pp   ISBN 978-0-922729-99-3

The Enemy Within
Encountering and Conquering the Dark Side
Mark L. Prophet and
Elizabeth Clare Prophet

The dark side. The not-self. The dweller-on-the-threshold. The enemy within is subtle—occasionally causing us to do things we regret. The authors unmask the dweller, bring spiritual tools to help us deal with it, and reveal our true nature.

Summit University Press books are available at your favorite neighborhood and online booksellers. Visit SummitUniversityPress.com to learn more.
For more information on Elizabeth Clare Prophet and the teachings of the ascended masters, contact info@SummitUniversityPress.com.

Elizabeth Clare Prophet is a world-renowned author, spiritual teacher, and pioneer in practical spirituality. Her groundbreaking books have been published in more than thirty languages and over three million copies have been sold worldwide.

For more information about Elizabeth Clare Prophet's work, including her Pocket Guides to Practical Spirituality and her series on the Lost Teachings of Jesus and the Mystical Paths of the World's Religions, visit Summit UniversityPress.com.

Printed by Libri Plureos GmbH in Hamburg, Germany